Montgomery Bell

Tennessee Frontier Capitalist

by

John P. Williams

Acclaim Press

MORLEY, MISSOURI

Praise for
MONTGOMERY BELL

"In this intriguing masterpiece, John Williams unlocks the untold, true story of the legendary Montgomery Bell. With words and thoroughly researched facts, Williams weaves a portrait of a great yet complex man, who was an industrial giant and a life-long philanthropist, supporting educational opportunities for youth. But the story of Montgomery Bell also reveals Bell's personal history and conflict with slavery, the overriding controversy during those turbulent times."

–Judge Hamilton Gayden (ret.),
former Davidson County Circuit Court Judge
and author of *Miscarriage of Justice*

"The ironworks of Montgomery Bell produced the cannonballs used to defeat the British at the Battle of New Orleans in 1815. Much later in his life, Bell emancipated a large number of his enslaved ironworkers and helped them establish themselves on the African continent. In this biography of Bell, John Williams covers these hallmarks of Bell's long life and a great deal more. This book is an important addition to the history of Tennessee."

–Paul Clements, Tennessee historian
and author of *Tell Them We Were Rising*

"The first full length biography of Montgomery Bell, John Williams' book paints a portrait of Bell that is sympathetic, thoroughly researched, and even-handed, reflecting Williams' background as a well-respected and versatile Nashville attorney. The focus is broad, making it a work that touches on a number of contextual topics. In addition to piecing together Bell's life and legacy, it offers valuable windows into an array of things, including the early nineteenth century iron industry, the American Colonization Society, and Tennessee slave codes regarding manumission."

–Clay Bailey, III, history teacher at Montgomery Bell Academy
and member of the Metro Nashville Historical Commission

"Through careful review and interpretation of what few records exist, John Williams has painted a surprisingly full portrait of frontier industrialist Montgomery Bell. Using public land records, newspaper ads and announcements, and research to explain 18th and 19th century manufacturing processes, Williams follows Bell from his birth in 1769 in Chester County, Pennsylvania to his time in the Lexington, Kentucky area at the end of the 18th century, and then on to the Middle Tennessee frontier where he became the region's leading iron producer. Bell's life provides a window through which one can view how ambition, teamed with a tenacious spirit, can bring dramatic change to an area in a very brief time."

–Robert N. Buchanan, III, Nashville attorney
and President of the Tennessee Historical Society (2014-2020)

P.O. Box 238
Morley, MO 63767
(573) 472-9800
www.acclaimpress.com

Book Design: Steward&Wise
Cover Design: Frene Melton

Pictured on the cover: Catoctin Furnace of Frederick County, Maryland was a steam operated cold-blast charcoal furnace operating when Montgomery Bell was alive. Photograph by E.H. Pickering, courtesy of the Library of Congress. Inset: At the age of about eighty, Montgomery Bell sat for this photo in Nashville. It is the only known photo of him.

ISBN: 978-1-956027-97-6| 1-956027-97-1
Library of Congress Control Number: 2024943079

First Printing: 2024
Printed in the United States of America
10 9 8 7 6 5 4 3 2 1

This publication was produced using available information.
The publisher regrets it cannot assume responsibility for errors or omissions.

Contents

Dedication

For Rick Hollis and Jay Swafford, whose knowledge and enthusiasm about Montgomery Bell have inspired me throughout my work on this book.

Preface

After forty-seven years of practicing law, I decided to ease into retirement in 2020. I was going to take all those road trips I had been planning and see all those places I had wanted to visit.

Then the COVID-19 pandemic hit.

I put my road trips on hold until it was safe to travel, dusted off the books on my coffee table and began to read like crazy.

I have always enjoyed biographies. As a kid, it was biographies of sports heroes like Babe Ruth and Lou Gehrig. As an adult, it is biographies of political, business and social leaders.

In 2021, I read biographies of 19th century business giants like John D. Rockefeller, Andrew Carnegie, and Cornelius Vanderbilt. I was especially interested in the life story of Mr. Vanderbilt, because I attended law school at Vanderbilt University, founded in 1873 with a large gift from Mr. Vanderbilt.

After reading the Vanderbilt biography, I began thinking about the other schools I had attended. I received my junior high and high school education at Montgomery Bell Academy (MBA), a private preparatory school in Nashville, Tennessee. Like Vanderbilt, MBA was established in the middle of the 19th century as the South was recovering from the Civil War. And like Vanderbilt, MBA was named for the man who had given a generous bequest for its founding — Montgomery Bell.

Surely, I thought, there must be a good biography of Mr. Bell. As I began digging, I was astounded at what I found. Very little.

There is a slim folder of material at the Tennessee State Library and Archives, the best repository of information on celebrated Tennesseans. The folder includes a handful of articles published in local newspapers over a period of more than 150 years since Mr. Bell's death in 1855.

The best of these articles is a twelve-part series by Ed Huddleston, published in the *Nashville Banner* in 1955. They reflect extensive research into Mr. Bell's long life. After reading these articles, I was even more surprised that Mr. Bell's accomplishments had not inspired some historian to chronicle his life story in a biography.

Although I am not a historian, I have done extensive writing in my career as a lawyer. I decided to follow the admonition of Nobel Prize-winning author Toni Morrison, who famously said: "If you find a book you really want to read but it hasn't been written yet, then you must write it."

So here it is. I hope my effort will fill a significant void in Tennessee and American history.

John P. Williams
August 2024

Introduction

*M*ontgomery Bell—*Tennessee Frontier Capitalist* is the first full-length biography of Montgomery Bell, written almost 170 years after his death in 1855. As I gathered material to write this book, it became apparent to me why no other historian has ever written his complete life story.

Biographies of 18th and 19th century Americans rely heavily on letters written by and to the subject of the story, and Montgomery Bell was apparently not much of a letter writer. With very few exceptions, the letters he wrote or received have not been preserved, to the extent they ever existed.

In addition, many 18th and 19th century Americans kept diaries.[1] Not Montgomery Bell. He was too busy running his iron furnaces and forges and tending to the rest of his businesses.

In the absence of letters or a diary, two sources have proved especially helpful in gaining information about Bell's life. To begin, he bought and sold many tracts of land that were described in deeds. Usually, these deeds were recorded at the local courthouse and are available to the public, even after 200 years.

Each deed stated the names of the buyer and seller, the amount of land being sold, the date of the sale, and sometimes additional information about the location of the land. Deciphering this information is often a challenge, as 18th and 19th century deeds were handwritten, and some handwriting is not easy to read.

The second source of information about Bell includes newspaper articles, notices and advertisements. From at least the beginning of the 19th century, businessmen placed ads and notices in newspapers on a regular basis. Business activities were also the subject of news articles, as they are today. Several newspapers were published in Nashville on a daily or weekly basis. There was no radio, no television, no internet … just newspapers.

Historians have come to rely on a website *(www.newspapers.com)* that is available to the public on a subscription basis. Through this website, a subscriber has access to articles, notices and ads in hundreds of newspapers throughout the country over a period of two centuries. The phrase "treasure trove" does not begin to describe the value of this website to historical research.

Montgomery Bell liked to place notices and ads in the newspaper. When he was considering a sale of any portion of his land or other assets, he would place a detailed notice in one or more Nashville newspapers. These notices provide the best evidence of the furnaces, forges, and properties that Bell owned at the time he placed them. Each notice was signed

VALUABLE IRON WORKS AND FARM FOR SALE.

OWING to the feebleness of the subscriber's health, he offers for sale his Iron Works and Farm:

1st. The Farm on which he now resides, in Williamson county, about 11 miles from Nashville, containing about 550 acres of land which cannot be surpassed for beauty or fertility of soil. As a "Grass Farm," it is too well known to require any description.

The buildings are of superior finish. There is plenty of stock water the whole year round—Little Harpeth river runs through it.

Also, the following tracts of land—ore banks, furnaces and forges:

1st.—JACKSON FURNACE—together with about 3,000 acres of land.

2nd—BELLVIEW FURNACE -with all its ore banks, and privileges, and timber, with between three and four thousand acres attached, well timbered and watered.

3d —VALLEY FORGE.—with upwards of 8,000 acres of land well timbered, and on it the best water power in this or any other country.

4th.—I will also sell a first-rate Water-Power at the Narrows of Harpeth, with a tunnel already excavated, and about 13 acres of land attached.

Also, all my Water Powers and Ore Banks on Mill Creek, in Hickman county.

I have also an Ore Bank on Duck River, which is very rich in quality and inexhaustible.

Any one wishing to purchase will please call upon the subscriber or address him at Good Spring P. O, Williamson county, when he will make known the terms, &c.

aug3—3m   MONTGOMERY BELL.

An example of a newspaper notice placed by Montgomery Bell. (Nashville Union and American, August 4, 1854)

"Montgomery Bell," verifying its authenticity. In the absence of letters that Bell wrote or a diary that he kept, the notices also provide a glimpse into Bell's mind, and I have therefore quoted extensively from them in this book.

Bell liked to advertise the iron products made at his furnaces and sold in his retail stores. These ads provide the best evidence of the location of his stores and the products he sold.

The notices and ads reproduced in this book retain the spelling of words as they appeared in newspapers at the time. In those days, there were no computers with spell-check to correct misspellings.

Bell was not alone among 19th century Americans in not being a perfect speller. The award-winning historian Stephen E. Ambrose quoted extensively from the diaries and papers of Meriwether Lewis and William Clark in his chronicle of the Lewis and Clark expedition to the Pacific Northwest in 1804-1806.[2] The spelling used by Lewis and Clark was truly atrocious, but typical of even famous people during this period of American history.

Although I am the first full-length biographer of Montgomery Bell, I am not the first person to write about Bell's eventful life. During his lifetime and after his death, he was occasionally the subject of newspaper articles and book chapters.

In the last year of his life, a five-page sketch of Bell was included in a mammoth four-volume set compiled by a New York lawyer named John Livingston, entitled *Portraits of Eminent Americans Now Living, with Biographical and Historical Memoirs of their Lives and Actions.*[3] This short summary of Bell's life, written in 1854, is largely accurate and presented Bell to a national audience while he was still alive.

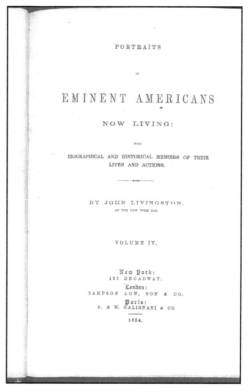

Cover of the 1854 book, courtesy of John Livingston.

In 1883, almost thirty years after his death, a lengthy feature article written by an anonymous author appeared in Nashville's *Daily American* newspaper. The article began with the following sentence: "There has been no man connected with the past progress of Tennessee, whose life is fuller of interest than that of Montgomery Bell."[4] That sentence surely got the attention of readers.

Montgomery Bell Academy, the school founded in 1867 with a bequest from Bell, established a publication known as the *Montgomery Bell Bulletin*. In 1901, a professor at that school, P.H. Manning, wrote a lengthy article about Bell's life in the *Bulletin*, which was later reprinted in *The Nashville American* newspaper.[5] According to Manning, the facts in his article were obtained from Alexander Hamilton Bell and his sister, Ann P. Hogan, both grandchildren of Montgomery Bell.

In the Montgomery Bell folder at the Tennessee State Library and Archives is a fifty-page narrative of Bell's life written by Nannie S. Boyd, a collateral descendant of Bell[6] who claimed to have spent forty years gathering information about his life. Her narrative was typed but contains many handwritten insertions and other edits to the typewritten portion. Mrs. Boyd had a sincere interest in telling Bell's life story, but she never converted her narrative into a book or even an article for publication. Mrs. Boyd came closer than anyone to writing the first biography of Bell.

A feature story by Christine Sadler appeared in the *Nashville Banner* in 1932.[7] According to this article, Bell had "four major titles to fame": the manufacture of cannon balls used in the Battle of New Orleans, the construction of the tunnel at the Narrows of the Harpeth River, the expenditure of a large sum of money to free his slaves and send them to Liberia, and the bequest of $20,000 to establish Montgomery Bell Academy.

The next effort to tell Bell's story was also in the *Nashville Banner* – a series of twelve articles by Ed Huddleston written in 1955 on the 100th anniversary of Bell's death.[8] These articles reveal extensive research by Huddleston and should have been expanded into a book, but were not.

Twenty-three years after Huddleston's articles were published, *The Tennessean*'s premier historical writer, Louise Davis, wrote a lengthy Sunday feature article about Bell, which included several details not mentioned in Huddleston's articles.[9] It is the second best effort by a journalist to tell the story of Bell's life.

Twenty-two years after Davis' article was published, Dale Graham wrote a series of nine articles that appeared in the *South Cheatham Advocate*, an excellent weekly newspaper that was published for thirty years in Kingston Springs, Tennessee.[10] Her articles drew heavily on Huddleston's articles, but also included information about Bell's life obtained from her interviews of several local

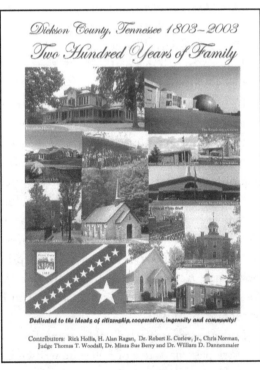

Cover of the Dickson County Bicentennial booklet, courtesy of the Dickson County Bicetennial Commission.

residents and from information supplied to her by Michael Holt, a local historian and genealogist who did extensive research on Bell and his enslaved workers.[11]

When Dickson County celebrated its Bicentennial in 2003, Rick Hollis chaired the Bicentennial Commission and helped put together a colorful booklet profiling many of Dickson County's prominent citizens over the years. Hollis wrote an excellent profile of Bell that was included in this booklet.[12]

Two respected Dickson County historians, Robert E. Corlew and George E. Jackson, wrote books containing useful information about Montgomery Bell. Corlew's 1956 book, *A History of Dickson County, Tennessee*, devoted seven pages (pages 22-28) to Bell, whose life story he described as "like a Horatio Alger novel."[13] Jackson's 1994 book, *Cumberland Furnace: A Frontier Industrial Village*, included much interesting information about Bell's involvement with his first iron furnace (pages 20-28).[14]

Two Master's Theses written by graduate students at Tennessee universities also proved enormously helpful. "Montgomery Bell, Tennessee Ironmaster" was written in 1970 by James Maurice Gifford to obtain his Master's degree at Middle Tennessee State University. "The Iron Industry in Dickson County, Tennessee" was written in 1970 by Buena Coleman Daniel to obtain her Master's degree at Austin Peay State University. With the universities' consent, these documents are available to the public.

Throughout this book, I have made reference to other books and historical journal articles that contain useful information about Bell and the iron industry. These books and articles are referenced in the endnotes.

Every biographer borrows from previously published material about the subject of the biography. Because of the great respect I have for the persons who have written about Montgomery Bell over the years, I think it important to acknowledge the help their work has provided in writing this biography.

I hope this will not be the last book written about Montgomery Bell. Just as he operated more than one iron furnace, his life merits more than one book. Perhaps other historians can use my book as a foundation to uncover additional information about his life and then write books that will add to the store of knowledge about this great Tennessean.

MONTGOMERY BELL

Tennessee Frontier Capitalist

CHAPTER ONE

Who Was Montgomery Bell?

In 2003, Dickson County, Tennessee celebrated its Bicentennial for which the County published a colorful booklet recognizing the people and places that have a special significance in the County's history. Many of the profiles in the booklet were written by Rick Hollis, a local historian and businessman who served as Mayor of Charlotte, Tennessee, from 1989 to 1993, and was Chair of the Bicentennial Commission in 2003.

The subject of his first profile was Dr. William Dickson, the physician and political leader for whom the County was named. His second profile was of "Iron Master Montgomery Bell", namesake of Montgomery Bell State Park, the County's principal tourist attraction.

The first paragraph of Hollis' profile of Bell captures the breadth and complexity of the man:

Tall. Handsome. Steely-eyed. Shrewd. Crafty. Firm. Energetic. Creative. Imaginative. Sophisticated. Unpretentious. Montgomery Bell was Tennessee's first capitalist and industrialist and the South's greatest Iron Master.[1]

In 1955, the *Nashville Banner* (Nashville's afternoon newspaper at the time) published a series of twelve articles on the 100th anniversary of Bell's death. Ed Huddleston, an ace *Banner* reporter, described Bell as a "Man of Mystery".[2]

According to Huddleston, "Montgomery Bell made money MOVE.... [H]e brought more money into the state, and into circulation, than any other Tennessean of his day."[3] In another article, Huddleston wrote: "Bell was no hoarder. Money was his willing servant, not his master.... His money kept moving, into productive holdings, better products, and back again… His dollars weren't dusty. He kept them shining from use."[4]

Louise Davis, a historical writer for the *Tennessean* (Nashville's morning newspaper), provided a striking description of Bell in a 1978 article: "Tough old Bell – rich and irascible, eccentric and brilliant – cared not a fig about his appearance."[5] Almost 100 years before Davis wrote those words, an article in another Nashville newspaper provided this flattering observation about the man: "The life of Montgomery Bell was such as should excite emulation and encourage the talent and perseverance required for a successful prosecution of any business in which a man is engaged."[6]

His gravestone contains a succinct statement of his importance in Tennessee history: "He was one of the earliest and most successful ironmasters in the State." This epitaph may have been written by Bell himself. He was not shy about touting the quality of his iron furnaces and products.

Bell was nationally recognized in his lifetime as well as after his death. In 1854 (the year before Bell's death), a New York lawyer named John A. Livingston wrote and published a four-volume set entitled *Portraits of Eminent Americans Now Living: Biographical and Historical Memoirs of Their Lives and Actions.*[7] At a time when the population of the United States exceeded 25 million, Livingston chose to profile only 112 persons in this monumental work. Montgomery Bell was one of thirteen Tennesseans that were included.

Livingston's five-page summary of Bell's life described him "as an industrious, economical, and useful citizen" who had "a wide-spread reputation for wisdom, energy, and industry."[8] Livingston said of Bell: "In appearance he is remarkably striking, and impresses all who see him with the idea that he is a man of decision, firmness, and intelligence."[9]

The best physical description of Montgomery Bell was supplied by Robert E. Dalton in a 1976 article in the *Tennessee Historical Quarterly*: "We know that he was a broad-shouldered man who stood over six feet tall, …with a broad forehead, firm mouth, strong chin, and youthful, penetrating eyes."[10]

Montgomery Bell was an American original. He refused to conform to the conventions and mores of the day. He marched to the beat of his own drummer. He lived life as he saw fit. And measured by any yardstick, he was enormously successful.

It is not possible to tell Bell's story without also telling the story of America in the late 18th and early 19th centuries. His long life was bookended by two American wars. He was born in 1769, six years before the start of the Revolutionary War, and died in 1855, six years before the start of the Civil War.

His life was essentially divided into three parts: his first twenty years were spent in eastern Pennsylvania, his next twelve years were spent in eastern Kentucky, and his last half century was spent in middle Tennessee.

Understanding Bell's life requires an understanding of the times in which he lived – times that are very different from the 21st century. This book provides context for each period of his life. Through this context, we gain insight into the history of this country we call the United States of America.

CHAPTER TWO

Chester County, Pennsylvania

Montgomery Bell was a native of Chester County, Pennsylvania and spent his formative years there. His early years in the Keystone State had a profound influence on the rest of his life.

Chester County was formed by William Penn in 1682 under a charter[1] granted by King Charles II of England.[2] Along with Bucks and Philadelphia Counties, it is one of Pennsylvania's three original counties.[3]

William Penn (Wikipedia)

English and Welsh immigrants settled in the central and southeastern parts of Chester County, while Scots-Irish immigrants settled in the western parts of the county.[4] Bell's father had come from Ireland, so the Bell family lived in West Fallowfield Township[5] in the western section of Chester County.

Map showing Chester County, Pennsylvania. (Wikipedia)

Chester County historic marker. (Author photo)

The soil of Chester County is very fertile. The early settlers grew corn, wheat, barley, oats, rye, buckwheat and flax. Milling was the county's first industry.

The county also had rich iron ore deposits and plentiful water power, so an iron industry quickly developed. Iron furnaces and forges were built at various locations in the county, including Coventry, Warwick, Valley Forge, Coatesville, and Phoenixville.[6]

BATTLE OF BRANDYWINE

On Sept. 11, 1777, an American force of about 11,000 men, commanded by Washington, attempted to halt a British advance into Pennsylvania. The Americans were defeated near Chadds Ford on Brandywine Creek by approximately 18,000 British and Hessian troops under Howe.

Battle of Brandywine historic marker. (Author photo)

The Revolutionary War came to Chester County in September 1777, when the British army invaded the county on its way to capture Philadelphia. The Battles of Brandywine and Paoli resulted in defeats for the Continental Army, and were followed by the Army's struggle to survive the bitter winter of 1777-78 in their Valley Forge encampment.[7]

During Bell's childhood, the population of Chester County was about 25,000, spread over an area of more than 1,000 square miles. By 2020, the county had a population of 534,413, but its geographical area had shrunk to 759 square miles (since portions of the original Chester County had been removed to form Lancaster, Berks, and Delaware Counties).[8]

Portions of Chester County are now suburbs of Philadelphia and Wilmington, Delaware. It is the fastest-growing county in the Delaware River Valley, and one of the fastest-growing counties in the northeastern United States. In 2010, Chester County had the highest median income of any county in Pennsylvania and the twenty-fourth highest in the United States. Forty-nine percent of its adult residents have college degrees; ninety-two percent are high school graduates.[9]

Chester County's best known agricultural product is the mushroom. Every September the County hosts the Mushroom Festival in the Borough of Kennett Square.[10]

As Montgomery Bell grew to manhood, what he saw was a largely rural landscape whose farms, mills, iron furnaces and forges operated within a largely self-sufficient economy in which surpluses were sent to market in Philadelphia. From the time he was eight years old, he also saw men preparing to fight a war, with all the devastation that war brings to people's lives. His early life must have been similar to the experiences of Ukrainian children after the Russian invasion in 2022.

There are several interesting historical facts worth mentioning about Chester County. After William Penn had acquired the grant of 45,000 square miles from King Charles II to establish Pennsylvania, a dispute arose regarding its southern border with Maryland, which had been established in 1632 by Cecilius Calvert, the second Lord Baltimore. The border dispute lingered for nearly a century until the Penn and Calvert descendants decided in 1763 to resolve the controversy.

They hired two English surveyors, Charles Mason and

The duo picked a clear geographical location due west of Philadelphia—the forks of the Brandywine Creek in Embreeville—and set up an observatory from which to make their observations. Using a device with a six-foot-long brass telescope that allowed them to establish their position relative to the stars, they observed the night sky from the observatory through frigid winters and oppressive summers for nearly five years. A marker, known as Star Gazers' Stone, was placed to mark the astronomical meridian line north of the observatory.

The marker and the Harlan House where Mason and Dixon stayed are listed on the National Register of Historic Places. Star Gazers' Stone is also designated a National Historic Civil Engineering Landmark, one of 125 sites in the country.

Mason and Dixon sign. (Author photo)

Marker for the Star Gazers Stone. (Author photo)

Jeremiah Dixon, who set up shop in Chester County on farmland owned by John Harlan. They placed a rectangular slab of white quartz in the ground as a reference point from which to run the boundary line. The quartz stone became known as the Star Gazer's Stone and the boundary line between the two colonies as the Mason-Dixon Line.[11] Other surveyors later extended the Line west to the Ohio River. The Mason-Dixon Line is now commonly thought of as the dividing line between North and South.[12]

Mason-Dixon Line historic marker. (Author photo)

When Abraham Lincoln decided to seek the Republican nomination for President in 1859, he was largely unknown outside Illinois. Jesse Fell, a Chester County native who was then living in Illinois, convinced Lincoln to provide sufficient information to allow Fell to write a short campaign sketch of Lincoln's life. Fell prepared a first draft, which was expanded into a 2,500-word essay by a Republican delegate from Chester County named Joseph J. Lewis. Lewis sent it to Samuel R. Downing, editor of *The Chester County Times*, which published the piece. It was widely circulated throughout Pennsylvania and later

The Star Gazers Stone. (Author photo)

Rock barrier around the Star Gazers Stone. (Author photo)

Lincoln University in Chester County, Pennsylvania. (Author photo)

the country, and became the basis for several campaign biographies. Pretty soon, everyone knew the life story of the Rail Splitter from Illinois.[13]

In 1854, a Chester County Presbyterian minister founded the Ashmun Institute, named for Jehudi Ashmun, an African American missionary who had dedicated his life to serving the interests of blacks that had been transported to Liberia by the American Colonization Society. After the assassination of President Lincoln, the Ashmun Institute was re-named Lincoln University and began offering an undergraduate curriculum, as well as expanding its seminary to include graduate programs in business, law, and medicine.[14]

Ashmun Institute was the first degree-granting Historically Black College and University (HBCU). Its most famous alumni include Supreme Court Justice Thurgood Marshall and poet Langston Hughes. The university currently has 2,000 students.[15]

CHAPTER THREE

Montgomery Bell: Child of the American Revolution

Montgomery Bell was born on January 3, 1769, the tenth child of John Bell and Mary Montgomery Patterson Bell.[1]

His father, born November 20, 1705, immigrated to America from County Donegal, Ireland in the early years of the 18th century. His mother, born in 1726, was a native of Pennsylvania, but had Scots-Irish ancestry. They were married on August 13, 1745.[2]

They lived in West Fallowfield Township[3] in the western part of Chester County. Their ten children were born over a period of twenty-four years, stretching from 1745 to 1769. There were six boys and four girls. They were a hearty group. In an era when children were frequently stillborn or died in childhood, the Bell children all lived to adulthood.

Their parents lived long lives. John Bell lived to be 91 years of age, dying on December 23, 1796, and Mary Patterson Bell lived until 1804, dying at the age of 78.

Below is a list of Montgomery's nine siblings:[4]

1) John Bell (1745-1831)
2) Zachariah Bell (1746-1804)
3) James Bell (1747-1800)
4) Grace Bell Williams (1747-1775)
5) Patterson Bell (1748-1833)
6) Elizabeth Bell Bean (1750-1809)
7) Jane Bell Luckey (1754-1818)
8) William Bell (1758-1807)
9) Mary Bell Haslet (1762-1797)

Little is known about John Bell's occupation or source of income. Like most residents of Chester County at that time, he was likely a farmer, albeit a very successful one. He acquired a significant amount of land. Chester County land records show him owning 194 acres in 1765 and 376 acres in 1795.[5] He built a comfortable home, which is still standing today at 467 Gum Tree Road in Cochranville. The family was modestly affluent by the standards of the day.

Gumtree Road marker. (Author photo)

Gum Tree Road existed at least as far back as 1775 and probably much earlier, according to records in the Chester County Archives.[6] It was one of the east-west routes from Philadelphia to Lancaster. Current residents who live on Gum Tree Road have explained that their houses were built in the late 18th century, like the Bells' house. One house

Montgomery Bell's childhood home in Chester County, Pennsylvania. (Author photo)

(at 339 Gum Tree Road) was used as a tavern and another house (at 359 Gum Tree Road) as an inn.[7] Montgomery Bell became accustomed to travelers passing by his family's home on horseback or in coaches.

Montgomery's childhood was disrupted by the war with the British. Two battles – the Battle of Brandywine and the Battle of Paoli – were fought in Chester County in the fall of 1777, when Montgomery was eight years old. Following those battles, the Continental Army made its winter quarters in Valley Forge, adjacent to Chester County.

The Bell family were staunch supporters of the Patriot cause. John and Mary Bell were friends with George and Martha Washington, who stayed in the Bell home on occasion.[8] John Bell, Jr. is credited with writing the first biographical sketch of George Washington. His article appeared in the August 1780 issue of the *Westminster Magazine* and was entitled "A Sketch of the Life and Character of General Washington".[9]

Although Montgomery was too young to fight in the Revolutionary War, four of his brothers saw service in the Continental Army. Patterson Bell was commissioned a Colonel in the 8th Battalion of the Chester County Militia in September 1777 and fought in the battles of Trenton, Brandywine,[10] and Monmouth. John, James and William Bell also served in the Continental Army.[11] It is local legend that Montgomery visited one of his older brothers in the encampment at Valley Forge.[12]

The most successful of Montgomery Bell's siblings was Patterson Bell. Before the war he received a B.A. degree from the College of Philadelphia (now the University of Pennsylvania) in 1771.[13] According to the July 11, 1771 edition of the *Pennsylvania Gazette*, he was one of several students chosen to address his class at graduation. He must have had a sense of humor, because the title of his address was "An Ironical Panegyric on the Effects of Drunkenness."

While serving as a Colonel in the Chester County Militia, Patterson Bell was appointed in 1778 by the Supreme Executive Council of Pennsylvania to seize and dispose of the Estates of Traitors to the Revolutionary cause, an important and sensitive responsibility during those turbulent times when many were still allied with the British.[14]

In 1778, Patterson Bell purchased a 220-acre tract of land in Lancaster County, just across Octorara Creek from Chester County. The next year, he married a wealthy widow named Mary Irwin Boyle. He later built a grand brick home known as Bellbank; the home is still in good condition and is often used for fundraising events today.

The Bells were staunch Presbyterians, the denomination of many Scots-Irish immigrants. Montgomery's father John Bell belonged to Faggs Manor Presbyterian Church, the third Presbyterian church established in the colonies before the American Revolution. It was built in 1730 on land that William Penn had left to his daughter Letitia in 1701 and was named Faggs

Patterson Bell's home, Bellbank. (Author photo)

Manor, because Sir John Fagg(e) had been William Penn's neighbor in England before Penn moved to Pennsylvania. Now known simply as Manor Presbyterian Church, the church has an active congregation to this day.

Manor Presbyterian Church. (Author photo)

After Patterson Bell moved to Lancaster County, he joined a Presbyterian church in that county, the Middle Octorara Presbyterian Church, also still active today. When John Bell died in 1796, Patterson chose to have his father interred in the small cemetery adjacent to that church.

Marker in Manor Presbyterian Church. (Author photo)

Middle Octorara Presbyterian Church. (Author photo)

The church cemetery in which John Bell is buried. (Author photo)

The moving tribute on John Bell's gravestone reads:

In Memory
of JOHN BELL who
departed this life Decm'r 23,
1796 in the 91st year of his
Age.
He was an affectionate Husband and
tender Father, a virtuous Man and a
faithful friend, his virtues are not
recorded on this perishable Stone, they are
written in the book of life and in the
hearts of his family and friends.[15]

The extent of John Bell's wealth can be measured in part by the bequests he made to his children in his Will.[16] He left to his wife Mary all his personal property, all the "rents and profits" from his property, and 100 pounds. To each of five sons (including Montgomery), he bequeathed 50 pounds. Two of his daughters received 40 pounds each, and another daughter received 70 pounds. One daughter had predeceased him. His sixth son, Zachariah, was executor of John's estate and received all of John's real estate.

Montgomery Bell's mother, Mary Bell, outlived her husband by eight years,

John Bell grave marker. (Author photo)

dying in 1804. Her place of burial is unclear. She may be buried next to her husband in the Middle Octorara cemetery, but there is no gravestone.

Because of the disruption caused by the war, Montgomery had little opportunity for formal education as a child. Even if life had been more normal, there were no public schools and few private schools in Pennsylvania at the time. Those that did exist were generally sponsored by churches. In fact, one of the first church-related schools in Chester County was Fagg's Manor Classical School, started in 1740 by Rev. Samuel Blair, the pastor of the church that John and Mary Bell attended.[17] It is not clear, though, that this school was operating during Montgomery's childhood.

Most children were homeschooled by their families. Bell was blessed in this regard. He had attentive parents and nine older siblings who undoubtedly taught him much.

By the time the Revolutionary War ended in 1783, Bell was fourteen years old. Two years later, he was apprenticed to a local tanner at a tanyard owned by his brother Patterson.[18]

Tanning is the process of treating skins and hides of animals to produce leather. The skins are first dehaired, desalted, degreased, and soaked in water, and then are processed at a tannery using tannin, an acidic chemical derived from the bark of certain trees.[19] Tanning was a lucrative business at that time because the primary mode of transportation involved horses, and there was a need for bridles and saddles.

The tanning business did not appeal to Montgomery Bell, probably for the same reasons it did not appeal to another famous American, Ulysses S. Grant. Grant's father operated a tannery in Ohio while Grant was a child in the 1820s. One of Grant's biographers described the impression it made on the future President: "The tannery…was a malodorous place that stank from lampblack and grease used to dress hides, and Ulysses, whose upstairs bedroom window stared out on the business, was revolted by the stench that regularly wafted across the street – a revulsion that lasted a lifetime."[20]

Bell was a tanner's apprentice for three years. Then he decided to become an apprentice to his brother Zachariah in the hat business.[21]

About this time, Montgomery made his "first attempt at trading" – something he would continue to do for the rest of his life. According to an early sketch of Bell, this trade "was a prototype of his future and more extensive speculations. He realized $100 and a silver watch by this trade."[22]

When he received word of the death of his brother-in-law William Bean in Kentucky in 1789, his life in Pennsylvania ended. He decided to move to Kentucky to care for his widowed sister Elizabeth and her six children.[23]

CHAPTER FOUR

Fayette County, Kentucky

In 1789, Montgomery Bell left Pennsylvania to help his widowed sister Elizabeth and her six children, who had recently moved from Maryland to Fayette County, Kentucky. Her husband, William Bean, had acquired 3,000 acres of land in Kentucky before his untimely death soon after they moved there. After arriving in Kentucky, Bell stayed for about twelve years and began his business career.

During his years in Fayette County, Kentucky became a state. Bell had a front-row seat to this unfolding chapter in American history, although there is no evidence that he played a role in the Kentucky statehood movement.

Kentucky Before Statehood

Like Tennessee, Kentucky was not one of the original thirteen colonies that became the United States of America after they declared independence from Great Britain in 1776. The land that is now Kentucky was the western part of Virginia.

The earliest settlers came to Kentucky shortly before the outbreak of the American Revolution.[1] The first permanent settlement in Kentucky was Harrodsburg, established by James Harrod in 1774.[2] The most famous early settlement was Boonesborough, established by Daniel Boone.[3]

The early settlers lived in "stations." A station usually consisted of one or more closely situated cabins for mutual defense from Indian attacks. When a community was established, the settlers would build a "fort," which provided better defense because it usually included a blockhouse and stockade.[4]

Such preparations were necessary because these settlers faced frequent attacks by Indians. 1782 was known as the Year of Blood in Kentucky. Many early settlers were killed in Indian raids.[5]

Despite these setbacks, settlers came to Kentucky in large numbers beginning in 1784. Virginia had paid its Revolutionary War soldiers with land warrants that entitled them to land in the area that is now Kentucky.[6]

In 1776, Virginia had created a county known as Kentucky County, encompassing what is now the State of Kentucky. By 1780, the population of Kentucky County had grown sufficiently large that it was divided into three counties – Fayette, Jefferson, and Lincoln. Six additional counties were subsequently created before Kentucky achieved statehood.[7]

Unlike the path that Tennessee followed to achieve statehood (discussed in a later chapter), Kentucky remained a part of Virginia until it became a state in 1792. Between 1784 and 1792, ten conventions were held in Kentucky to discuss and plan for statehood.[8]

Virginia did not oppose the separation of Kentucky into a new state. In fact, the Virginia General Assembly passed an Enabling Act setting forth the conditions of separation. Virginia's main concern was to protect the land grants that Virginians had received.[9]

Congress, of course, had to approve the admission of Kentucky into the Union, and it did so on February 4, 1791. Kentucky's first constitution was drafted at its tenth convention and approved by the delegates in April 1792.[10]

Kentucky became the 15th state on June 1, 1792. Its first governor, Isaac Shelby, served from 1792 to 1796 and again from 1812 to 1816.[11] Members of the Kentucky legislature were also elected, and they in turn chose John Brown and John Edwards as the state's first U.S. Senators.[12]

Creation of Lexington and Fayette County

Montgomery Bell spent the last decade of the 18th century in Kentucky. During that time, the population of the state almost tripled, growing from 73,000 to 221,000. Slightly less than 20% of the population during this period consisted of enslaved persons.[13]

Bell's time was spent mostly in Fayette County, which had been established in 1780 while Kentucky was still a part of Virginia.[14] The county was named for the Marquis de Lafayette, the famous Frenchman who helped Americans win the Revolutionary War.[15] The county seat of Fayette County has always been Lexington. Its name was chosen by early settlers encamped at McConnell's Spring in 1775 when they learned that the Battle of Lexington had been fought in Massachusetts in April of that year. They thought Lexington a good name for their planned settlement.[16]

Although the name Lexington was chosen in 1775, the Indians drove off the earliest settlers with encouragement from the British. It was not until 1779 that a permanent settlement was established at Lexington.[17]

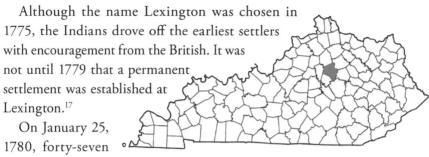

Map showing Fayette County, Kentucky. (Wikipedia)

On January 25, 1780, forty-seven residents of Lexington signed a document known as the Articles of Agreement, which set forth the manner in which the community would be governed by elected Trustees. Later that year, the Virginia legislature officially created Fayette County and designated Lexington as the county seat.[18]

In 1781, the Trustees adopted a plan laying out streets and lots for the Town of Lexington. Daniel Boone, the first Representative from Fayette County to serve in the Virginia legislature, introduced a bill to formally create the Town of Lexington, and its Charter was approved on May 6, 1782.[19]

A history of early Lexington contains a plat showing the lots as laid out by the Trustees in 1781. There were eighty-seven "in-lots" (each a half acre in size) along a "commons" on Water Street and 112 "out-lots" (each five acres in size) located north and east of the "in-lots."[20] Montgomery Bell would later acquire two of the "in-lots" (Nos. 39 and 47) and one "out-lot" (No. 91). The names of the streets as shown on the original plat are mostly unchanged over the ensuing two centuries.

Lexington and Fayette County During and After Bell's Stay

Montgomery Bell arrived in Lexington about 1790 and lived there throughout the last decade of the 18th century. The town was already beginning to grow. "During the decade of the 1790s, merchants advertised an amazing assortment of merchandise, and tradesmen offered a multiplicity of services."[21] Lexington tax records for 1795 list twenty-six stores, nine "ordinaries" (taverns and restaurants), and several inns and boardinghouses.[22] The list of businesses included all the following:

> **hemp, baggage and rope factories or "walks"; a brewery and distillery; brickyards; tanning yards; a nail plant (evidence**

that frame buildings were succeeding logs); wheel, cabinet and furniture makers; a variety of "smiths" — blacksmith, whitesmith, coppersmith, locksmith, clocksmith, silver and goldsmiths — as well as a hatter, glover and saddler; shoe and boot makers; a weaver, dressmakers and tailors; and, in what was to become the "**Horse Capital of the World**," the first livery stable.[23]

The "hatter" referred to in this list of businesses existing in Lexington in 1795 was Montgomery Bell's hat business.

During Bell's years there, Lexington was a thriving frontier town of more than 2,000 residents.[24] It was the largest city in what was then America's West.[25]

In the 19th century, the best known resident of Lexington was Henry Clay, long-time U.S. Congressman and Senator from Kentucky and unsuccessful Presidential candidate in 1824, 1832, and 1844. Henry Clay moved to Lexington from Virginia in 1797 and immediately set up a law practice. There is evidence that Bell and Clay engaged in land transactions, and even opposed each other in lawsuits. Henry Clay's home, known as Ashland, has been preserved and is open to the public as a museum *(www.henryclay.org)*.

The second most well-known person from Lexington was Mary Todd, who married Abraham Lincoln in 1842. Her father, Robert Todd, was a successful banker in Lexington, and the Lincolns visited Lexington on several occasions. The Todd home is a museum open to the public *(www.mtlhouse.org)*.

Although Kentucky remained neutral during the Civil War, Lexington became active as a slave market during the 1840s and 1850s and by the beginning of the War was the largest slave market in the Upper South.[26]

The law office of Henry Clay in Lexington, Kentucky. (Author photo)

The Mary Todd Lincoln House in Lexington, Kentucky. (Author photo)

Kentucky had the third largest number of slaveholders in the country, behind only Virginia and Georgia.[27] Ironically, Lexington was also a haven for free blacks during that same period of time, and free blacks constituted almost 10% of the town's total population by 1850.[28]

Lexington is now Kentucky's second largest city, with a population of more than 300,000. In 1974, Lexington and Fayette County adopted a consolidated city-county government similar to that of Nashville and Davidson County, Tennessee.[29]

Lexington has a very diverse economy today, but is best known for its horse farms, the Keeneland Race Course, and the Kentucky Horse Park, which tells the story of horses. It is also the home of the University of Kentucky and its legendary basketball teams.

CHAPTER FIVE

Montgomery Bell: Hatter

Montgomery Bell and his nine siblings were a close-knit group. In the turbulent years of the early frontier, they had to look out for each other.

His sister Elizabeth married a man named William Bean (sometimes spelled Bain). In the 1780s, they made their home in Cecil County, Maryland, just over the border from Chester County, Pennsylvania, and had six children.

In 1789, Bean acquired from Dr. Benjamin Say, a prominent Philadelphia physician, a tract of 3,000 acres located on Licking River north of Lexington, Kentucky. William and Elizabeth and their six children moved to Kentucky, but soon after they arrived, William met an untimely death.

Faced with an uncertain future in an unfamiliar land and the prospect of raising six children by herself, Elizabeth called on her family for assistance. Ever the loyal brother, Montgomery agreed to help his sister. He made the arduous journey over the mountains to Lexington in 1789.[1]

Travel from Pennsylvania to Kentucky at that time was no easy feat. "There were no railroads, no steamboats, no stages, no macadamized roads, and west of the mountains scarcely any roads at all…Kentucky was not yet a state."[2] George Washington had just assumed office as America's first President.

After Montgomery Bell arrived in Lexington, he rented a house and "took his sister and her children to live with him, supported and educated them, and ministered to all their wants, as a kind and indulgent father would have done."[3]

During his years in Kentucky, Bell's business career began in earnest. Using the skills he had learned while serving as an apprentice to his brother, he opened a hat-making business in Lexington. It became "the largest hat shop west of the Alleghenies".[4]

In the latter years of the 18th century, hats were big business. In fact, the hat business was one of the first industries in the newly formed United States. Although Americans imported most of their other apparel from Europe, they wore domestically made hats.[5]

The tricorne cocked hat was the most popular hat worn by men in

A Tricorne hat (Wikipedia)

the 18th century. In the 1790s, the bicorne hat began to replace the tricorne.[6] The tall black polished felt hat was prescribed by Congress in 1810 as the military hat for the American army.[7] In the early years of the 19th century, the high beaver hat was the fashionable headpiece, with a crown of varied shapes.[8]

Beaver fur was the most popular material for making hats.[9] The huge demand for beaver hats caused the fur trade to boom in the 18th and early 19th centuries.[10] The fur of the beaver had little barbs which, when pressed, would lock together and make a solid fabric known as felt.[11]

It may surprise readers to learn that making hats was a hazardous occupation in the 18th and 19th centuries because it involved the use of chemicals, one of which was mercury. Hat-makers added small amounts of mercury nitrate to hot water to cause the animal hairs to pack together more easily.[12] The toxic mercury fumes created health problems for hatters working in poorly ventilated rooms, giving rise to the phrase "mad hatters."[13]

Beaver was not the only fur used to make hats. To keep costs down, hatters sometimes substituted raccoon, otter, muskrat, and other animals for beaver. An inferior grade of felt was also made of wool and vegetable fibers.[14]

In the 18th and early 19th centuries, the process of making a beaver felt hat was a long and complicated process involving about thirty steps, requiring multiple artisans, and taking about seven hours to complete.[15]

Bell employed twenty men in his hat business in Lexington.[16] He placed advertisements in *The Kentucky Gazette*[17] from time to time seeking animal skins with which to make hats. The following ad was placed in the *Gazette* on February 11 and 25 and March 17, 1792:

FURRS
The highest price given for BEAVER,
OTTER, RACOON, FOX, WILD-CAT
and MUSKRAT skins. By MONTGOMERY
BELL, at his Hat Manufactory in Lexington.

On October 19 and November 16, 1793, Bell placed the following ad in
the *Gazette*:

The subscriber has on hand a very
Elegant Assortment of Lady's
And Gentleman's
HATS
Which he is determined to
dispose of on the most reasonable
terms for cash.
He is also wanting an APPRENTICE
to the Hatting business, that can
come well recommended.

Montgomery Bell

On December 20, 1794, Bell placed the following ad in the *Gazette*:

The Highest Price Given for all kinds of
F   U   R   S
By the subscriber at his Hat-Manufactory
in Lexington.

Montgomery Bell

Bell's business career in Kentucky involved more than just hat-making.
He acquired several hundred acres of land, located in Fayette County at the
time he acquired it. Because an 1803 fire at the Fayette County courthouse
destroyed many of the deeds and other records prior to that year, the location
and number of acres of property he purchased is not completely known.[18]
One of his largest purchases was a tract of 1,000 acres located on Stephens

Creek on the north side of the Kentucky River, which he bought in 1800 from Nathaniel Rochester for $4,100.[19]

In 1798, a new county known as Jessamine County[20] was carved out of Fayette County, and much of the land that Bell owned was at that time placed in the new county. He lived on a farm in Jessamine County during part of his time in Kentucky. He built and operated grist mills, lumber mills, and a distillery on his property, with considerable financial success.[21]

In addition to the land in Jessamine County, Bell acquired several lots in the town of Lexington in 1798 and 1799.[22] The 1803 fire at the Fayette County courthouse may have destroyed deeds to other Lexington properties that Bell owned.

He sold three of his Lexington lots in 1800, always for a profit.[23] In 1802, he sold a prime lot on Water Street to George Trotter and Alexander Scott.[24]

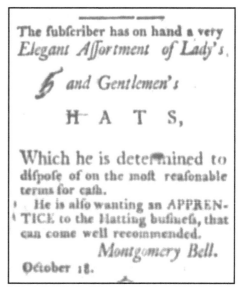

This notice about hats made and sold by Montgomery Bell appeared in the Kentucky Gazette, November 16, 1793.

Center right: Historic marker for Jessamine County, Kentucky. (Author photo)

Bottom right: Map showing Jessamine County, Kentucky (Wikipedia)

Bell placed an advertisement in *The Kentucky Gazette* on December 11, 1801, as he was preparing to move to Tennessee. The ad refers to his holdings in Jessamine County:

TO BE RENTED
ON VERY MODERATE TERMS:

The Farm whereon I live in Jessamine
County, about two and a half miles
from the Court House, and about five
miles from Boler's Ware House, on the
Kentucky river; with fifty acres of Wheat
in the ground. A merchant mill, forty-
five by fifty-five feet, three stories high,
calculated for three pair of stones, and
staves taken out for twelve or fifteen
hundred flour barrels.

Also a saw-mill, with log carriage and
Oxen; a small grist mill, that runs a great
part of the year; and a distillery sixty by
thirty four feet, with stills and boilers for
a house of that size; a black smith's shop
and tools. They will be rented separately
or together, as may suit, for one or
more years. Will likewise be hired, on
the premises, the first day of January next,
for one year, if not hired by private contract
previous to that time, fifteen negroes:
Men, Women, and Boys.

Bond with security will be required. I
will lease a considerable part of the above
tract of land five years, for improvement.

MONTGOMERY BELL

This ad attracted a response from Daniel McViars. On February 8, 1802, Bell leased to McViars "the merchant mill built by said Bell on Hickman Creek, and the houses adjoining on the west side of the creek" for a term of five years at a rental fee of $500 annually. The lease was recorded in Fayette County, even though the property was located in Jessamine County.[25]

The exact date of Bell's move to Tennessee is not known, but on September 19, 1802, Bell gave his Lexington friend Cuthbert Banks a broadly worded Power of Attorney allowing Banks to collect all debts due or which might become due to Bell, as well as giving him full authority to sell and convey, lease and rent, or otherwise dispose of, Bell's real, personal or mixed estate, to receive payment therefor and give discharges, and to do all other related matters. This document was recorded in Fayette County.[26]

Bell disposed of most of his Jessamine County property before completing his move to Tennessee. In July 1803, he sold 150 acres to John Kay,[27] 190.5 acres to Thomas R. Gatewood,[28] and 114 acres to Anthony Samuel.[29] In September 1803, he sold 131 acres to John Jeffreys[30] and 164 acres to Henry Clay.[31] In October 1803, he sold 175 acres to John Jordan, Jr.[32] These tracts were all part of the 1,000 acres he had bought from Nathaniel Rochester in 1800.

After he had moved to Tennessee, he sold the remainder of his Jessamine County property. In August 1804, he sold 174 acres to Hezekiah Harrison[33] and 125 acres to John Jordan, Jr.[34]

In June 1805, he sold his best tract of land in Jessamine County to Morgan Brown, a Tennessean from whom he had just purchased the Yellow Creek Iron Furnace in Montgomery County, Tennessee. The deed stated that this 228.75-acre tract (described as a "valuable tract of land") was "commonly known by the name of Bells Mills" on Hickman Creek. According to the deed, the conveyance to Brown included "the merchant mill, sawmill, tub mill & distillery thereon situated", as well as "all trees, woods, ways, watercourses, profits, commodities, advantages, emoluments, hereditaments and appurtenances whatsoever."[35] This was the property that had been most extensively developed by Bell in Jessamine County.

Morgan Brown sold the property he had acquired from Bell to Robert Crockett in 1816 for $10,000. In 1821, Crockett sold the property for $20,000 to three Lexington investors, who changed the name of the mills to Union Mills – the name by which the area is known today.[36]

❖ ❖ ❖

Of most importance, Bell gave his hat business to his nephew, Patterson Bain, his sister's son.[37] Lexington's first City Directory, showing businesses active in 1806, lists Patterson Bain as one of seven hatters active in the city in that year.[38] (Throughout his career, Bell's nephew used the surname Bain rather than Bean.) The hatters active in Lexington in 1806 were said to "employ upwards of fifty hands and manufacture about $30,000 worth of fur and wool hats annually."[39]

Notices in Lexington newspapers provide evidence that for more than thirty years Bain operated the hat business started by his Uncle Montgomery. In 1807, Bain formed a partnership with Thomas S. Holloway to operate the business. A notice Bain placed in the *Kentucky Gazette and General Advertiser* on June 16, 1807, stated: "Merchants may be supplied with Hats of all kinds on the shortest notice and on a liberal credit." Bain and Holloway added John Steele to their partnership in 1812, according to a March 17, 1812, notice in the *Kentucky Gazette*.

In 1834, Bain entered into a new partnership with William F. Tod, Jr. to run the hat business. Throughout Bain's ownership, the shop remained at the corner of Main and Cross Streets in downtown Lexington – the same location where Montgomery Bell had established it in the 1790s. An ad placed in the *Kentucky Gazette* on May 17, 1834, by Bain and Tod promised "Hats made to order, of any size, form, or quality, both Wholesale & Retail, with Punctuality and Despatch." Patterson Bain clearly had his uncle's flair for colorful rhetoric in advertising!

At the end of 1836, Bain conveyed his interest to his partner Tod, who pledged to "continue the business in all its various branches." Bain and Tod dissolved their partnership in an amicable manner. According to a December 1, 1836, notice in the Louisville *Courier-Journal*, the business had received for sale "Easter Fall and Winter Fashions for Gentlemen's HATS and Ladies' Fur and Satin Beaver BONNETS." This was an upscale hat shop.

Like his uncle in Tennessee, Bain was a leading citizen of Lexington throughout his business career. According to a January 8, 1819, notice in the *Kentucky Gazette*, he was a

A Beaver hat (Wikipedia)

director of the Farmers and Merchants Bank, which he had helped to found in 1818. An April 18, 1827, notice in the *Kentucky Gazette* listed Bain as a member of the Building Committee raising funds for the construction of a medical school building at Transylvania University in Lexington. He operated a tavern known as the Washington Hotel, which he advertised for sale in a November 11, 1829, ad in the *Kentucky Reporter.* He even dabbled in local politics, becoming a candidate for the Lexington City Council, according to a December 21, 1837, notice in the *Kentucky Gazette.*

During his Kentucky years, Montgomery Bell "rubbed shoulders" with the most prominent citizens of Lexington. Cuthbert Banks, to whom Bell gave his Power of Attorney, was a prominent businessman who had been commissioned as a Notary Public in 1798.[40] In 1800, he became involved in the iron business.[41] In 1802 he helped to establish the Kentucky Insurance Company to "insure shipping on board boats plying the western waters."[42] This company was extremely successful and expanded into the banking field.[43]

Banks also operated the Eagle Tavern[44] and an inn known as Traveler's Hall, which hosted a reception for William Clark, of Lewis and Clark fame, during Clark's 1809 visit to Lexington.[45] Banks was elected Secretary of the Jockey Club in 1797 and Master of the Masonic Lodge in 1802.[46] Like his friend Montgomery Bell, Banks had his fingers in a lot of pies.

Not surprisingly, Bell crossed paths repeatedly with Kentucky's most prominent citizen, Henry Clay. Clay's purchase of 164 acres from Bell in 1803 was more than a simple land transaction. Clay paid $1,000 for the property, but he also entered into a written agreement with Bell by which Clay "delivered to the said Bell one horse and mare" and covenanted to pay, on Bell's behalf, $100 to John Jordan, Jr. and $500 to Rice Jones (to satisfy a judgment that Clay the attorney had obtained against Bell on behalf of his client Jones, the Attorney General of the Indiana Territory).[47] In 1803, Clay the attorney also obtained judgments against Bell for three clients for unpaid debts.[48]

The published Papers of Henry Clay include the text of an August 1804 letter from Bell, sent to Clay from Cumberland Furnace, Tennessee. Bell told Clay that he had "made a purchase of a most valuable tract of land" since his arrival in Tennessee, referring to the Cumberland Iron Furnace property that he had purchased from James Robertson in June 1804. In the letter, Bell authorized Clay to represent him in settling his "business" with the Estate of

George Nicholas (the man for whom the county seat of Jessamine County is named). Amusingly, Bell also encouraged Clay to sell Bell's Jessamine County mills in exchange for 27,000 gallons of whiskey "delivered in good barrels at Bolers warehouse, if a sale of that kind can be affected by you."[49]

Clay the businessman later recovered a judgment of $750 against Bell on a note on which Bell had served as a surety. This case went twice to the Kentucky Court of Appeals before the final ruling against Bell was handed down by the appellate court, so it appears that relations between the two men had soured.[50]

Montgomery Bell's interest in funding the creation of educational institutions began in Kentucky. In 1799, he and several other wealthy landowners in Jessamine and Fayette Counties donated money for the establishment of Transylvania University, thereby creating the first law school and the first medical school in what was then the American West.[51]

The most fascinating endeavor undertaken by Montgomery Bell during his Kentucky years was a collaboration with a man named James W. Stevens to establish a "Young Ladies' Academy" for the education of girls. Perhaps he was concerned that the female children of his sister get a proper education. The details of their project were presented to the public in the following advertisement published in *The Kentucky Gazette* on February 21 and March 14, 1798:

YOUNG LADIES' ACADEMY

**In conformity to the wishes and
solicitations of several gentlemen of
respectability, the subscriber proposes
to establish an institution in Lexington,
called the YOUNG LADIES' ACADEMY,
for the purpose of conferring
the degrees of a classical education;
wherein will be accurately taught
Orthography, Reading, Writing,
Arithmetic, English Grammar,
Geography, Composition, and other branches
of useful and ornamental literature.**

The subscriber conceives that any
eulogium upon the importance and
utility of female education would be to
arraign the discernment of the public
who are competent judges of the
incalculable benefits resulting from an
institution of this nature, when conducted
upon proper principles; being intended
as well to inculcate the important
precepts of virtue, and science as
to prevent an indiscriminate intercourse
of the sexes so injurious to the morals,
and incompatible with the delicacy
of the fair.

The subscriber can produce
unexceptionable testimonials of integrity,
and he trusts his unremitted exertions
to do ample justice to his pupils,
will render unequivocal satisfaction to
those Ladies and Gentlemen who shall
deign to patronize the institution.

Future intimation will be given of
the time and place of opening the
Academy.

The price of tuition will be ten dollars
per annum to be paid quarterly.

Application to be made to Mr.
Montgomery Bell.

JAMES W. STEVENS

Further research has not revealed whether the Young Ladies' Academy
came to fruition, but it is an early indication of Montgomery Bell's interest

YOUNG LADIES' ACADEMY.

IN conformity to the wishes and solicitations of several gentleman of respectability, the subscriber proposes to establish an institution in Lexington, called the YOUNG LADIES ACADEMY, for the purpose of conferring the degrees of a classical education ;— wherein will be accurately taught, Orthography, Reading, Writing, Arithmetic, English Grammar, Geography, Composition, and other branches of useful and ornamental literature.

The subscriber conceives that any eulogium upon the importance and utility of female education, would be to arraign the discernment of the public who are competent judges of the incalculable benefits resulting from an institution of this nature, when conducted upon proper principles ; being intended as well to inculcate the important precepts of virtue, and science as to prevent an indiscriminate intercourse of the sexes so injurious to the morals, and incompatible with the delicacy of the *fair.*

The subscriber can produce unexceptionable testimonials of integrity, and he trusts his unremitted exertions to do ample justice to his pupils, will render unequivocal satisfaction to those Ladies and Gentlemen who shall deign to patronize the institution.

Future intimation will be given of the time and place of opening the Academy.

The price of tuition will be ten dollars *per annum* to be paid quarterly.

Application to be made to mr. Montgomery Bell.

*31f   **JAMES W. STEVENS.**

Article advertising Montgomery Bell's Young Ladies' Academy from the March 14, 1798 edition of Kentucky Gazette.

in supporting an educational institution and his belief that girls were entitled to a proper education, as later demonstrated by his decision to send his daughter Evelina to the Nashville Female Academy.

His nephew, Patterson Bain, had the same commitment to female education. In 1835, Bain was involved in a group of Lexington citizens proposing the opening of "a permanent institution for the education of Young Ladies," according to a July 18, 1835, notice in the *Kentucky Gazette.* Almost forty years after Montgomery Bell sought to create a school to educate young women, his nephew sought to do the same.

The ties of the Bell family to Kentucky were extensive. At the time of their deaths, four of Montgomery's nine siblings were living in Kentucky. William was living in Montgomery County when he died in 1807. Elizabeth and Jane were living in Fayette County at the time of their respective deaths in 1809 and 1818. John was living in Jefferson County when he died in 1831.

CHAPTER SIX

Iron

No biography of Montgomery Bell would be complete without a thorough discussion of iron. After all, Bell made his fortune by building and operating iron furnaces and forges in which iron ore was refined and made into many useful objects.

The Importance of Iron

Iron has been called "the common man's gold."[1] It is the most important and most prevalent of all metals and the fourth most abundant element, by mass, in the Earth's crust (behind oxygen, silicon, and aluminum). It is the 26th element in the Periodic Table.[2]

Approximately five percent of the Earth's crust is iron. The atomic symbol for iron is **Fe,** derived from the Latin word "ferrum," meaning "firmness." The word "iron" has always been a symbol of strength.

Iron is essential for all forms of life. Human beings use iron to make hemoglobin, a protein in red blood cells that carries oxygen from the lungs to all parts of the body, and to make myoglobin, a protein that provides oxygen to muscles. Humans need 8-18 milligrams of iron every day. Most people get all the iron they need by eating a balanced diet. A lack of iron causes anemia to develop. Iron is also an important component of chlorophyll in plants.[3]

Iron is a shiny, greyish metal that rusts easily in damp air. It is never found in its pure state, but always exists in combination with other elements such as sulfur, phosphorus, manganese, and silica.[4] To be used commercially, iron must be separated from these impurities. The most common iron-containing ore is hematite, but iron is also found in magnetite, taconite, and other ores.[5]

The importance of iron to the development of the United States in the 18th and 19th centuries cannot be exaggerated. Molten iron could be cast into almost any form. Well-made iron tools lasted for many years. The rise of factories and the advent of railroads required an enormous amount of iron, which savvy entrepreneurs like Montgomery Bell were only too happy to supply.[6]

Today, iron is commercially produced in a blast furnace by heating hematite or magnetite ore with coke (a form of coal) and limestone to form pig iron, which is then used to make steel. About 1.3 billion tons of crude steel are produced worldwide each year.[7]

A History of Iron

Iron has been utilized by humans for at least 4,000 years and is frequently mentioned in the Bible. The use of iron was common in Asia and northern Africa as far back as 1500 B.C.E. The Hittites of Asia Minor (today's Turkey) were the first to smelt iron from its ores.[8]

We know from the poems of Homer that iron was used by the Greeks. Iron is frequently mentioned in the early history of Rome, where it was used for tools, agricultural implements, and weapons of war.[9]

During the first Millennium, the country that dominated the iron industry was Spain. Iron was so prominent in that country that Spanish ironworkers were sought by other countries, and Spain's dominance continued until the closing years of the 17th century. Eventually, Germany and Great Britain surpassed Spain in the quantity of iron manufactured because these two countries adopted more effective manufacturing methods.[10]

The manufacture of iron products in Britain began at the beginning of the first Millennium, during the Roman occupation. In the 15th and 16th centuries, the manufacture of iron in Britain was greatly improved, due largely to the introduction of blast furnace technology.[11]

Blast furnace technology was dependent on the use of charcoal for fuel, however, and eventually Britain began to experience a shortage of timber used to make charcoal. By the middle of the 18th century, coke began to be used as fuel in blast furnaces rather than charcoal. By the end of the 18th century, charcoal furnaces had been largely replaced in Britain by furnaces that used coke.[12]

Throughout the 19th century, Britain led the world in the manufacture of iron. It replaced Spain in the top spot.[13]

Iron in the New World

The Native Americans who first inhabited North America were not acquainted with the use of iron. They used stone, rather than metal to make their tools.[14]

The Europeans who settled the New World brought iron technology with them to North America.

The first permanent English colony was established at Jamestown in 1607. The next year, a ship returned from Virginia to London carrying, among other goods, iron ore from which was smelted seventeen tons of metal. This was the first iron made by Europeans from American iron ore.[15]

In 1619, the Virginia Company of London sent a number of skilled iron-workers to Virginia to build "iron works" on Falling Creek, a tributary of the James River, near Richmond. Unfortunately, these workers were slain during an Indian massacre in 1622, and the iron works were destroyed and never re-built. Thus, the first attempt to make iron in America failed.[16]

The next effort to establish iron works in the Colonies was near Lynn, Massachusetts. Eleven "English gentlemen" advanced 1,000 pounds to establish an iron foundry on the west bank of the Saugus River in 1643. The Saugus Iron Works ceased producing iron in 1668,[17] but was successfully reconstructed in the 20th century and is now a National Historic Site open to the public (*www.nps.gov/sair*).

The success of the Saugus facility led to the establishment of a second iron furnace and forge at Braintree, Massachusetts, ten miles from Boston. Other iron enterprises quickly followed, and Massachusetts became the chief seat of iron manufacture in America in the 17th century.[18]

In Pennsylvania, the manufacture of iron began in 1692 during the time of William Penn. The first iron forge was located on Manatawny Creek, about three miles from Pottstown. The next iron enterprise in Pennsylvania was Coventry Forge on French Creek in northern Chester County – the county where Montgomery Bell was later born. The Coventry Forge was very successful and continued making iron for more than a century and a half, until 1870.[19]

The rapid development of the iron industry in America created an adverse reaction in Great Britain, which quickly came to view the Colonies as a competitor in the iron business. To protect its own manufacturing facilities, the British Parliament passed laws in 1750 that restricted the Colonies to making only pig iron and bar iron, which had to be shipped to England. Finished iron products sold in America had to bear the words "Made in England." These laws were honored more in the breach than in the observance, and they helped foster the Americans' desire for independence from Britain.[20]

By the beginning of the Revolution, Pennsylvania had replaced Massachusetts as the colony with the most iron works. By 1800, there were more than one hundred iron facilities in Pennsylvania. The three counties with the most facilities were Chester, Lancaster, and Berks.[21] Montgomery Bell undoubtedly became familiar with the iron industry during his childhood in Chester County.

Many Pennsylvania furnaces and forges are historically significant. The celebrated Franklin stove, invented by Benjamin Franklin in 1742, was manufactured in large quantities at the Warwick Furnace on French Creek in Chester County. The Warwick Furnace operated continuously from 1738 through 1867.[22]

The most successful iron manufacturer in Pennsylvania in the first half of the 18th century was Thomas Potts, whose family dominated the iron industry in that state for many years.[23] One of Thomas' sons was John Potts, for whom the Borough of Pottstown[24] was named after he had laid it out in 1752. (Pottstown is the childhood hometown of Beth Halteman Harwell, who moved to Nashville, Tennessee in the 1970s to attend college and later entered politics. She served thirty years in the Tennessee House of Representatives, where she was the first female Speaker of the Tennessee House. She has also served on the Board of Trustees of Montgomery Bell Academy, where her sons attended school.)

A third generation of the Potts family was historically significant during the 18th century. John Potts' son, Joseph, owned an iron forge on Valley Creek known as Valley Forge (also known as Mount Joy Forge). This facility was burned by the British in September 1777, during the early stages of the Revolution.[25]

Isaac Potts, another son of John Potts, owned a stone house on the other side of Valley Creek from the forge. Isaac's house was used by General George Washington as his headquarters during the winter of 1777-1778, when the Continental Army was encamped for six months in the community known as Valley Forge.[26]

Another important iron facility in Pennsylvania was the Cornwall Iron Furnace in Lebanon County, built by Peter Grubb in

Isaac Potts house in Valley Forge National Historic Park. (Author photo)

1742 and operated until 1883. This furnace cast cannon, shot, and shells for the Continental Army during the Revolutionary War. An iron ore mine just south of the furnace continued to operate until 1973.[27] The Cornwall Furnace is now a National Historical Landmark and a state historic site

Cornwall Furnace marker (Author photo)

and is open to the public as the best remaining example of a charcoal-burning iron furnace still standing in its entirety (*www.cornwallironfurnace.org*).

The Hopewell Furnace in Berks County has also been preserved and is open to the public as a National Historic Site (*www.nps.gov/hafu*). Built by Mark Bird in 1771, the Hopewell Furnace produced iron until its final closure in 1883.[28] It was sold to the federal government in 1935 and stabilized by the Civilian Conservation Corps during the Great Depression. It is managed by the National Park Service.

The top of the Hopewell furnace pit. (Author photo)

The bottom of Hopewell furnace pit. (Author photo)

Caledonia Forge, located about ten miles from Chambersburg in Franklin County, was owned by Radical Republican Congressman Thaddeus Stevens. His furnace and forge were burned in 1863 by the Confederate army as they marched toward Gettysburg.[29]

Pennsylvania's prominence in the iron industry in the 18th and 19th centuries was surely an important factor in Montgomery Bell's decision to make iron his life's work. By the time he made that decision, "iron had become America's first heavy industry."[30]

Operation of Iron Furnaces and Forges in 19th Century America

Montgomery Bell moved to Tennessee at the beginning of the 19th century. For a man who had decided to enter the iron business, he was in the right place at the right time.

Three raw materials were needed to operate an iron furnace in the United States in the 19th century: iron ore, timber to make charcoal, and limestone. Tennessee had all three in abundance.

Charcoal

By the beginning of the 19th century, Britain had moved away from charcoal as a source of fuel for its iron furnaces due to a diminishing supply of timber to make the charcoal. But in America virgin forests were limitless, especially in a largely unsettled state like Tennessee. So charcoal was the fuel of choice for making iron during the first half of the 19th century.[31]

21st century Americans think of charcoal briquettes as the fuel used to fire their grills, and they go to Target or Walmart to buy bags of charcoal. For 19th century Americans, there was no such ready supply of charcoal. They had to make it from scratch.

A charcoal blast furnace consumed from 150 to 1,500 acres of timber per 1,000 tons of iron produced, depending on the efficiency of the furnace and the quality of the charcoal.[32] Vast tracts of woodland were needed close to the furnace.[33]

Various types of wood were used to make charcoal, including hickory, oak, beech, walnut, ash, chestnut, elm, and pine. The quality of the wood determined the quality of the charcoal.[34]

Woodchoppers felled the trees with axes and bundled them into "cords." An acre of timber yielded from thirty to forty cords. Each cord measured eight feet by four feet by four feet, and yielded about forty bushels of charcoal. These cords of wood were hauled to dry, level sites and stacked.[35]

The men who made the charcoal from this wood were called "colliers." They created a level circular spot from thirty to fifty feet in diameter, known as the pit or hearth. They formed a circle of sticks in the center of the hearth to compose the "chimney," which was six to eight feet tall. Around the chimney the cords of wood were arranged to form a cone about twenty-five feet in diameter at the base.[36] It looked like an Indian wigwam.

After the cone was built, a layer of damp leaves and loose earth was placed on the pile. Wood chips, dry leaves, and other flammable material were placed into the chimney and lighted from the top. Holes were drilled in the sides to draw air. The smoking pile of wood being charred gave off a dark heavy smoke with a disagreeable odor.[37]

After the pile was lit, it had to be watched carefully to ensure that the entire pile did not go up in flames. This process produced just enough heat to drive out all the water, tar, and other substances from the wood, leaving behind nearly pure carbon. It took from ten to fourteen days to char the entire pile.[38]

The charcoal burners lived in huts close to the pile so they could watch the charring pile day and night. Their homes were crude pole huts, about ten feet high and eight feet wide, with a door, a wood stove, and a log bunk. They lived like hermits.[39]

After the pile was completely charred, the colliers raked the charcoal into small piles, so that the whole mass would not be ignited through spontaneous combustion. After the small piles had cooled, the charcoal was then hauled by "teamsters" in wagons to a thick-walled stone charcoal house where it was stored, sometimes for extended periods, until used in the furnace.[40]

The charcoal made through this process burned in the blast furnace at a temperature between 2,650 and 3,200 degrees Fahrenheit, hot enough to melt the iron ore.[41] The amount of charcoal consumed by the furnaces was enormous. Every ton of iron that was produced required more than 400 bushels of charcoal. Every day that a blast furnace was in operation, an acre of trees in the form of charcoal was consumed.[42]

Iron Ore

The supply of iron ore available to Montgomery Bell was plentiful in the areas he selected for his furnaces. One historian has described the iron ore mined by Bell in the following manner:

Typical hut in which colliers lived. (Author photo)

54

A wgaon in which charcoal was hauled to the cooling shed. (Author photo)

The ore in Dickson County does not occur in stratified beds, but rather in irregular shaped masses of loose particles near the surface. The particles vary from shot-size to boulders ten to fifteen feet in diameter. These ore banks were usually found to occupy a high position, being located on the borders or near the crests and spurs of the plateau-ridges; they tended to adapt to the upper hill slopes, lying in a horizontal position. Other deposits occurred toward the level of valleys, but these low-lying deposits were found to be inferior, having a substantial thickness of chert between the ore and underlying rocks. The existence of good ore was often indicated by the presence of a fine gravel or "shot ore" scattered over the surface and embedded in the subsoil. Ledges of chert-gravel cemented by brown iron oxide were found on the hillsides, but these masses were no richer in content than the low-lying deposits. The iron ore found in the area was usually covered with soil, clay, gravel, sand, and other foreign matter which had to be removed before mining began.[43]

The ore was scraped from the beds using bars and pick-axes. In effect, the ore was quarried rather than mined.[44]

Before going into the blast furnace, the ore "had to be as free from foreign matter as possible. This was accomplished by the washer."[45] A washer was "a large perforated iron cylinder where water was sprayed on the mass of iron as the cylinder revolved," washing away the clay and other impurities.

Brown hematite ore containing approximately sixty percent iron was the primary ore used in Bell's furnaces.[46] For every ton of iron produced, two tons of ore were needed.[47]

Limestone

Limestone was used as a "flux" to remove impurities from the iron ore, both chemically and by physically sticking to the dirt and stones in the ore. The principal impurities in the ore were clay, chert, sand, and gravel.[48] Limestone was especially good as a flux because of "its affinity to combine with sand and clay forming a molten slag."[49]

Approximately thirty to forty pounds of limestone were fed into the furnace for every 400 to 500 pounds of iron ore and fifteen bushels of charcoal.[50] When the limestone combined with the impurities in the iron ore, the resulting product was called "slag."[51]

Along with iron ore and trees to make charcoal, beds of limestone were readily available in Tennessee. Like the iron ore, limestone was easily quarried.[52]

Blast Furnaces

Bell operated several "blast furnaces." A blast furnace was used to separate the iron from the ore by forcing a blast of air under pressure from a water-powered bellows or "blowing tub" into the mix of ore, charcoal, and limestone. The process produced liquid iron and slag.[53]

The blast furnace was usually built into the side of a small hill so that the ore, charcoal, and limestone could be placed into the "stack" through a door at the top of the stack. Such furnaces were known as "hillside furnaces" because "the wagons loaded with ore, limestone, and charcoal could be unloaded directly into the furnace, thus solving the problem of elevation to the top of the stacks."[54]

The bottle-shaped stack was approximately twenty-five to thirty feet high. It was narrow at the top, about two feet wide. In the middle, the stack widened to about nine feet in an area called the "bosh." It narrowed again to about three feet in the area known as the "crucible." At the bottom of the stack was the "casting bed" where the molten iron from the hearth ran into sand molds.[55]

There was a wooden bridge at the top of the furnace which the "fillers" continually crossed bearing their baskets loaded with iron ore, charcoal, and limestone to feed the furnace. Alternate layers of ore, charcoal, and limestone were fed continuously into the stack. 800 pounds of iron ore, eighty pounds of limestone, and twenty bushels of charcoal constituted the proper mix of these ingredients.[56] This process was called "charging" the furnace. The person who oversaw these activities was called the "founder.[57]

On one side of the furnace at the bottom was a small aperture in which was inserted a "tuyere" (i.e., blower pipe) through which air

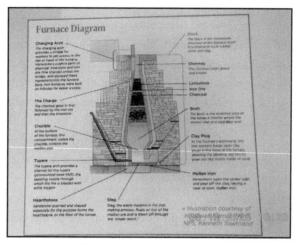

Iron Furnace diagram prepared by Kenneth Townsend of the National Park Service, courtesy of the Catoctin Furnace Museum.

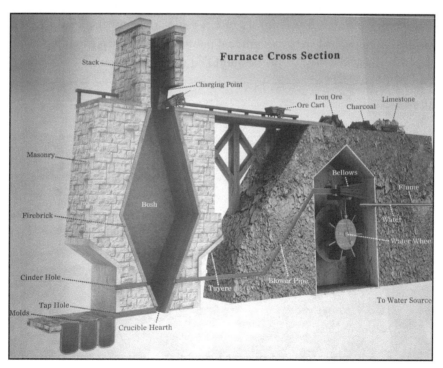

Furnace cross-section, courtesy of the Clement Railroad Hotel Museum.

was injected into the furnace. The blower pipe was connected to the large water-driven bellows or tubs which furnished the blast.[58]

The large double bellows were made of wood and leather and were driven by huge water wheels. The bellows measured twenty to twenty-five feet in length and several feet in width. The air was conveyed to the hearth through the tuyere. The bellows were eventually replaced by closed blowing tubs, also powered by water wheels, which provided a more uniform blast than the bellows.[59]

The ore melted when it reached the level of the tuyere and dropped to the hearth below. The slag which floated on top of the molten iron was the result of the action of the limestone flux on the impurities in the iron ore and was drawn off from time to time. The molten iron was removed from the hearth twice a day and allowed to run into the casting bed of sand through a process called "tapping." The persons who oversaw this activity were called "gutter-men." Each tapping produced about one to one-and-a-half tons of pig iron.[60] The slag was drained into a container lined with bricks called a "hot pot."[61]

The main channel running from the crucible at the bottom of the furnace into the casting bed was called the "sow." The side gutters were called "pigs."[62] Thus the term "pig iron," which consisted of long narrow pieces of crude iron that were five to ten feet long, six inches wide, and four inches thick and weighed from thirty-five to one hundred pounds each.[63] The pig iron produced at a blast furnace was quite brittle and filled with impurities.

Waterwheel used to power the Hopewell furnace. (Author photo)

In addition to using the molten iron to make pig iron, the molten iron was sometimes delivered into large ladles, then poured into smaller ladles, and finally into molds for casting. Thus the term "cast iron." The molds allowed the molten iron to be shaped into pots, pans, skillets, kettles, Dutch ovens, and stove plates.[64]

Iron Kettle from the 1800s. (Wikipedia)

The workers who ran the furnace included "founders" (in charge of the overall smelting process), "keepers" (in charge around the bottom of the furnace), "fillers" (who filled the stack with ore, charcoal, and limestone), "potters" or "molders" (who made the ironware), and a few other laborers. The founders and the molders were considered *skilled* workmen. All these laborers worked in two 12-hour shifts.[65]

Refinery Forges

The rough pig iron bars created at a furnace were taken to a refinery forge, where they were re-heated to soften them and burn off the carbon before they were placed under weighty trip hammers driven by a water wheel to hammer out the impurities. The pig iron was converted into "wrought iron" at the forge. The wrought iron bars thus created were called "anconies" and were usually re-heated at the forge and hammered again into long iron bars of varying length and width. These finished bars were then sold to blacksmiths, locksmiths, coopers, wheelwrights, millwrights, and others to be made into finished products.[66]

The forge hammers were massive pieces of cast iron weighing several hundred pounds and mounted on oak beams. The water wheels which furnished the power to drive the hammers measured twenty-five feet in diameter. Even larger water wheels provided power for the bellows or blowing tubs that furnished the blast for the fires at the forge's hearth. Operation of the hammers required both skill and strength.[67]

The bar iron produced at the forges was then shaped into finished products by blacksmiths who created axes, saws, hoes, shovels, knives, hooks, chains, scythes, wagon wheels, gates, horseshoes, and other articles essential to agriculture and other facets of daily life in frontier Tennessee.[68]

Stamping Mills

Recycling and reuse were an important part of the iron industry at that time. The cinders and slag from the furnace were taken to "stamping mills," which recovered as much iron as possible for re-use in the furnaces.[69]

Slitting Mills

At "rolling and slitting mills," wrought iron was prepared for making nails of all sizes. The iron bars from the forge were cut into strips by water-powered shears. The strips were divided into rods called "slit iron," which was used to make nails at the mill or sold to blacksmiths or even farmers who made the nails themselves.[70] Making nails was an important part of the daily operations at Thomas Jefferson's Monticello[71] and other Southern plantations.

Transportation

Once the iron bars were created at the forges, they had to be transported to persons who would turn them into finished products. Pack horses and wagons carried the iron bars over the mountains. They were sent downriver on boats where possible.[72] Not until the middle of the 19th century were railroads readily available as a means of transportation.

Iron Communities

Iron communities, often known as iron plantations, sprang up near the furnaces and forges. There were few material comforts. Life was cheerless for those who toiled long and hard in hazardous working conditions to produce the iron that was rapidly becoming essential to life in the early years of the 19th century.[73]

The American frontier was not a hospitable environment for immigrant workers and their families.[74] They tended to stay in the cities. Because the production of iron required large numbers of workers, the use of enslaved persons and indentured servants was common in Tennessee and other states, both Northern and Southern, in the 19th century.[75]

For enslaved workers at Montgomery Bell's furnaces and forges, the work was hard, but it gave them an opportunity to develop skills that some of them were able to put to good use after they were emancipated by Montgomery Bell or after the end of the Civil War.

CHAPTER SEVEN

Dickson County, Tennessee

From the time Montgomery Bell moved to Tennessee at the beginning of the 19th century, he lived in and near Dickson County. In fact, he helped to create the county.

Tennessee Before Statehood

In the 1760s, the first settlers moved to what is now eastern Tennessee.[1] At that time, the area was part of the North Carolina colony.[2]

By 1779, James Robertson and a few of these early settlers were ready to move further west. Described by one historian as a "latter-day Moses," Robertson led a party of approximately one hundred men through the Cumberland Gap along the Wilderness Trail that had been blazed by Daniel Boone. They reached the area that is now Nashville on Christmas Day 1779.[3]

John Donelson, whose daughter Rachel would later marry Andrew Jackson, assembled a flotilla of riverboats to transport the families of the men who had gone with Robertson. After navigating the Holston, Clinch, Tennessee, Ohio, and Cumberland Rivers, this second group reached Nashville on April 24, 1780.[4]

The leaders of this new settlement drew up the Cumberland Compact to govern the settlement. The 256 signers of the Compact included in it a Statement of Principles, created a militia composed of all men above the age of

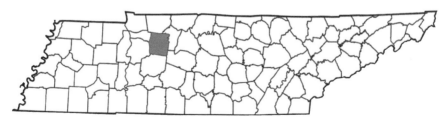

Map showing Dickson County, Tennessee. (Wikipedia)

sixteen, and set up a tribunal of twelve "notables" to administer the functions of the new government.[5]

During the years 1780 through 1783, the Cumberland settlements were under constant attack by Indians, who resented the settlers' intrusion into lands they had occupied for hundreds of years. The settlers needed help, so they petitioned North Carolina for official recognition and protection.[6] By then the Revolutionary War had ended and the colony of North Carolina was now a state.

The North Carolina general assembly responded by making the entire Cumberland country into a single county – Davidson County.[7] Magistrates were appointed to perform the duties of a typical North Carolina county court – a body that had legislative, executive, and judicial powers. This body elected James Robertson and Anthony Bledsoe to represent Davidson County in the North Carolina general assembly.[8]

In addition to creating Davidson County, North Carolina designated a Military Reservation within the area of the Cumberland settlements, for the benefit of North Carolina soldiers who had fought in the American Revolution and been paid with land warrants. These land warrants could be traded freely, thereby opening the Cumberland settlements to land speculation. Many soldiers elected to stay east of the Appalachian Mountains but sold their warrants to men who wanted to move to the Cumberland settlements.[9]

Settlers poured into Davidson County. In 1786, the North Carolina general assembly subdivided Davidson County, creating Sumner County from the northern portion of Davidson County. In 1788, Tennessee County was created from portions of Davidson and Sumner Counties. For the purpose of holding courts of law and equity, these three counties were combined into a district known as the Mero District.[10]

In 1787, the thirteen states that had defeated the British in the Revolution were operating under the Articles of Confederation that had been adopted in 1777. After the new Constitution was drafted in Philadelphia during the summer of 1787, it was sent to all the states for ratification.

North Carolina was slow in ratifying the Constitution, but finally did so on November 21, 1789. One of the first actions the North Carolina general assembly took after joining the United States of America was to cede all its lands west of the Appalachian Mountains to the new federal government in December 1789.[11] The fate of what is now Tennessee was thereby placed in the hands of the newly elected First Congress of the United States.

The cession legislation approved by the North Carolina general assembly protected the rights of property owners and claimants to the lands being ceded to the federal government. The legislation also provided that Congress could not ban slavery in the ceded territory.

Congress acted quickly to accept the ceded territory. On April 2, 1790, President George Washington signed the bill accepting the cession. On May 26, 1790, President Washington signed a second bill creating "the Territory of the United States South of the River Ohio." This territory included the entire 43,000 square miles that would in 1796 become the State of Tennessee.[12] From 1790 to 1796, it was commonly referred to as the Southwest Territory.

Southwest Territory

The 1790 act provided that the inhabitants of the Southwest Territory would enjoy all the privileges and benefits that had been set forth in the Ordinance of 1787 creating "the Territory Northwest of the River Ohio."[13]

President Washington appointed William Blount to be the governor of the Southwest Territory.[14] Governor Blount organized four existing counties (Washington, Sullivan, Greene, and Hawkins) into the Washington District – the eastern part of the Southwest Territory. He organized three existing counties (Davidson, Sumner, and Tennessee) into the Mero District – the western part of the Southwest Territory. He appointed numerous officials to serve these two Districts.[15]

The first census of the Southwest Territory taken in 1791 showed 28,649 residents in the Washington District and 7,042 residents in the Mero District.[16] These residents cleared land and built homes. They opened retail establishments, inns, and taverns. They established cities and towns.

One historian observed that "the most ambitious undertaking was the ironworks." He noted that "the most extensive [iron facility], belonging to Virginia businessman David Ross…[was] set up near the west end of the Long Island of Holston between the North Fork and Reedy Creek." He also mentioned "Nicholas Tate Perkins' ironworks near Bull's Gap in Greene County and James King's ironworks in Sullivan County."[17] These early ironworks were all located in east Tennessee.

Largely because of the unrelenting Indian attacks during the existence of the Southwest Territory, Governor Blount and the Territorial general assembly[18] decided to seek statehood. They would be the first *territory* to propose statehood under the terms of the Northwest Ordinance of 1787 (which governed the Southwest Territory).[19] It was a bold move, since there was no precedent for such an action.

The Northwest Ordinance specified that there must be at least 60,000 inhabitants in a territory before it could seek statehood. By 1795, there were 77,263 inhabitants in the Southwest Territory.[20] Thus, it was eligible for statehood.

In January 1796, five representatives from each of the by-then eleven counties in the Southwest Territory met in Knoxville to write a constitution for the proposed new state. It didn't take long. The delegates finished writing the constitution in less than a month and approved it unanimously on February 6, 1796.[21] Because they chose the name Tennessee[22] for their new state, they divided Tennessee County into two counties, to be named Robertson and Montgomery.[23]

The next step was to submit to Congress their newly drawn state constitution and their request to be admitted to the Union. On June 1, 1796, President Washington signed the act admitting Tennessee as the 16th state.

John Sevier was elected Tennessee's first governor, and Andrew Jackson was elected its first Congressman. Under the U.S. Constitution, the newly elected Tennessee General Assembly had the responsibility of appointing the state's two U.S. Senators. They chose William Blount and William Cocke.[24]

Creation of Dickson County

At the time Tennessee achieved statehood, there were only four counties in Middle Tennessee – Davidson, Sumner, Robertson, and Montgomery. Soon thereafter, several additional counties were carved out of these original counties – Smith, Wilson, and Williamson in 1799, Jackson in 1801, and Rutherford and Stewart in 1803.

When the Tennessee General Assembly convened in 1803, they considered a petition filed by 257 residents of Robertson and Montgomery Counties asking the legislature to create another new county. The proposed boundaries of the new county were Montgomery County on the north, Davidson and Williamson Counties on the east, Stewart County on the west, and the Territory of Alabama on the south. This would be a very large county.

On October 25, 1803, the legislature adopted legislation creating Dickson County.[25] The county was named for William Dickson, a young Nashville physician who was serving in Congress at the time. Ironically, Dickson never lived in the county which bears his name.[26]

The first members of the Dickson County Court of Pleas and Quarter

Sessions (its legislative body) met on March 19, 1804, at the home of Robert Nesbitt on Bartons Creek (the creek near which the Cumberland Furnace was located). Montgomery Bell was one of ten men that constituted the initial Dickson County Court. During their two-day session, they appointed all the county officials.[27]

3E 9

ROBERT NESBIT

The former home of this pioneer is 0.2 miles north. Here, March 18, 1804, the first County Court of Dickson County met with Lemuel Harvey presiding. Other members were Montgomery Bell, Richard Napier, Jesse Craft, William Doak, William Teas, Gabriel Allen, William Russell and Sterling Brewer, with David Dickson, clerk.

Later that year, the Tennessee General Assembly approved legislation naming five men as Commissioners empowered to purchase forty acres on which to lay out a town that would be

Historic marker for the Robert Nesbitt home. (Author photo)

the county seat of Dickson County and would be named Charlotte, after the wife of James Robertson, the man who had built Cumberland Furnace in northern Dickson County. This law specified that two of the forty acres would be a public square on which would be a courthouse and a jail.[28]

Montgomery Bell, a newcomer to Tennessee, must have made a favorable impression on the leaders of the Tennessee legislature and of Dickson County because he was one of the five men designated by the legislature to perform this critical task of finding a proper location for the new county seat.[29] Their task was made easy when a large landowner named Charles Stewart agreed to sell fifty acres for the county seat.[30] The Commissioners of the new Town of Charlotte paid Stewart "Five Thousand Silver Dollars" for the fifty acres.[31]

The General Assembly imposed one more responsibility on Montgomery Bell with respect to the new county. During the first decade of the 19th century, the legislature established "academies" (i.e., schools) in each of the state's existing counties. The General Assembly passed legislation appointing Bell and four other Dickson County residents to serve as Trustees of Tracy Academy in Dickson County.[32] In essence, Bell was a member of the initial Dickson County Board of Education.

The first post office opened in the new county seat in 1806 after the completion of a mail road from Nashville to Charlotte. The Nashville sections of this early road are still referred to as Charlotte Pike. Prior to the Civil War, roads running west toward Memphis and Clarksville went through Charlotte, which "became one of the busiest county seats in Middle Tennessee," according to one historian.[33]

Montgomery Bell lived and worked primarily in or near Dickson County during the first half of the 19th century. During that half century, the population of the county almost doubled, from 4,500 to 8,500. About 25% of the population were enslaved persons.[34]

Like most residents of Tennessee during that time period, the majority of Dickson Countians were farmers. Many raised corn, wheat, hemp, flax, cotton, and vegetables, but the principal *cash* crop was tobacco.[35] Many raised horses, mules, oxen, sheep, and swine, as well as turkeys and chickens.[36]

Iron was the principal *industry* in Dickson County between 1800 and 1850. Dickson County was the center of Tennessee's Western Iron Belt, which was "an area fifty miles wide, running north to south through the state"

Map of Highland Rim (U.S. Geological Survey Bulletin 795-D, 1927)

and comprising "an

area of 5,400 square miles lying between the Central Basin and the Tennessee River.[37] The Iron Belt included all or part of thirteen Tennessee counties.[38]

When James Robertson discovered iron ore in the area that would become Dickson County, "the area was a dense forest from which the Indian war cry could still be heard."[39] Despite the area being wilderness, it had "an inexhaustible supply of iron ore" and "the combination of limestone, water power, and timber for charcoal which were the other essentials for the iron industry."[40] "[T]he demand for iron products on the frontier was tremendous."[41] "[T]he frontiersman…could not possibly survive without agricultural implements, a gun, cooking utensils, horse-shoes, and horse-shoe nails."[42]

For fifty years Montgomery Bell was considered the most prominent of Dickson County's ironmasters. As one historian said: "He was the first to utilize Tennessee's streams for water power, and he developed ingenious methods of operation which set off a revolution in the iron industry all over the South."[43]

Other businessmen were prominent in the Dickson County iron industry during the first half of the 19th century. Anthony Van Leer, who also hailed from Pennsylvania, purchased the Cumberland Furnace from Bell in 1825 and was very successful in the iron business in Dickson County for more than thirty years. Four members of the Napier family operated iron facilities in Dickson County, including Laurel Furnace, located in the part of the county that is now Montgomery Bell State Park.[44]

According to a report prepared by Gerard Troost, the Tennessee State Geologist, there were six blast furnaces and ten refining forges in operation in the state in 1832. By 1835, the number of furnaces had increased to twenty-seven. Six of these were in Dickson County, and six were in neighboring Montgomery County.[45] Several of these furnaces were operated by Bell.

Since the death of Montgomery Bell in 1855, Dickson County has remained a rural county, although

Frank Clement (Tennessee State Library and Archives)

by 2020 its population had grown to more than 54,000. Charlotte, still the county seat, has remained small, with a population of only 1,600 in 2020. The largest city in the county is Dickson, with a population of 16,000 in 2020.[46]

Other than Montgomery Bell, the most famous person in Dickson County history is Frank G. Clement, who served as Tennessee's governor for ten years (1953-1959 and 1963-1967). He was a racial moderate during a turbulent period in Southern history and made significant accomplishments in the areas of mental health, education, and road construction.[47]

Oscar Roberston of the NBA's Milwaukee Bucks. (Wikimedia Commons)

Another well known native of Dickson County is Oscar Robertson, the college and professional basketball star who was born in Bellsburg, a community named for Montgomery Bell and located on Highway 49 near the Montgomery Bell Bridge over the Harpeth River. Robertson is the grandson of Mr. and Mrs. Early Bell, descendants of enslaved persons that worked for Montgomery Bell.[48] He still returns to Dickson County on occasion to visit his cousins and friends who live there.

CHAPTER EIGHT

Montgomery Bell: Ironmaster

Montgomery Bell moved to Tennessee about 1802 to go into the iron business. Perhaps he had grown tired of making hats. More likely, he knew there was more money to be made in iron. He quickly became Tennessee's best known ironmaster.

Bell's primary residence was in Dickson County, although he had houses in at least two other counties. Until 1835 the deeds by which he bought and sold property described him as a resident of Dickson County. After 1835 the deeds described him as a resident of Davidson County or Williamson County.

Bell owned land and did business in several counties. His first iron furnace was the Cumberland Iron Works (later known as Cumberland Furnace), built by James Robertson about 1796. At that time, the furnace was located in Tennessee County, which was divided into Montgomery and Robertson Counties at the time Tennessee achieved statehood. After Dickson County was created in 1803, the furnace was located in Dickson County.

Bell may have worked for Robertson at the furnace when he first moved to Tennessee. He bought the Cumberland Iron Works and surrounding 640 acres from Robertson in 1804 for $16,000.[1] The land surrounding the furnace was rich in iron ore and limestone and had a vast amount of timber which could be used to make charcoal.[2]

Because the operation of Cumberland Furnace required so much timber, Bell had to buy additional land containing stands of timber as well as iron ore and limestone. In September 1804, he bought 520 acres from Daniel Ross. The deed expressly provided that his purchase included "all Woods Waters Mines & Minerals."[3]

Four years later, Bell purchased a nearby tract of 100 acres from George Ross[4] and another nearby tract of 260 acres from John Davis and Jonathan Frier Robertson.[5] But he was not through buying land near the Cumberland Furnace. In 1810 he purchased 120 acres from Richard Napier, one of his main competitors in the iron business.[6] This tract (which was located in the middle of his furnace property) and the tracts he previously bought were all on or near Bartons Creek, where Cumberland Furnace was located.

In 1811, Bell bought three additional tracts located near the furnace. He purchased 960 acres from James Robertson, his original benefactor.[7] From Thomas Batson, he acquired 114 acres.[8] From Nathaniel Perry, he acquired 640 acres.[9]

Bell's insatiable quest for land near Cumberland Furnace did not end with these acquisitions. In 1813, he bought 640 acres from Edward Gwinn.[10] In 1817, he purchased 255 acres from John Young[11] and 640 acres from David Erwin.[12]

His largest acquisition of land near Cumberland Furnace was a purchase of 4,800 acres located on both sides of Bartons Creek for $4,800 in late 1817.[13] The seller was Dr. Hugh Williamson, a signer of the U.S. Constitution, who had received the land for his service as North Carolina's surgeon general during the Revolutionary War.[14]

Through these purchases, Bell acquired almost 10,000 acres in the vicinity of Cumberland Furnace. This estimate is based solely on the deeds recorded at the courthouse. He likely owned additional property acquired through deeds which he did not record.[15]

Despite his purchase of these large tracts of timber land, they did not fully satisfy the needs of Cumberland Furnace for wood from which to make charcoal. From time to time, Bell advertised in local newspapers that he wished to buy cords of wood. On March 28, 1815, for example, he placed an ad in the *Nashville Whig* stating: "I will give fifty cents, per cord, for chopping wood; a preference will be given to those that will contract for the largest quantity."

The Manufacturers Census for 1820 lists Cumberland Furnace as consisting of "one water wheel 36 feet in diameter…2 blowing tubs 6 feet in diameter, 5 feet 10 inches high worked in fender posts and gates with a lever to each." The annual output of the furnace was reported as "300 tons of hollowware, 50 tons of pig metal, and 6 tons of machinery."[16]

The Cumberland Furnace also produced munitions for the young nation's military. Montgomery's brother Patterson Bell helped him obtain a contract with the federal government. On April 16, 1809, Patterson wrote a letter to Tench Coxe of the Quartermaster's Department, recommending that the government contract with his brother for the manufacture of cannon balls. On December 2, 1809, Montgomery wrote to the Secretary of Navy, stating that he had molds to cast 32-, 24-, and 18- pound balls and could deliver them to New Orleans at $92 per ton.[17]

He was successful at obtaining a contract with the federal government, under which he supplied not only cannon balls but also gunpowder and whiskey.[18] During the War of 1812, Cumberland Furnace supplied General Andrew Jackson with "two-ounce canisters to thirty-two pounders, double-head and single-head cannon shot"[19] which was used to defeat the British at the Battle of New Orleans in 1815. It must have given Bell enormous satisfaction to know that he played a role in defeating the British who had made his childhood so miserable in the 1770s.

For twenty-one years (1804-1825), the Cumberland Furnace was Bell's principal ironworks. But it was not his only facility. In 1805, the year after he bought the Cumberland Iron Works from James Robertson, Bell bought an iron furnace (Yellow Creek Furnace) in Montgomery County from Dr. Morgan Brown for $25,000. Dr. Brown was a leading citizen of Montgomery County, who had moved to Tennessee from South Carolina in 1795 and served as chairman of the Montgomery County Court of Pleas and Quarter Sessions from 1800 to 1808.[20]

The Yellow Creek Furnace was located about 3.5 miles from the mouth of Yellow Creek, a major tributary of the Cumberland River.[21] According to the deed from Dr. Brown, Bell acquired 2,474 acres, including "orchards, houses, mills, forges, and furnaces" on the property.[22] By buying the Yellow Creek Furnace, he also eliminated a competitor.[23]

A successful ironmaster could never have enough land from which to cut timber for charcoal. In 1808 Bell acquired two tracts totaling 445 acres, located near the Yellow Creek Furnace, from Samuel Peters and John Stinnett.[24] In 1814 he bought an additional 400 acres from John Hamilton.[25]

Bell operated the Yellow Creek Furnace for about fifteen years and eventually sold the furnace and surrounding property in 1819 to Thomas Watson and John Marable for $44,000.[26] Bell realized a gain of $19,000 on the sale of this property. The Yellow Creek Furnace was destroyed by a flood in 1836, rebuilt by subsequent owners, and later destroyed by Union troops during the Civil War.[27]

By 1818, Bell was working on his Tunnel project at the Narrows of the Harpeth River in Davidson County (this project is described in detail in

Chapter Ten).[28] Although Bell eventually constructed an iron forge at this site, that did not occur until 1832, after he finally abandoned his effort to sell the property to the federal government for an armory.

After 1817, Bell decided to build additional furnaces and forges in Dickson County. In 1818, he acquired 705 acres on Jones Creek from Christopher Strong.[29] On this tract he built Jones Creek Forge. In 1823, he bought 182 acres on Turnbull Creek from George W.L. Mann.[30]

About 1824, Bell built Bellview Furnace (also known as Bellevue or Mammoth Furnace) on Jones Creek.[31] This furnace operated from 1825 to 1834.[32]

Although the furnace is no longer there, the Rock Church (a still active Church of Christ) stands on the site and meets in a building which was once part of Bell's furnace operations. The building was used for the storage of ingots of cast iron.[33] Near the entrance to the church is a stone marker which reads: "**M Bell A.D. 1826**".

Montgomery Bell rock marker at the entrance to Rock Church of Christ. (Author photo)

Rock Church of Christ (Author photo)

When the United States experienced its first major economic recession, commonly referred to as the Panic of 1819, the iron business was especially hard hit. The country's iron production decreased from 54,000 tons in 1810 to 20,000 tons in 1820.[34]

Bell survived the recession, but his expansion plans had created a need for additional funds.[35] He decided to sell some of the real estate he owned in Nashville. On May 4, 1819, he advertised for sale the Elk Tavern on College Street (now Third Avenue North), a two-story brick house on Market Street (now Second Avenue North), and thirty unimproved lots adjoining these two tracts. In the ad, Bell said he was "determined to vest the proceeds [from these sales] in the Harpeth works,"[36] referring to his Tunnel under construction at the Narrows of the Harpeth.

By 1825, Bell was in serious need of additional funds to accomplish his expansion plans. He placed a notice in two Nashville newspapers advertising for sale virtually all his holdings. At the time he wrote this ad, he decided to cast a wide net for potential buyers. He had never given up his contacts in Pennsylvania, so he placed this same ad in the *Pittsburgh Weekly Gazette*.

The ad was classic Bell in every respect.[37] The top line of the ad is an exhortation: **"Men of capital and Manufacturers, Attend!!"** The next lines describe generally what he is selling: **"IRON WORKS, Scites for Forges, Mills, Factories, &c. &c. FOR SALE"**.

The ad explains that Bell is "desirous of repose from the active pursuits in which he has been engaged" and that he "proposes to sell on a *liberal credit*, the following property". Bell was fifty-six years old at the time he placed this ad. It is unlikely that he was ready to retire. More likely, he wanted potential buyers to believe that he would not remain a competitor.

The ad demonstrates the marvelous sales ability of Montgomery Bell and is a thorough summary of Bell's holdings in 1825:

Two Blast Furnaces, on the Iron-ore
Fork of Barton's creek, in Dickson County,
40 miles west of Nashville, and 10
South of Cumberland river, with about
12,000 acres of well timbered land, one
half of which is fit for cultivation, with
fine streams and several springs of
excellent water. The ore bank from which

these Furnaces are supplied, is about
half a mile from each, the ground descending
to the Furnace, and is not inferior
to any in this, or perhaps any other
country; the ore is believed to be
inexhaustible, & is easily raised from the bank.

Also, a fire forge on Jones' creek, about 8 miles
from the Furnace, having the advantage
of the most modern improvements.
Also, a good scite for a Forge on the same
creek, one mile above this establishment.
To each of the last named places is attached a Grist mill.

Also, a very good scite for a Forge, on the main Turnbull
creek, which affords water at all seasons
for all kinds of machinery. Also, a scite
for a Furnace on the Beaverdam Fork
of Turnbull creek, with a good Ore bank
about one mile distant, (This ore bank
ranks in quality with the Salisbury ore,
on trial at the Springfield armory.) The
surrounding country is thin land handsomely
timbered, and well watered with springs.

The above scites are also situated
in Dickson county, about 25 miles
from Nashville, and 8 from the Narrows
of Harpeth. There is attached to them
about 1000 acres of well timbered land.

Also, 3 other interesting scites, on Mill
creek, a branch of the Piny river, in
Hickman county, about 6 miles from Duck
river, with an inexhaustible bank of approved
ore, and from 9 to 10,000 acres of
land of inferior quality, but well timbered.

Also, the justly celebrated scite of The
NARROWS OF THE HARPETH.
This scite I am constrained to believe
combines more power and safety than
any other on the western waters, and is
better calculated for the preparation of
steam engine materials, the making of
arms, or building of steam boats, than
any other within my knowledge in the U.
States. The NARROWS OF HARPETH
embrace a bend in that river of about 8
miles in its circuit, and coming within the
distance of 60 yards at the conclusion of
its circle; a tunnell has been excavated
through the point, a distance of 96 yards,
which is 15 feet wide and 6 feet high by
means of which a natural fall of water is
gained of near 19 feet. The river is here
bottomed on a smooth sound rock, on
one side is a solid bed of rocks of 250 feet
in height, on the other the bank is
of stiff blue clay twenty-two feet high
and would admit the raising of a
dam 12 feet high with perfect safety,
thereby affording a head and fall of 30
feet of water. The river Harpeth is
navigable to this point in keel boats from
3 to 6 months in the year. The power
and advantages of this scite are almost
incalculable, and hold forth the strongest
inducements to men of capital and enterprize,
not only in the Manufacture of
Iron and Iron implements, but also to the
Manufacturer of Cotton and Wool. This
scite is about 29 miles from Nashville,
and 6 from Cumberland river.

In addition to the above, the subscriber
also offers for sale on the same terms
6000 acres of Land in White's bend, from
6 to 12 miles below Nashville, on the
margin of Cumberland river, well watered
with numerous springs --- Also, 800
acres opposite the Harpeth Island, 28
miles below Nashville; 400 of which is
low ground of first quality, with good
springs on the upland. --- Also, 657 acres
including the mouth of Harpeth, with a
handsome improvement thereon, with
100 acres of cleared land, and first rate
Springs. Also, 640 acres of broken land,
Including what is called Weakley's ferry.
--- Also, 400 acres including Hamilton's
ferry, 300 of which is of superior quality,
with 80 acres cleared and a good spring.
---Also, 2000 acres including Well's ferry,
One half bottom lands, no improvements.
---All of which lie on the margin of
Cumberland river. Also, 640 acres on
the east fork of Yellow creek, of superior
quality, 4 miles from the river.

Should these works and scites not be
disposed of before the 1st of March, I
will then receive proposals of partnership
for improving and carrying on
unimproved scites.

The subscriber will also hire out by the
Year, a set of Furnace hands, well skilled
in all the different branches of the business;
also a considerable number of Forge
hands.

**Letters addressed to me on the above
subject, at Nashville, will be promptly
attended to.**

MONTGOMERY BELL

In Bell's own words, the ad reveals the property characteristics most important to a successful ironmaster:

1) Well-timbered land
2) Adequate water supply
3) Inexhaustible supply of iron ore
4) Navigability of nearby streams
5) Access to ferries
6) Proximity to Nashville
7) Trained work force

With respect to his site at the Narrows of the Harpeth, Bell also suggested its appeal as a site for the processing of cotton and wool as well as iron, thereby broadening the pool of potential buyers.

In creating the ad, Bell was his own wordsmith.[38] With no assistance from an advertising agency, he painted a glowing picture of the sites he wanted to sell: *Well timbered land. An ore bank not inferior to any in this or perhaps any other country. Water at all seasons for all kinds of machinery. An inexhaustible bank of approved ore. The power and advantages of this site are almost inexhaustible.*

As it turned out, Bell did *not* sell most of the property mentioned in the ad. But he did sell the Cumberland Furnace and much of the surrounding land to Anthony Van Leer for $50,000.[39] The deed recites the tracts being purchased by Van Leer, which constitute most of the property near Cumberland Furnace that Bell had acquired between 1804 and 1819.

Bell had paid $16,000 for the Cumberland Furnace and surrounding 640 acres when he bought it from James Robertson in 1804. He later spent approximately $20,000 to buy additional timber land near the furnace. By selling

Cumberland Furnace and the surrounding land to Van Leer for $50,000, Bell realized a substantial profit.

The sale of the Cumberland Furnace to Van Leer is interesting because Van Leer was one of Bell's most prominent competitors. Raised in Pennsylvania, Van Leer had heard of Bell's success in the iron business and had come to Tennessee several years earlier, hoping to achieve the same success Bell had achieved. Now he had his chance.

Despite the statement in the 1825 ad that he was "desirous of repose from the active pursuits in which he has been engaged," Bell was getting his second wind. He was producing iron at the Bellview Furnace on Jones Creek, which he had built about 1824. He needed a forge to which he could send the pig iron produced at his Bellview Furnace.

In about 1829, he built Valley Forge, located about a quarter mile below the junction of two branches of Jones Creek. He built a dam at the junction of the two branches and a second dam in the valley where he built an iron forge. By building this dam, he obtained a fall of 28 feet 9 inches to propel the machinery at the forge. The forge was just a few miles away from Bellview Furnace and received much of its pig iron from that furnace.

Valley Forge was located about four miles from Charlotte. It is believed that Bell named this forge for the Revolutionary War encampment of the Continental

Valley Forge in modern times. (Author photo)

Army near his childhood home in Pennsylvania. Since the forge was located in a steep valley, the name was also a logical name given the geography.

An article in the *Tennessee Historical Quarterly* describes the Valley Forge dam in the following words:

> "The massive hand-hewn limestone wall of the … Valley Forge dam is perhaps the most stunning achievement of Bell's expert corps of craftsmen. Almost thirty feet tall at the center and extending for more than 400 feet, the finished dam totally enclosed a small valley. After water was diverted from nearby Jones Creek by a low barrier and channeled into the natural depression, the pressure produced by the considerable change in elevation of the large volume of water captured in the reservoir was more than enough to power the four huge tilting hammers and the rest of the subsidiary equipment … at this forge."[40]

In order to build and operate Bellview Furnace and Valley Forge, Bell had to acquire additional land in Dickson County on or near Jones Creek. He made the following purchases:

1. Robert Larkins – 350 acres – 1827[41]
2. Edward C. Watson – 3,200 acres – 1828[42]
3. James Walker – 315 acres – 1830[43]
4. Christopher W. Dickson – 200 acres – 1836[44]
5. Michael M. Dickson – 340 acres – 1836[45]

Bell also received several grants of land on Jones Creek from the State of Tennessee through deeds signed by the Tennessee Governor at the time of the purchase:

1. Governor Newton Cannon – 201.5 acres – 1837[46]
2. Governor James K. Polk – 70 acres – 1839[47]

All traces of Valley Forge itself have disappeared, but the 28-foot-high dam in the valley is intact and stands today as a towering monument that was one of Bell's most significant achievements.

In 1830, Bell built Jackson Furnace in the southern part of Dickson County. Located on the Beaver Dam Fork of Turnbull Creek, it was the tallest furnace in the state at forty-seven feet high.[48] To build and operate that furnace, Bell acquired two tracts of land on or near Turnbull Creek from the State of Tennessee (through deeds signed by the governor at the time of the purchase):

1. Governor Sam Houston – 600 acres –1826[49]
2. Governor Newton Cannon – 600 acres – 1837[50]

Like modern businessmen, Bell knew how to appeal to state government officials for assistance to his businesses. Bell also acquired twenty acres on Turnbull Creek from Jacob Puckett in 1828.[51] At present, nothing remains of the Jackson Furnace.

In 1825, Bell acquired from Isaac West, Sr. a tract of 160 acres in Dickson County containing a rich vein of iron ore known as the Mother Ore Bank.[52] In 1839, Bell received a grant from the State of Tennessee of 5,000 acres next to the Mother Ore Bank on Pine River.[53] In 1844, he built Worley Furnace on this tract of land.

Worley Furnace was the last furnace Bell built. It was the first of Bell's furnaces in which he used steam power to propel the machinery. He named the furnace for his trusted slave and long-time business companion, James Worley.[54]

The importance of Worley in Bell's life is recognized by a historic marker erected by the Tennessee

> **3E   15**
>
> ## JAMES WORLEY
>
> On this site, in 1844, Montgomery Bell named his last furnace for his faithful slave, James Worley. He aided Bell in selecting ore banks and water powers, as well as in all his iron operations. As Bell's agent, he carried ironware to Cincinnati and New Orleans. Bell credited most of his success to Worley. A resident of New Orleans once offered a large sum of money for Worley. Bell's reply was: "Not for all of New Orleans."
>
> TENNESSEE HISTORICAL COMMISSION

James Worley historic marker in Dickson County. (Author photo)

Historical Commission (Marker No. 3 E 15) on Old Furnace Road in Dickson County. The marker contains these words:

> On this site, in 1844, Montgomery Bell named his last furnace for his faithful slave, James Worley. He aided Bell in selecting ore banks and water powers, as well as in all his iron operations. As Bell's agent, he carried ironware to Cincinnati and New Orleans. Bell credited most of his success to Worley. A resident of New Orleans once offered a large sum of money for Worley. Bell's reply was: "Not for all of New Orleans."

Worley Furnace was operated by Bell's nephew/son-in-law, James L. Bell, in the 1850s and, after the Civil War, by other owners. In the 1870s, Worley Furnace was one of only two operating iron furnaces in Dickson County. It was finally shut down in 1880.[55]

Bell never operated any furnaces or forges in Hickman County. But in 1821, Bell ventured into Hickman County to buy several tracts of land from Thomas Hardin Perkins and Daniel Perkins for $15,000.[56] Hardin Perkins had built two iron forges on this land. According to an early history of Hickman County, Hardin Perkins was Bell's "most formidable competitor in the manufacture of iron" and by making this purchase, Bell "intended to monopolize the entire iron trade of Middle Tennessee, West Tennessee, and portions of Kentucky, Mississippi, and Alabama."[57] While this statement may be a bit of an exaggeration, Bell was, like any good businessman, always interested in cornering the iron market to the extent he could.

As soon as he acquired the two forges from Perkins, Bell shut them down. His attempt to stifle competition from Perkins did not work, though. Perkins "in a short time erected two forges between those two he had sold to Bell and commenced to operate them."[58] If this transaction had occurred in the 21st century, Bell would surely have required Perkins to sign a non-competition agreement as part of the deal.

During the years that Bell was operating his furnaces and forges, the demand for iron products on the frontier was tremendous.[59] The pig iron and the cast iron products produced at his furnaces and the wrought iron produced at his forges were transported "with ox teams and later with six-mule teams to Betsytown on the Cumberland River" where they were "then loaded on flatboats and shipped down the river to market."[60]

Bell wanted to promote the sale of his products, so he got into the retail end of the iron business. He operated a retail store on College Street (now Third Avenue North) in Nashville, where he sold kettles, stoves, cups, saucers, dishes, and other iron utensils made at his furnaces and forges.[61] The store later moved to Market Street (now Second Avenue North). His forges also supplied iron gates and ornamental balcony railings for fine Southern homes.

One of Bell's specialty products was iron kettles. "He made kettles so excellently thin that they would float. These were used on the sugar plantations of the South and for soap making, washing, and numerous other 'kettle' activities of that day."[62]

Bell was an unabashed self-promoter. To distinguish his iron from that of other ironmasters, Bell had his name "imprinted on each bar."[63] He "vowed to make better iron than can be made at any other establishment in the state."[64]

He placed advertisements in local newspapers publicizing his retail stores and the goods he sold there. In 1824 and 1825, ads appeared in the *Nashville Whig* and the *Nashville Gazette* entitled "Iron and Castings." These ads reveal the colorful sales pitch Bell used to describe his products.

An ad in the *Nashville Whig* of July 12, 1824, said Bell "will keep up a constant supply at the works, as well as in the house lately occupied by Messrs. Norvell and Hill, College street, Nashville." The ad said, "he will sell Iron and Castings at the most reduced prices, and will attend to the business in Nashville himself." The ad said these iron goods "will hereafter be known by his name being impressed on each bar." Finally, the ad stated that he "trusts those wishing to furnish themselves with the above articles, will not regret giving him a call." A 21st century advertising executive would be impressed by the advertising slogans and arguments Bell used to attract customers.

By January 1825, Bell had moved his Nashville store from College Street to Market Street. An ad placed in the *Nashville Whig* on January 24, 1825, varied his sales pitch a little. He said he will "keep a large and general assortment of Iron and Castings at the store." According to the ad, Bell "confidently believes he can make better Iron than can be made at any other establishment in the state" and "is determined to sell at a lower price than they ever have been sold in this place." He continued placing this ad in the local papers throughout 1825.

These advertisements must have earned Bell a steady stream of customers to his retail store in Nashville because he did not continue placing the ads after 1825.[65] Beginning in 1842, though, he began placing the ads again. By then, he had moved his retail store back to College Street.

An ad placed in the *Republican Banner* on July 20, 1842, entitled "Hammered Iron and Castings," asserted that Bell's iron goods "he can warrant equal to any manufactured in this or any other country." The ad touted the superiority of the iron ore from which he made his goods: "There is a peculiar quality in the ore that gives pleasure in every stage of its refinement in the furnace, forge, and workshop, and from its malleability and fine texture is a most desirable article." One can imagine Montgomery Bell drawing immense pleasure from the wording of these ads. Modest he was not!

By 1844, Bell was seventy-five years old. He was considering retirement and decided to sell most of his holdings. On April 3, 1844, he placed an ad in Nashville's *Republican Banner* headlined **"VALUABLE WATER POWER, IRON WORKS & IRON MINES FOR SALE"**, stating that he was "admonished by my infirmities to retire." Unlike 1825, Bell meant it this time.

This advertisement is important as a statement of Bell's holdings in 1844:

1. The Jackson and Bellevue Furnaces, together with their "inexhaustible" ore banks and "all the lands to them belonging". He wanted $10,000 for the Jackson Furnace and $12,000 for the Bellevue Furnace, payable one-third when conveyed, one-third in 12 months, one-third in 2 years". The ad stated that these "furnaces were located and erected after an experience of 30 years in the Iron business...[and] are not inferior to any in this country."

2. At the Bellevue Furnace, "a splendid set of iron flasks and patterns, a spacious stone warehouse, brick office, and large comfortable stone moulding rooms." (This building is now the Rock Church of Christ.)

3. The Valley Forge site "built with eight fires and four hammers, under a head of 28 feet", together with the surrounding lands situated 2 miles from Bellevue. The ad said "there is, in my estimation, no more desirable water power on any stream of same magnitude".

4. The Patterson Iron-Works at the Narrows of Harpeth, "with the fertile farms and timbered lands thereunto belonging".

5. A "furnace that I am at present engaged in building at the

mother ore bank, for the use and benefit of Patterson works". (He was referring to the Worley Furnace.)

6. 6,525 acres in White's Bend. The ad said Bell will sell this land "in full form" or "will divide it into lots to suit purchasers". The ad described this property as located "on the Cumberland river, commencing about six miles below Nashville. In this Bend there is an immense source of wealth; exclusive of its rich soil, it possesses a water privilege of incalculable power, procurable at a very moderate expense in labor, which has long lain unnoticed." (This area of Davidson County is currently known as Bells Bend.)

7. Three good "water powers, with ore banks attached to each" situated on Mill Creek in Hickman County.

8. Some "small tracts...with an ore bank" on Yellow Creek in Montgomery County.

In this ad, Bell used the following language to attract buyers: "Gentlemen disposed to continue in the iron business, or to embark, have now an opportunity....I invite examination – they will appear for themselves, and exceed any expectations that could be formed from any description that could be given of them." He said these assets "will be sold on most favorable terms, together with all my stock of every description."

Bell really was planning to retire. His intention was made clear by the following sentence in the ad: "I would willingly barter a 640-acre tract at the mouth of Harpeth, and a 320 acre tract three miles below, for a comfortable residence in Nashville." He wanted to leave his rural homes in the woods and live in a comfortable home in the city. He was able to fulfill this wish seven years later when he purchased a fashionable brick home in Williamson County, just south of Nashville, where he lived from 1852 to 1854.

Before he could complete his move to Williamson County, though, Bell had a serious accident which almost ended his life. After eating dinner in Nashville, he was headed to his home in Whites Bend when "his horse became frightened, ran away, threw him out of the buggy, and down a precipice, breaking his shoulder bone, and severely injuring his neck. He lay helpless for several hours, before any assistance came to him." He was rescued from this precarious condition by a passing African American woman who heard his cries and called for help.[66] He eventually recovered from his injuries.

As he prepared to move to his newly purchased home in Williamson County in 1852, Bell took a dramatic step affecting his iron empire. He gifted a major portion of his properties to his nephew/son-in-law James L. Bell, who had been assisting him in business for many years.

In September 1851, his two most active iron facilities were the Worley Furnace in Dickson County and the Patterson Forge at the Narrows of the Harpeth in Davidson County. Montgomery Bell signed a "deed of gift" conveying these two facilities and all the land surrounding them to James L. Bell. The deed describes the tracts of land being conveyed to his nephew/son-in-law. The total acreage at Patterson Forge was 10,603.5 acres, and the total acreage at Worley Furnace was 8,055 acres.

Montgomery Bell had purchased this land and built these iron facilities over a period of more than thirty years and was now trusting his nephew/son-in-law to administer them properly. This must have been a very tough decision for a man of eighty-two years, who had accomplished so much in his long life.

He was still the detail-oriented businessman, though. The deed, which was recorded in both Dickson and Davidson Counties,[67] expressly *reserved* from the gift "all the metal now on hand at said establishment, and that may be made at them, and the privilege of collecting the same in blooms until and before the delivery of this deed to the said James L. Bell." Montgomery Bell did not intend to "leave any change on the table."

The deed contained another reservation from the gift which is even more interesting. Bell reserved the *second* tunnel he had built at the Narrows of the Harpeth, which the deed stated "has not yet been occupied, together with ten acres of land on the west side of the river for a residence, garden, etc. for those who may employ said tunnel, for the necessary buildings and improvements for the use of the water power there, together with free access to the same, for the purpose of carrying on any manufactory that may be erected at said tunnel."

What did Bell have in mind when he added this exclusion to his deed of gift? Perhaps he was worried that he would be bored leading the life of a country squire at his Williamson County home. If he did get bored, he would have the option of getting back into business at the Narrows of the Harpeth, with a source of water power for whatever he decided to build.

Bell did not like living in Williamson County. He spent less than three years at the fine home he had bought there. By 1854 he was ready to move again. He still owned several iron facilities that he had not conveyed to his nephew/son-in-law.

On August 4, 1854, at the age of eighty-five years, Montgomery Bell placed the following ad in the *Nashville Union and American*. The ad contains a summary of his holdings at that time, less than a year before his death:

VALUABLE IRON WORKS AND FARM FOR SALE

Owing to the feebleness of the subscriber's health, he offers for sale his Iron Works and Farm.

1st. The Farm on which he now resides, in Williamson County, about 11 miles from Nashville, containing about 550 acres of land which cannot be surpassed for beauty or fertility of soil. As a "Grass Farm," it is too well known to require any description. The buildings are of superior finish. There is plenty of stock water the whole year round – Little Harpeth river runs through it.

Also, the following tracts of land – ore banks, furnaces and forges:

1st. – JACKSON FURNACE – together with about 3,000 acres of land.

2nd. – BELLVIEW FURNACE – with all its ore banks, and privileges, and timber, with between three and four thousand acres attached, well timbered and watered.

3rd. – VALLEY FORGE – with upwards of 3,000 acres of land well timbered, and on it the best water power in this or any other country.

4th. – I will also sell a first-rate Water-Power at the Narrows of Harpeth, with a tunnel already excavated, and about 13 acres of land attached.

Also, all my Water Powers and Ore Bank on Mill Creek, in Hickman County.

I also have an Ore Bank on Duck River, which is very rich in quality and inexhaustible.

Any one wishing to purchase will please call upon the subscriber or address him at Good Spring P. O., Williamson county, when he will make known the terms, etc.

MONTGOMERY BELL

Despite his enticing sales pitch, Bell was not able to dispose of any of his iron properties before his death in April 1855. Within a couple of years after his death, his empire had disappeared.

First to go were the Patterson Forge and the Worley Furnace. Bell's nephew/son-in-law did not have the same zeal for making iron products that his uncle/father-in-law had. In May 1856 – just over a year after his uncle's death – James

L. Bell sold to Sylvester L. Finley the two tracts that Montgomery had gifted to him in 1851: nearly 10,000 acres at Patterson Forge and about 8,000 acres at Worley Furnace.[68] The purchase price was not stated in the deed.

The iron properties that Montgomery Bell still owned at the time of his death had to be disposed of by his Executors. They placed an ad in the *Nashville Union and American* on March 12, 1856, offering to sell at a public sale about 7,000 acres attached to Valley Forge and Bellview Furnace. The ad also stated that several properties would be sold at private sale:

1. Jackson Furnace and the lands appurtenant, which had been recently re-built, located on Beaver Dam Creek and on the line of the Nashville and Northwestern Railroad;
2. The Duck River Ore Bank in Hickman County;
3. 5 acres, including the Upper Forge, on Mill Creek;
4. 11 ¼ acres, below the Upper Forge, on Mill Creek;
5. 1 acre on Mill Creek;
6. 3 acres, including the Town Ore Bank, near Mill Creek;
7. 2 acres on Mill Creek, including an Ore Bank; and
8. The Town Tunnel at the Narrows of the Harpeth. (This is the property Montgomery Bell had excluded from his gift to James L. Bell in 1851.)

The ad stated that the properties would be sold on "one and two years credit" and "a lien retained on the land until the purchase money is paid in full."

The ad attracted some buyers. Bell's executors sold 654 acres on Jones Creek to Robert Oakley in April 1856 for $884.[69] The same month, the Executors sold 392.5 acres on Jones Creek to Robert McNeilly for $1,505.[70] These sales likely included Bellview Furnace and Valley Forge.

In November 1856, the Executors sold sixteen tracts totaling 1,845.5 acres to a group of five persons (Moses Tidwell, F. M. Caslin, John W. Sullivan, T. K. Grigsby, and W. M. Larkins) for an undisclosed sum.[71] This property was located on the Beaver Dam Fork of Turnbull Creek and included the Jackson Furnace.

With these sales, Montgomery Bell's iron empire came to an end. The work product of Tennessee's most celebrated ironmaster was dispersed to several different owners, who would never again achieve the output that Bell had achieved during the first half of the 19th century.

CHAPTER NINE

Cumberland Furnace

Cumberland Furnace was the first iron furnace in Middle Tennessee. It was built by General James Robertson, the founder of Nashville.[1] In 1793, Robertson acquired the land on which the furnace was built. The date of its construction is uncertain, but one leading historian has said that "the furnace probably went in blast for the first time in 1796, or surely no earlier than the latter part of 1795 or no later than the first part of 1797."[2]

The area that is now Tennessee was originally a part of North Carolina. In 1782 the North Carolina General Assembly passed a resolution authorizing the distribution of lands to Revolutionary War soldiers. The size of the grant varied with the rank of the soldier. The smallest grant was 640 acres, given to soldiers who had been discharged from the Continental Line (i.e., the Army) with the rank of Private.[3] 640 acres is equivalent to one square mile of land.

These land grants resulted in an influx of settlers to the area that is now Tennessee. Robertson was one of these settlers. He surveyed much of Middle Tennessee and discovered rich deposits of iron ore in the Highland Rim area.[4]

In 1793, Robertson and his silent partner, William Sheppard of North Carolina, purchased 640 acres from James Campbell, a Private in North Carolina's Continental Line who had received the land as a grant for his wartime

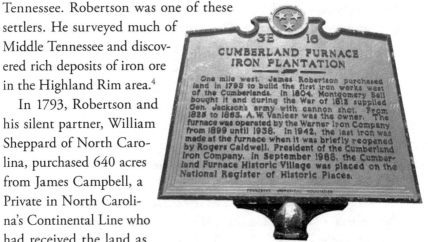

Cumberland Furnace historic marker. (Author photo)

service. On this tract of land, Robertson built an iron furnace, first known as Cumberland Iron Works and later as Cumberland Furnace.[5]

The furnace was located on the west branch of Bartons Creek, known then as Iron Fork and now called Furnace Creek. These ironworks were about eight miles north of the present town of Charlotte, Tennessee and about ten miles from the Cumberland River.[6] The community which grew up around the furnace became known as Cumberland Furnace and is today an unincorporated rural community of about 3,600 residents.

James Robertson (Tennessee State Library and Archives)

The furnace that Robertson built was "a small, crude contrivance that could scarcely turn out a ton of pig iron a day."[7] But the location of the furnace was ideal. It was near a big spring, the iron ore was dug from surrounding hills, limestone was secured from a nearby bluff, and the forests supplied wood for charcoal.[8]

Robertson also built an iron forge at a site near the mouth of Bartons Creek and later built a second forge closer to the Cumberland River. From the site of the second forge, the iron products created there "had only a short distance to the river port of Fayetteville, Dickson County's first platted town," which had been laid out by William Betts in 1797 or 1798. Fayetteville later became known as Bettstown and was commonly called Betsytown.[9] This river port was a direct outgrowth of the Cumberland Furnace and was used for years by the successive owners of the furnace to get their products to market via the Cumberland River.

In the early days of the Cumberland Furnace, Robertson was serving as Brigadier General of the Mero District, a post to which he had been appointed by President George Washington. He was also the leading surveyor of lands in Middle Tennessee. Even though he had assistance in operating the furnace,[10] he did not devote adequate time to its management. He needed help to develop it to its full capacity.[11]

Enter Montgomery Bell. While Robertson was building his furnace in the 1790s, Bell was living in Lexington, Kentucky, making and selling hats and engaging in other profitable business ventures. By the end of the decade, Bell was looking for new challenges.

He was attracted to Tennessee because he wanted to get into the iron business – an industry that he had become familiar with during his early years in Pennsylvania. He knew that Middle Tennessee offered water power and rich deposits of iron ore.

Bell probably worked for Robertson at Cumberland Furnace sometime during the years 1800 through 1804. At any rate, Bell purchased Cumberland Furnace and the surrounding 640 acres from Robertson and his partners for $16,000 in June 1804.[12] Thus began the long and prosperous career of Montgomery Bell as Tennessee's most prominent ironmaster.

Soon after acquiring the property, Bell abandoned the furnace built by Robertson and erected a new Cumberland Furnace.[13] To increase the output at the furnace, Bell needed to acquire additional woodland for charcoal, so he began buying surrounding properties. His largest purchase came in 1809, when he bought 4,800 acres from Dr. Hugh Williamson, who had received the largest military grant in Dickson County for his service as North Carolina's surgeon general during the Revolutionary War.[14]

On December 2, 1809, Montgomery Bell wrote a letter to the Secretary of the Navy offering to provide iron munitions to the federal government – a letter which is maintained today in the National Archives.[15] The letter stated:

> I have furnished myself with Iron moulds for casting 32, 24 & 18 lb balls. Should you want any of those sizes delivered at New Orleans or any port above N. Orleans and below the mouth of Cumberland River, I will furnish on the shortest notice, at Ninety-two dollars per Ton.
>
> I am Sir, respectfully,
Your obedient servant,
Montgomery Bell

Bell entered into a contract with the federal government to supply cannonballs, gunpowder, and whiskey. During the War of 1812, Bell was one of the chief suppliers of heavy ammunition for the Army and the Navy. Cumberland Furnace supplied the two-ounce canisters, 32-pounders, and single-head and double-head cannon shot used by General Andrew Jackson in the Battle of New Orleans.[16] These iron munitions were loaded onto flat-bottom boats at Clarksville and shipped to New Orleans in November 1814.

Sometime before 1820, Bell built a more modern Cumberland Furnace near the original furnace. According to the federal manufacturer's census of 1820, the new furnace's annual production was 300 tons of hollowware, fifty tons of pig iron, and six tons of machinery, with seventy men working at the furnace.[17] Among Bell's most prominent customers were members of the Harding family, who purchased iron for the blacksmith shop at the Belle Meade Plantation in Nashville.[18]

As for so many businessmen, the economic recession that began in 1819 created problems for Bell. He advertised the Cumberland Furnace and other properties he owned as being for sale.[19]

On July 25, 1825, Bell deeded the Cumberland Furnace and several other tracts of land to Anthony Van Leer and his two partners, Isaac H. Lanier and Wallace H. Dickson, for $50,000.[20] Like Bell, Van Leer was a Pennsylvania native who had moved to Tennessee from Chester County several years earlier. He was familiar with Bell's success in the iron business and hoped to duplicate that success.

In 1833, Van Leer bought the interests of his two partners for $70,000. He dismantled the original furnace built by Robertson and re-built the furnace built by Bell. He introduced steam power to the operation of the furnace.[21] He continued to acquire ore and timber land surrounding the furnace. At the time of his death in 1863, he owned 20,000 acres.[22]

Van Leer kept Cumberland Furnace as a family business. In 1839, he turned over management of the furnace to Hugh Kirkman, who had married Van Leer's daughter Eleanora.[23]

By 1840, Tennessee had become the third largest iron-producing state in the country. More than ninety-five percent of the state's pig iron was produced in Middle Tennessee, with Dickson County the leading producer.[24]

By 1850, there were 121 workers at Cumberland Furnace producing 1,400 tons of pig iron and 200 tons of iron castings annually. In 1860, there were 100 workers at Cumberland Furnace producing 1,831 tons of pig iron. Hugh Kirkman and Robert B. Stone managed the furnace.[25]

The Civil War resulted in some changes in the operation of the furnace. Key personnel passed from the scene. Hugh Kirkman died in November 1861, and his father-in-law Anthony Van Leer died in July 1863. According to one historian, the furnace shut down after the fall of Fort Donelson in February 1862 and did not reopen while the war was raging.[26] But the published papers of Andrew Johnson, Military Governor of Tennessee during the war, tell a slightly different story.

Anthony Van Leer's two grandchildren, Van Leer Kirkman and Mary Florence Kirkman, inherited Cumberland Furnace upon their grandfather's death in 1863. One of Anthony Van Leer's business associates, Daniel Hillman, became Trustee for the two Kirkman heirs and assumed management of the furnace. It continued to operate for several months but eventually shut down for the remainder of the War, probably because the furnace workers had been pressed into military service.[27]

Mary Florence Kirkman shocked her family by marrying a Union captain, James P. Drouillard, in 1864. After the war ended in 1865, the Drouillards lost no time in reopening the furnace, hiring the former manager Robert Stone to run it. In 1870 Mary Florence Drouillard bought her brother's interest in the furnace and surrounding 15,000 acres. By 1880, Cumberland Furnace's 250 workers were producing twenty tons a day. The acreage surrounding the furnace had increased to 17,000 acres.[28]

In 1881, J.B. Killebrew, the Tennessee Commissioner of Agriculture, Statistics and Mines, wrote a tract entitled *Iron and Coal of Tennessee*. He stated that Cumberland Furnace "is a very old furnace and has been run more regularly and profitably than any other in Tennessee."[29] He included in his tract an elaborate description of the furnace built by Bell before 1820 and modified by Van Leer in 1833.

According to Killebrew:

> The stack is of limestone thirty feet square at the base, thirty-five feet high and twenty-four feet square at the top. The hearth is six feet high, twenty-six inches diameter at bottom and thirty at the top. The tuyeres come in thirty inches from the bottom; the bosh is four feet high and ten and a half feet diameter, from thence to top the in-wall is a regular slope to a mouth twenty-eight inches in diameter.[30]

He described the furnace as "a perfect type of an old style charcoal furnace."[31] He said the primary ore bank "is on a ridge facing south, half a mile west of the furnace" and "has been worked for seventy-eight years, but exhibits no sign of exhaustion."[32] He called the Cumberland Furnace property "historical" because "[h]ere the first ore was dug and the first iron made west of the Cumberland Mountains."[33]

The furnace prospered under the Drouillards' ownership. Initially they

The Drouillard house (Author photo)

operated it as a family business. They were community-minded and built a church and a school. Mary Florence Drouillard also built a large mansion on a hill overlooking the community, which became a showpiece in Dickson County and is still standing.[34]

In 1882, the Drouillard Iron Company was formed, bringing stockholders into ownership of Cumberland Furnace for the first time, although James Drouillard and Robert Stone were the largest stockholders. The newly formed company paid James and Mary Florence Drouillard $170,000 for the furnace and surrounding land.[35]

In 1889, the Drouillard Iron Company sold out to Southern Iron Company, an Alabama company, for $140,000. Southern Iron Company replaced the charcoal-fired furnace with a more modern coke-fired furnace in 1893, and a newly built rail line enabled coke and iron ore from other areas to be brought to the furnace.[36]

As the new owners were modernizing the furnace operation, a recession hit – the Panic of 1893. Southern Iron Company had to declare bankruptcy. The Warner family of Nashville reorganized the company as Buffalo Iron Company, but it also went out of business two years later.[37]

Determined to stay in the iron business, though, the Warner family in 1899 formed the Warner Iron Company,[38] which operated the furnace until 1917. In that year, the furnace and surrounding property were conveyed to Joseph Warner, who managed to increase production by updating the ironworks.[39]

Unfortunately, Joseph Warner became involved in a patent dispute with Jeff Gray in the mid-1920s over the right to manufacture ferrophosphorus iron. The seven-year legal dispute depleted Warner's finances, and he was forced into receivership in 1938.[40] The Receiver appointed by Chancellor S. A. Marable was E.H. Stone, the son of Robert Stone, who had managed Cumberland Furnace from the 1860s through the 1880s when the Drouillards owned it.[41] While the receivership proceedings were pending, Joseph Warner died in 1939.[42]

On July 12, 1940, the Dickson County Chancellor Court entered a Decree[43] allowing the Receiver to lease the furnace to Cumberland Iron Company, a corporation headed by Nashville businessman Rogers Caldwell, who obtained a loan from the Reconstruction Finance Corporation allowing the furnace to re-open in 1942. For several months during World War II, the furnace operated 24 hours a day, seven days a week, employing 250 people and producing eighty tons of pig iron daily. Due to financial irregularities, the government closed the furnace later in 1942. That was the final closure of this historic iron furnace.

Rogers Caldwell, courtesy of Kenny Davis.

In October 1943, Sol Chazen, a Chattanooga scrap dealer, bought the property from the Reconstruction Finance Corporation for $25,000. The furnace was dismantled, and the scrap was sold as part of the World War II scrap drive.[44]

That was the sad end of 150 years of iron production at Cumberland Furnace, which had operated longer than any iron furnace in the United States. The furnace supplied iron for munitions used in every war our nation has fought from the War of 1812 through World War II.[45]

The present-day community of Cumberland Furnace is a quiet rural community of 3,600 residents in northern Dickson County. The iron furnace no longer exists, but the village, including more than thirty buildings and sites associated with the iron industry, was placed on the National Register of Historic Places in 1988 as a Historic District.[46]

The most impressive of the historic buildings in Cumberland Furnace is the luxurious mansion built in 1870 by Mary Florence Drouillard, which was modeled on the homes that Mrs. Drouillard had visited in Newport, Rhode Island. The Drouillard House was added to the National Register of Historic Places in 1977, eleven years before the entire community was added to the Register by the National Park Service.[47] This magnificent home stands as a testament to the era when the iron furnace and surrounding community flourished.[48]

An interesting legacy of the furnace is Promise Land, a small community located five miles south of Cumberland Furnace. Referred to by some as an Emancipation Community, Promise Land was established by formerly enslaved persons shortly after the end of the Civil War. Many of these settlers had worked at the furnace before the War, and some continued to work there after the War. Promise Land is maintained by the Promise Land Heritage Association as a historic site which tells the story of African Americans in Dickson County during the Reconstruction era and the early 20th century (*www.promiselandtn.org*).[49]

CHAPTER TEN

The Tunnel

The most unique and enduring accomplishment of Montgomery Bell is the tunnel he created at the Narrows of the Harpeth River. At the time it was built about 1819, there was no precedent for such an engineering marvel.

It is the oldest existing full-size tunnel in the United States, and it represents the first application of rock tunneling technology to the field of water power. As constructed, the tunnel is 290 feet long (about the length of a football field), eight feet high, and fifteen feet wide. It is taller and wider at the entrance and exit portals.[1]

The entrance to and exit from the tunnel are both located on the Harpeth River, a Tennessee Scenic River which originates in Rutherford County and flows for 115 miles through the hills of Williamson, Davidson, Cheatham, and Dickson Counties before

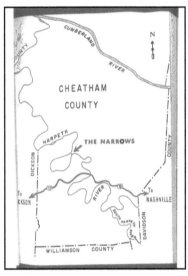

Map of the Narrows of Harpeth, by Robert E. Dalton.

emptying into the Cumberland River near Ashland City. Approximately twenty-two miles upstream from the mouth of the river, the Harpeth reverses course in a graceful seven-mile oxbow

Water exiting the Tunnel. (Author photo)

Looking into the Tunnel entrance during a period of low water. (Author photo)

Water gushing through the Tunnel following a period of heavy rains. (Author photo)

that encircles a limestone bluff. The steep neck of land running between these two river segments varies in height from 60 to 250 feet and in width from 180 to 450 feet.[2]

Bell purchased 343.5 acres, including the Narrows of the Harpeth tract, for $1,374 in 1814 from Jacob Battle of North Carolina. The tract was part of a 640-acre grant by the State of North Carolina to James Robertson in 1792.[3] Bell saw its potential as a source of water power to turn the wheels and lift the hammers of an iron forge he intended to build.

By this point in his life, Bell had been in the iron business for more than ten years. He knew what it takes to operate iron furnaces and forges, and he knew the importance of water power for a successful iron facility. But no other ironmaster in the United States had tried to harness the power of a river by creating such a tunnel.

The closest historical analogy to what Bell envisioned is the Roman aqueduct system, which brought drinking water to Romans through 200 miles of underground tunnels.[4] Perhaps Bell had read about the aqueducts.

More likely, though, Bell had heard of plans to build the Auburn Tunnel on the Schuylkill Navigation Canal in eastern Pennsylvania near Bell's childhood home. The Auburn tunnel was begun in 1818 but not finished until 1821.[5] By then, Bell had completed his tunnel at the Narrows of the Harpeth.

There is no existing documentation as to the method of excavation Bell used in building his tunnel. But it is almost certain that he used the method known as hand drilling.

Holes were hammered into the face of the limestone rock using hand-held hammers and chisels. One worker would hold a metal rod with a sharpened edge (the "drill") against the rock while another worker hammered the end of the drill. The drill holder would pivot the drill after each blow so that the edge of the drill would make contact with a different portion of the hole. The drill holder would periodically pour a small amount of water into the hole to reduce the heat being transferred to the drill by successive contacts with the rock.

The number of blows required to drill a hole to the proper depth varied with the hardness of the rock, the sharpness of the drill, and the force of the hammering. Newly sharpened drills had to be brought frequently to replace the drills that had become dull.

After a number of holes were drilled in this manner, the holes had to be cleaned out and dried. The next step was the placement of black powder explosive in the holes, which were then packed tight with clay. A fuse leading to the powder was ignited, causing the rock to fracture or break away.[6]

The work was slow and arduous. Completion of the 290-foot-long tunnel took at least a year. Most of the work was performed by the eighty-three enslaved workers Bell owned at the time. Their work was supervised by Samuel W. Adkisson, a young mechanic and stonecutter who later achieved prominence in Tennessee as a turnpike builder.[7]

At the mouth of the tunnel, there was a sixteen-foot fall of water that could be utilized to power the water wheels and lift the hammers of an iron forge. The flume could be used for other industrial purposes as well.

After the tunnel's completion, Bell was apparently running low on funds to build a forge. Like all successful businessmen, he did not hesitate to seek financial assistance from the government when it was available.

In 1822, he sought a loan from the State of Tennessee to enable him to build the forge.[8] His request was referred to a legislative committee, which reported that "the committee think it unwise and unsafe for the General Assembly to exhaust the resources of the Bank of the State of Tennessee by large loans of money upon any security whatsoever at this time", although the committee report noted that "the manufactory and works intended to be erected by the petitioner, Montgomery Bell, would be of great and incalculable public benefit."[9] The request for the loan was referred by the committee to the full House of Representatives, which voted 18-16 not to approve it.[10] It is apparent from the closeness of the vote that Bell had a great deal of support in the General Assembly, despite the negative recommendation from the committee.

Bell next proposed to the *federal* government that the tunnel and surrounding land would be the perfect site for a new armory that had been authorized by Congress in 1823. In his sales pitch to Congress, Bell said: "There is not a site on the western waters that combines as much power and safety as the Narrows of Harpeth."[11]

Bell convinced his friend Andrew Jackson to write a letter of endorsement to Secretary of War John C. Calhoun.[12] Bell also convinced the Tennessee legislature to reserve large tracts of adjacent land that could be used for the armory.[13] With the full support of Governor William Carroll, the General Assembly passed a bill reserving "all the vacant lands within five miles of the Narrows of Harpeth"[14] until the Congress made a decision about the location of the armory.

The Congressional selection process dragged on for several years in the 1820s.[15] Meanwhile, the completed tunnel sat idle. Bell grew frustrated.

In 1825, Bell advertised in a Nashville newspaper his intention to sell all his holdings, including the Narrows of the Harpeth site. He may have been suffering from the aftereffects of the economic recession known as the Panic of 1819. Yet he did not follow through on the sale of the Narrows of the Harpeth property.[16] In 1829, he submitted a written petition to the Tennessee legislature offering to sell the Narrows property to the State if the legislature determined to build either an armory or a prison.[17]

In 1830, Bell began acquiring additional property near the site of his tunnel. He purchased 250 acres from Benjamin Woodward for $2,250[18] and 130 acres from Sterling Fowler for $1,100.[19] He built a sawmill and a gristmill on the property.

Finally in 1832, Bell decided to build his own iron forge, which he named the Patterson Forge. His mother's maiden name was Patterson.[20]

Since it had become clear that Congress was not going to authorize an armory to be built at the Narrows of the Harpeth, the Tennessee General Assembly had to decide what to do with the land it had reserved for use in connection with such an armory. Bell wanted to get his hands on this land, and in 1831 he filed a written petition with the legislature asking that they repeal the 1823 law by which the land had been reserved.[21] In November 1833, the legislature passed a statute creating a process allowing persons to apply to buy this land. Bell was given "the preference of entry" for up to 10,000 acres of this land.[22]

A man named Willoughby Williams acquired two tracts totaling 6,830 acres from the State in 1834. Bell wanted this property, so the next year he bought the two tracts from Williams for $2,000.[23] After this purchase, Bell owned about 8,000 acres near his tunnel at the Narrows of the Harpeth. In 1848, Bell made one final purchase of 1,200 acres along the Harpeth River from Turner J. Evins for $600.[24]

The operation of the forge Bell built at the Narrows was described by Robert E. Dalton in a 1976 article in the *Tennessee Historical Quarterly*:

> A dam built downstream of the entrance insured that water always flowed through the tunnel; a headgate controlled the amount. A second dam on the output side raised the water level to provide a good head to operate the works. Sluices, with gates to control the flow, channeled the water to at least eight ponderous wheels. Many of the structures, perhaps most, were elevated to protect them from the seasonal floods, but the forge buildings also required heavy rock foundations,

sturdy enough to withstand the weight of the anvil and the relentless pounding of the hammer. The hammer weighed several hundred pounds, and usually two fires were needed to supply the heated iron. Two wheels powered each forge. One operated connecting rods which moved the pistons in the blowing cylinders which supplied a constant stream of air to keep the forge fires hot enough to superheat the pig iron. The stout handle of the hammer was mounted parallel to the large shaft of the second wheel, and cogs on the shaft lifted the hammer. The deafening staccato sounds of the hammers could be heard for miles, and Bell kept the four hammers at Patterson Forge operating constantly.

Pig iron bars, five or six feet long and six inches wide, cast at Bellview Furnace [one of Bell's furnaces] or—because of its excellent quality—purchased from Richard Napier's nearby Laurel Furnace, were forged at the Patterson Forge. Brawny finers heated the pig and worked it into a half bloom, and holding the red hot lump with tongs, the hammermen pounded out the carbon and other impurities. After cooling, the iron was further refined by reheating and rehammering; it was then shaped into an ancony, a bar which was wide at each end and narrow in the middle. Anconies were sold to the manufacturers of steam boilers and other heavy equipment. Heated a third time in a chafery forge, the iron was then hammered into bars, cut to various lengths, and sold to blacksmiths, locksmiths, and gunsmiths.... Bell likely had a small army of blacksmiths who fashioned axes, rakes, hoes, shovels, hinges, chains, and other implements and tools for the local farmers.[25]

Another historian has provided an equally colorful description of the operation of the Patterson Forge:

The water was conducted about twenty feet, from the fall to the top of twin water wheels, by the use of wooden troughs. The weight of the water caused the wheels to revolve on their axles. The axles were made of large poplar logs near the ends of which were driven two protruding pins of white oak, called lever trips. As the axles revolved, these trips pressed down and released a long lever on the end from which hung a huge hammer. The heated iron was held with tongs on top of a long anvil; it received two hammer blows with every revolution of the two water wheels, each of which operated a hammer.[26]

The wrought iron created at the Patterson Forge was either hauled to Nashville or Franklin by wagon or shipped down the Harpeth and Cumberland Rivers to Clarksville, where it was shipped to Natchez and New Orleans via the Ohio and Mississippi Rivers.[27]

About the time the Patterson Forge began operation in 1832, Bell began excavating a second tunnel at his Narrows property, located about 226 feet downstream from his first tunnel. On February 28, 1832, he placed an ad in the *Pittsburgh Weekly Gazette* stating his intention to "lease, for a term of years, at low rent, the FURNACE and FORGE he is at present building, with a good grist and saw mill attached ... also, a well-regulated TAN YARD, with a tolerable stock of leather and bark." The ad suggested that this project would be finished "in three or four months." Although the site had a good iron ore bank, Bell suggested in the ad that it was also suitable for the manufacture of cotton or wool products because of the "extraordinary water power."

He never completed this second tunnel, for reasons that are not clear. The entrance to the second tunnel was visible as late as 1882, but the annual floods on the Harpeth have since filled it.[28]

With the help of his nephew/son-in-law James L. Bell, Montgomery Bell

continued operating Patterson Forge until giving it to his nephew by deed in 1851, four years before Montgomery's death. In May 1856 — a year after his uncle's death — James L. Bell sold to Sylvester L. Finley the two tracts that Montgomery had gifted to him in 1851, including nearly 10,000 acres at Patterson Forge.[29] The land containing the tunnel and forge changed hands several times after that and was eventually acquired by wealthy Nashville businessman Justin Potter. In 1943, the site was conveyed to Commerce Union Bank, acting as Trustee for the Justin Potter, Jr. Boy Scout Endowment Fund.[30] The Boy Scouts used the site near the Tunnel as a campground for many years.

Justin Potter, courtesy of Bill Carey and the family of David K. Wilson.

The State of Tennessee acquired 101 acres from Commerce Union Bank in 1978, and it became the Harpeth River State Park.[31]

The tunnel and adjacent forge site were listed on the National Register of Historic Places in 1971. The American Society of Civil Engineers designated the tunnel as a historic civil engineering landmark in 1981.[32] The U.S. Department of Interior designated the tunnel as a National Historic Landmark in 1994.

In 1996, the State of Tennessee acquired an additional thirty-three acres to add to the Harpeth River State Park.[33] At the time of that acquisition, the Commissioner of the Tennessee Department of Environment and Conservation was Justin Wilson, the grandson of Justin Potter. Commissioner Wilson told a Nashville newspaper that his grandfather had told him stories about Montgomery Bell, whom he described as "a great example of a self-made businessman, an innovative fellow who worked hard to accomplish his dreams."[34]

Montgomery Bell had a sentimental attachment to the Narrows of the Harpeth. He built a home on a ridge northeast of the tunnel, where he allegedly could oversee the activities of the workers at his Patterson Forge.[35] Bell is buried in a small cemetery located within sight of the tunnel.[36]

Two centuries after it was built, the tunnel is in fine shape, although nothing remains of the forge or related structures. On U.S. Geological Survey maps, the land encompassed in this bend in the river is still known as Bells Bend.

Rock climbing is a popular pasttime at the Tunnel exit. (Author photo)

Those who visit Harpeth River State Park can hike to the small pool of water lying below the mouth of the tunnel, can view the entrance to the tunnel, and can climb to the top of the narrow isthmus between the two segments of the Harpeth. In periods of abundant rainfall, visitors wade and even swim in the pool below the mouth of the tunnel (notwithstanding the "No Swimming" signs erected by the State). In periods of dry weather, when little or no water exits the tunnel, intrepid visitors have been observed climbing along the rock ledge near the top of the tunnel. On either side of the tunnel, canoeists and kayakers are regular travelers on the Harpeth River.

Montgomery Bell would undoubtedly be proud that his engineering creation is still a source of interest to Tennesseans 200 years after it was built.

The greatest tribute to Bell's genius, though, is found in a book published by the Society of Mining, Metallurgy & Exploration in 2017. It is an oversized book, 552 pages in length, filled with color photographs and text describing all the major tunnels built in this country from 1820 to 2017. The book begins with a four-page foldout entitled "Tunneling Milestones in the U.S." Listed are 130 tunnels built over two centuries for railroads, highways, and water projects. The very first milestone on the Society's list is the "Montgomery Bell (or Patterson Forge) Tunnel, TN – water power for local iron industry."[37] Montgomery Bell was indeed ahead of his time.

CHAPTER ELEVEN

Montgomery Bell: Land Developer

It is not surprising that Montgomery Bell became a large landowner and land developer. In the 18th and 19th centuries, land ownership was the measure of a person's wealth. By that yardstick, Bell was a wealthy man, indeed.

He bought and sold thousands of acres. He needed timber land to provide charcoal for his iron furnaces and forges. But he also bought properties with the intent to develop or use them for business and residential purposes.

In deciding what properties to buy, Bell understood the importance of buying land containing rivers and streams. He utilized water power at his iron furnaces and forges. He also recognized the importance of water in operating gristmills and sawmills.

In the 18th and 19th centuries, a gristmill ground grains such as wheat and corn into flour. It was usually built close to a stream, which was impounded to create a small millpond that supplied water to operate a large waterwheel. The waterwheel powered the large flat millstones that ground the grain into flour.[1] A sawmill was often built near a gristmill because water power was also essential to its operation.

Bell owned gristmills and sawmills during his years in Kentucky and Tennessee. They were an additional source of income for him, as well as a service to the community. Even more importantly, the gristmills helped him feed his enslaved workers, and the sawmills enabled him to cut the wood needed to make charcoal and to build houses for his workforce.

An examination of deeds and other property records from several counties in two states gives a sense of the breadth of his land holdings, but it does not tell the full story of his land ownership for several reasons. Sometimes Bell did not record his deeds at local courthouses. The availability of business records for the early 19th century is often limited. The deeds were all written by hand in those days and are hard to decipher.

His land purchases began in the last decade of the 18th century while he was living in Kentucky. During the years he operated his hat business in Lexington, he started buying lots in the city. At the time he was preparing to move to Tennessee, he sold at least three of these lots.[2]

Although Bell lived and worked primarily in Lexington during his Kentucky years, he acquired and eventually sold property in Jessamine County, a county which was carved out of the southern portion of Fayette County in 1798. His largest purchase was a tract of 1,000 acres located on Stephens Creek on the north side of the Kentucky River, which he bought in 1800 from Nathaniel Rochester for $4,100.[3] He built a "merchant mill" and several houses on that property. As he prepared to move to Tennessee in 1802, he leased the mill and homes on the property to Daniel McViars for $500 annual rent.[4] As described in more detail in another chapter, Bell sold the rest of his Jessamine County property in the years 1803-1805.

By 1803, Bell's move to Tennessee was almost complete. With the exception of the spa ownership in Mercer County, Kentucky (described in another chapter), most of his subsequent land development activities occurred in Tennessee.

Because Bell's furnaces and forges were located primarily in Dickson County, his land transactions in that county consisted mainly of the purchase of vast tracts of timber land he needed for making charcoal. But he also bought some properties with the intent of development or re-sale for profit. He had purchased an enormous amount of land on Bartons Creek near the Cumberland Furnace, and he eventually began to sell some of this land.

In 1822, he sold 640 acres on Bartons Creek to Walter Bell[5] and 100 acres to Jacob Evans.[6] In 1825, Bell made an interesting agreement with Christopher Robertson. He sold Robertson 875 acres but reserved the right to build on the property a warehouse for the storage of his iron and castings.[7] In 1825, Bell sold land on Bartons Creek to the Bartee brothers — 100 acres to Jesse Bartee[8] and 100 acres to William Bartee.[9]

In 1834, Bell sold several tracts of land totaling 813 acres, plus two lots in the Town of Charlotte, to Christopher Robertson and Benjamin C. Robertson.[10] Christopher Robertson was the nephew of General James Robertson, and Benjamin was Christopher's only son. Two years after buying this land from Bell, Christopher Robertson drowned in the Harpeth River.[11]

Bell purchased two large tracts on the south side of the Cumberland River near the mouth of the Harpeth River —

Pardue Recreation Area (Author photo)

743 acres from Thomas Whitmill in 1821[12] and 868 acres from Christopher Robertson in 1830.[13] Bell developed this property into a community he named Bellville. Today we would call such a development a large subdivision.

In 1835, Bell began selling lots he had laid out in Bellville. He sold Silas Harris Lot No. 23, which had a frame house on it.[14] He sold Elisha Hall an acre of land consisting of two lots (Nos. 43 and 77).[15] He sold Andrew Stewart several lots with improvements on them.[16]

He continued selling the Bellville lots in 1836. He sold Lot No. 42 to William Eatherly.[17] He sold Lot No. 40 to Jonathan D. Stewart.[18] He sold a half-acre lot, Lot No. 10, to Duncan Bethune.[19] In 1843, he sold two Bellville lots (Nos. 65 and 79) to Robert Duke.[20]

By 1853, Bell was anxious to dispose of his remaining lots in Bellville. He sold four lots (Nos. 25, 26, 27, and 58), each containing a half-acre, to Benjamin C. Robertson.[21] He sold six half-acre lots (Nos. 3, 4, 5, 6, 22, and 24) to Elizabeth B. Pardue and Rachael A. Hinton.[22] He sold 7 and 27/160 acres to O. Simpkins for $143.38, which (according to the deed) represented a purchase price of $20 per acre.[23]

By the middle of 1853, Bell decided to give the remainder of the unsold Bellville lots to four of his relatives.[24] This deed of gift stated that the original Bellville "subdivision" included 525 acres – a large residential subdivision at that time.

There is no historic marker or other recognition of the long-ago existence of Bellville — one of Bell's proudest land development accomplishments. Bellville once lay at the mouth of the Harpeth River, where it joins the Cumberland River. In that area now is the Pardue Recreation Area on Cheatham Lake, operated by the U.S. Army Corps of Engineers. Dozier's Boat Dock is a favorite boat-launching ramp for those engaged in water recreation on that portion of the Cumberland River, which is now Cheatham Lake, created by the completion of the Cheatham Dam in 1952.

While he was operating the Yellow Creek Furnace in Montgomery County from 1805 through 1819, Bell bought several lots (Nos. 5, 55, and 58) in the Town of Clarksville.[25] One lot that he acquired from Samuel Peters and John Stinnett had a tavern on it — a source of revenue for Bell. In this same transaction, he acquired the right to operate a ferry to transport people and freight across the Cumberland River at Clarksville — another source of revenue for Bell.[26] The Montgomery County Court granted Bell a license to operate the ferry in December 1809.[27] Bell always had many "irons in the fire."

Even after he sold the Yellow Creek Furnace in 1819, Bell invested heavily in real estate in Montgomery County. It is not clear whether he developed houses on the property he acquired.

In 1821, he acquired from Alexander Porter a one-half interest in 3,923.25 acres on the north side of the Cumberland River.[28] Perhaps Bell was not able to develop this tract, because he conveyed his interest in the property to Sanford Wilson in 1836 by quitclaim deed.[29]

In 1833 he received two tracts totaling 1,969 acres on the Cumberland River from the heirs of Jenkins Whitesides.[30] Three years later, Bell sold this property to Sanford Wilson for $4,000.[31]

In 1838 he acquired from the Powell heirs three tracts of 640 acres each.[32] This purchase was made with the intention of re-selling the property for a profit. The following year, Bell sold portions of this property to three individuals. Hardiman Stone bought 160 acres,[33] John Rye bought 300 acres,[34] and James T. Wright bought 160 acres.[35] Bell also donated three acres of this property to the United Baptist Church.[36]

Bell also bought considerable property in Davidson County, some of it in downtown Nashville. He used the downtown property to establish his retail outlet where he sold iron products made at his furnaces and forges.

He bought Lot No. 164 in Nashville from three owners (J. Whitesides, M. Tannehill, and James Stewart) in 1817.[37] Later that year, he purchased from William Carroll (soon to be Governor of Tennessee) a portion of Lot No. 10, on which was located a brick house,[38] later used by Bell for sale of his iron goods. In the same year, he purchased from William Carroll a portion of Lot No. 128, located on Mechanic Alley.[39]

Bell and Carroll were friends. In 1810, Carroll had moved to Nashville from Pennsylvania to open the first nail store in Tennessee, and in 1818 he brought to Nashville the first steamboat on the Cumberland River. He served six two-year terms as Governor (1821-1827 and 1829-1835).[40] Known as Tennessee's "Business Governor", he was a staunch advocate for public funding of internal improvements such as roads and bridges, needed by Bell to transport his iron products to market.

William Carroll (Tennessee State Library and Archives)

Two things are notable about Bell's downtown land purchases. Nashville's early leaders had carefully laid out plots of land and had given them Lot Numbers, which are mentioned in Bell's deeds.[41] More significantly, the prices Bell paid to acquire these Lots greatly exceeded the amounts he had paid for his furnace properties located in rural areas. One can hear the modern real estate chant "Location, location, location"!

After these purchases in 1817, Bell bought additional property in downtown Nashville during the next two years. In 1818, he bought Lot No. 20 at a Sheriff's sale.[42] From Alpha Kingsley in 1819, he bought six acres located in the "College Lands".[43] In 1820, he had to mortgage the latter property to Thomas H. Perkins and Daniel Perkins, but he received it back from the two Perkins brothers when he re-paid them later that year.[44] This deed notes that the Kingsley property was located next to the property Bell had bought from William Carroll and included the Elk Tavern — undoubtedly another source of revenue for Bell.

In 1821, Bell acquired from David Irwin a 1/3 interest in Lot Nos. 6, 7, and 8 in downtown Nashville, totaling 7.33 acres.[45] This is the final recorded deed by which Bell purchased land in downtown Nashville, although he may have acquired other tracts and elected not to record the deeds at the courthouse.

Bell sold several of his lots in downtown Nashville during the years 1819 through 1821. He may have been feeling the effects of the Panic of 1819.[46]

One land "flip" on which Bell lost money was his purchase in 1822 of 796 acres on the north side of the Cumberland River, two miles above the mouth of the Harpeth River. He sold this property nine years later at a loss of $1,000.[47]

Bell's largest land acquisition in Davidson County was his purchase of 5,932.75 acres in the western portion of the county in an area known as Whites Bend. He and Jenkins Whitesides bought this land in 1817 for $23,731 from the Estate of William Tait, intending to develop and sell portions of it in the future.[48] On this property, he built a sawmill and gristmill on the banks of the Cumberland River.

On May 19, 1834, Bell placed the following Notice in the *National Banner and Daily Advertiser*:

> To Thomas Whiteside, James Whiteside, Richard C. Whiteside, William Whiteside, James Lafferty, Jane Lafferty, John Lafferty, Isaac Parker, and Mary his wife, James McGoldrick and Isabella McGoldrick, heirs at Law of Jenkins Whitesides, deceased, and to all others whom it may concern.
>
> Take notice, that I shall present a petition to the county court of Davidson, at its October term 1834, for an order to divide and make partition of a tract of land lying in the county of Davidson, on the north side of Cumberland river, below the mouth of White's creek, and including White's bend, containing 5932 3/4 acres, which land was conveyed to said Whitesides and myself jointly, by the Executors of William Tait, deceased, and which has never been divided between us. Attend if you please.
>
> MONTGOMERY BELL

In January 1835, Bell placed the following Notice in two different newspapers (*The Tennessean* and the *National Banner and Nashville Whig*) on five separate days:

WHITE'S BEND FOR SALE

The above tract of land will forthwith be laid off into lots to suit purchasers, and sold on accommodating terms, for the culture of grain and grass, it is confidently believed there is no better soil on

Cumberland or any other river in the western country, and a more luxuriant growth of timber perhaps has not been seen. — Lots can generally be laid off to front on the river. — The subscriber residing on the premises six miles west of Nashville, will show the land, and make the terms known.

M. BELL

At the time he placed this Notice, Bell was apparently living on his property in Whites Bend, "six miles west of Nashville." The Notice stated that Bell was "residing on the premises" and "will show the land and make the terms known" to prospective purchasers.

Still standing on this property is a house (referred to as the John Bell house) which was probably built by Montgomery Bell and his nephew John J. Bell and lived in by Montgomery Bell during the years 1835 to 1851. The house was less than a mile from Bell's mills.

Another newspaper ad confirms that Bell was still living on his Whites Bend property in January 1850. B.D. Harris placed an ad in the *Daily Nashville Union* seeking the public's help in locating a runaway slave named Wiley, who was (according to the ad) "lurking about the plantation of Mr. Montgomery Bell, some six or eight miles below Nashville." The property referred to in the ad was Bell's Whites Bend property.[49]

Bell sold his sawmill to J. Thomas, who made improvements to the sawmill and then placed a "Notice to Builders and Architects" stating that he was "now prepared to furnish Building Timber of every description, at the shortest notice and lowest Prices." This Notice appeared in *The Tennessean* on August 31,1853 and described the sawmill as "formerly owned by Montgomery Bell, some six miles from the city of Nashville." Montgomery Bell had operated the sawmill for about fifteen years before selling it to Thomas. It was undoubtedly a good source of revenue for Bell.

As Bell neared the end of his life, he decided to sell this huge tract of land in Whites Bend that he had owned for more than thirty years. He sold the property to two brothers, James and George Anderson, in 1850 for $85,000 — more than three times what he had paid for it in 1817.[50]

If Montgomery Bell had not been so busy operating his iron furnaces and forges, he would have had more time to devote to his land development activities. This was a segment of his business career that he thoroughly enjoyed.

CHAPTER TWELVE

Montgomery Bell: Spa Owner

A frontier capitalist like Montgomery Bell was always looking for good investment opportunities. In 1809, he found a unique one in Harrodsburg, Kentucky, located about forty-five miles southwest of Lexington.

Harrodsburg was the first permanent settlement west of the Appalachian Mountains,[1] founded by James Harrod in 1774.[2] One of the early residents of Harrodsburg was Captain Lucas Van Arsdal, a Revolutionary War veteran, who in 1793 received a land grant of 228 acres adjacent to the town limits of Harrodsburg on the Salt River.[3]

In 1806, it was learned that Van Arsdal's property contained mineral springs, thought to have beneficial medicinal qualities. The discovery was made by the Reverend Jesse Head, a cabinet-maker and circuit-riding Methodist minister who lived in nearby Springfield, Kentucky and was conducting services in Harrodsburg at the time he became aware of the springs.

According to a recently published history of Harrodsburg, Rev. Head was in poor health and became convinced that he received immediate benefits from the springs on Van Arsdal's property. He was "enthusiastic about the curative powers of the iron and saline water," which he characterized as "the best mineral water in any state bordering on the Ohio River".[4]

Like many persons in Montgomery Bell's life story, Rev. Head is a noted historical figure, albeit for a reason unrelated to his discovery of the mineral springs. As a circuit-riding minister, he conducted marriage ceremonies for many couples. In the same year that he

Map showing Mercer County, Kentucky, of which Harrodsburg is the county seat. (Wikipedia)

discovered the mineral springs on Van Arsdal's land, he officiated at the wedding ceremony of Thomas Lincoln and Nancy Hanks — a union which produced the sixteenth President of the United States, Abraham Lincoln.[5]

Upon his return to Springfield, Rev. Head told his friend Felix Grundy about the healing properties of the mineral springs in Harrodsburg. At that time, Grundy was a young lawyer who had just been appointed to the Kentucky Court of Appeals and would become Chief Justice in 1807.[6] Apparently, Rev. Head painted such a glowing picture of the springs that Grundy decided to contact Van Arsdal about investing in the property. In the summer of 1806, Grundy purchased a "moiety" (an undivided one-half interest) in the 228 acres for $1,900.[7]

In the early 19th century, these so-called "healing springs" became very popular. The recently published history of Harrodsburg contains this colorful description:

> Taking the waters became popular for social as well as medical reasons, and attracting guests from far and wide became a competitive business. Not everyone who summered at a watering place was ill. Far from it. If one person in a family felt indisposed and the entire family could afford it, they would pack up — servants and all — and go to take the waters. If no one was ill, the springs were thought of as first-rate preventive medicine environment, particularly during cholera, yellow fever and other epidemics. But many people shamelessly went to spas to have a good time....
>
> Most of the watering places appealed to all members of the family. While they offered brilliant dancing balls and excellent "wining and dining," with plenty of opportunity for romance and matchmaking, they also provided such family diversions as croquet, horseshoes for the gentlemen, lawn tennis and other games all ages could enjoy. The personality of the resort host, his management practices, his imagination and skill in providing amenities and entertainment determined the atmosphere of the watering place and the type of guests who returned year after year.[8]

The two partners (Grundy and Van Arsdal) used Grundy's purchase money ($1,900) to "begin a frenzied building program," which included twenty-one new cottages and a large new framed house or tavern that "offered commodious quarters for a great many guests".[9] Grundy, Van Arsdal, and Rev. Head went to Springfield to recruit Daniel Jennings, a well-known tavern owner, to move to Harrodsburg where he would run the tavern and serve as proprietor of the facility, which they named Greenville Springs.[10]

GREENVILLE SPRINGS

Last remnant of medicinal springs prevalent in Mercer County during 1800s. Healing properties were discovered by Rev. Jesse Head in 1806. First of the famed spas in Harrodsburg. Gazebos covered the springs & cabins rented to those who came to take the waters. Dr. C. C. Graham purchased it in 1827 & later developed Graham Springs.

The word must have spread rapidly because hundreds of people from throughout the state visited Greenville Springs during the "watering season" of 1807, which lasted from June through mid-September.

Greenville Springs marker (Author photo)

Many Harrodsburg families "rented" beds and bedclothes to the owners, and Rev. Head the cabinet-maker built furniture for the guest rooms.[11]

Greenville Springs turned out to be a good investment for Felix Grundy, but his judicial post did not produce much income, so he decided in late 1807 to move to Nashville, Tennessee, where he could establish a law practice and make substantially more money.[12] Grundy sold his undivided one-half interest in the Greenville Springs property to Daniel Jennings, who had been serving as proprietor of the facility for more than a year, for $2,500.[13] In little more than a year, Grundy had realized a gain of $600.

As the new owners of Greenville Springs, Van Arsdal and Jennings drew up an agreement by which Jennings would pay two-thirds of the expenses and draw two-thirds of the profits, with Van Arsdal paying and drawing the other one-third. In the summer of 1808, business continued to be good. More than 1,500 people visited Greenville Springs that summer, and the partnership "took in 734 pounds, fourteen shillings, eleven pence and 500 pounds in bonds."[14]

Despite the success of Greenville Springs, Van Arsdal and Jennings did not get along. Van Arsdal was the "strait-laced Dutch Reform member of the partnership [who] did not approve of the billiard table, the bar room, and the worldly ways of Jennings and some of his guests."[15] Van Arsdal decided to sell his one-half interest in the property to Thomas Eastland, who took over management of Greenville Springs in early 1809. The verbal contract between Van Arsdal and Eastland ultimately became the subject of acrimonious litigation that reached the Kentucky Court of Appeals.

Unfortunately, the new joint owners of Greenville Springs, Eastland and Jennings, could not work together either. Jennings wanted out. In August 1809, Jennings decided to sell his one-half interest to Montgomery Bell for $2,500 — the amount that Jennings had paid Grundy when he acquired his interest the previous year. Unlike the deeds by which Grundy and Jennings had acquired their one-half interest, Montgomery Bell wisely recorded his deed from Jennings.[16]

Historic marker for Greenville Springs spa (Author photo)

Bell and Eastland were now the joint owners of Greenville Springs. Since Bell was busy running his iron furnaces and forges in Tennessee, Eastland continued as host and proprietor of Greenville Springs. Eastland wanted to expand the Springs facilities, so he mortgaged his one-half interest to Bell in order to get some ready cash from Bell.[17]

Eastland and Bell were both businessmen looking for ways to maximize the return on their investments. They decided to establish a "rope-walk" on twelve acres of the property. A rope-walk was a factory for making hemp rope, which was used to "bag" cotton bales. "This factory quickly brought in the needed cash and more buildings were erected, lavish parties and balls were given, and visitors came in increasing numbers to enjoy this expanding and fashionable summer resort."[18]

Unfortunately for Bell, ownership disputes soon emerged, resulting in prolonged litigation in Mercer County Circuit Court. Van Arsdal refused to follow up on his verbal agreement with Eastland because the items that Eastland had promised to give Van Arsdal as consideration for the one-half interest in the property were actually not owned by Eastland. So, Van Arsdal contended that he still owned one-half interest in the property, and the court sustained Van Arsdal's contention.[19]

Since it was determined that Eastland did not own the one-half interest, he could not mortgage it to Bell, so Bell's deed from Eastland was not valid. Bell brought suit against Eastland, but did not recover anything because the court found that Bell had made so much money from the rope-walk.[20]

During the years that the suit was pending and until 1819, Greenville Springs was successfully operated by Henry Palmer, a Justice of the Peace and former Mercer County Sheriff. Business was still booming.[21]

After the lawsuit was concluded in 1814, Van Arsdal sold his one-half interest to Thomas Deye Owings, a Lexington iron manufacturer, who in turn sold the one-half interest to two Harrodsburg businessmen, Harrison Munday and John Hanna, in 1818. So that these two owners could be the *sole* owners of Greenville Springs, Montgomery Bell agreed to sell them the one-half interest he had acquired from Jennings in 1809 and had held since then. Bell received $10,000 for this one-half interest in the property — more than four times what he had paid in 1809.[22] Montgomery Bell had received a nice return on his investment!

Unfortunately for the new owners of Greenville Springs, though, they were about to face competition from mineral springs on the property of David Sutton, a Harrodsburg hat manufacturer, located less than a half mile from the Greenville Springs.[23]

Munday sold his interest to his partner Hanna and a man named William Fulkerson. Hanna now owned a three-quarter interest in the Greenville Springs property. Poor management and a variety of other factors forced Hanna to mortgage the property to Robert Boyce for $13,000.[24] Montgomery Bell had not been paid in full by Hanna when Bell sold Hanna and Munday his one-half interest. So, Boyce and Bell both sued Hanna in 1822, threatening to foreclose.

Bell was able to "buy in" the property, so no foreclosure sale took place. Bell leased the property to Hiram C. Bennett and John Trimble, two out-of-town managers who ran Greenville Springs.[25] Still the legal owner of the property, Hanna could not pay his debts, and the property was finally sold by the Mercer County Sheriff at a foreclosure sale in November 1826 for $4,843.52 to Dr. Christopher Columbus Graham. Dr. Graham acquired 227 acres, the tavern, all the other buildings, the name Greenville Springs, and all the actual springs for that price.[26]

Dr. Graham was the son-in-law of David Sutton, the owner of the springs that competed with Greenville Springs. Sutton's springs were known as Harrodsburg Springs and were managed by Dr. Graham. After buying the Greenville Springs property, Dr. Graham had no intention of continuing to operate both springs.[27]

Dr. Graham sold the tavern and other buildings, the rope-walk, and twenty-four acres of the Greenville Springs property for $1,000 to Rev. William D.

Jones to be used for a Female Seminary of Learning. In 1834, Jones sold that property to Harrodsburg lawyer James Harlan, the father of future U.S. Supreme Court Justice John Marshall Harlan, who lived there for seven years as a boy.[28]

When the Harlan family moved to Frankfort in 1841, the property was leased and later sold to Professor Samuel G. Mullins for a girls school called Greenville Institute. Fire destroyed the old buildings in 1851, but they were replaced by substantial brick buildings. These buildings were used as the site of Daughters College from 1856 to 1893. In 1894, the name was changed to Beaumont College.[29]

When the college was closed in 1917, the new owner Annie Bell Goddard opened an inn known as Beaumont Inn, which is still open to the public more than 100 years later.[30]

Although not a part of Montgomery Bell's story, it is worth noting that the rival springs on the property of David Sutton in Harrodsburg were developed into a celebrated spa by Sutton's son-in-law, Dr. Christopher Graham, the man who had bought Greenville Springs

John Marshall Harlan (Wikimedia Commons)

Beaumont Inn in Harrodsburg, Kentucky. (Author photo)

at the foreclosure sale and then closed it. Known initially as Sutton Springs and then as Harrodsburg Springs, it was eventually named Graham Springs and remained open to the public as a spa until 1853, often hosting 4,000 to 6,000 guests per year during the height of its popularity.[31]

"Taking the waters" at thermal mineral springs became a popular tradition for wealthy Americans in the first half of the 19th century. Enthusiasts believed that soaking in and drinking mineral water could cure a number of ailments, especially sore muscles and joints stiff from arthritis and injuries. In many instances, though, people just wanted a change of scenery, a rest, and some fun.

Montgomery Bell was obviously aware of this new desire of wealthy Americans. His decision to invest in Greenville Springs was a smart decision, which yielded a good return on his investment during his fifteen years of ownership. His development of the "rope factory" on the Greenville Springs property is a further example of his entrepreneurial skills.

CHAPTER THIRTEEN

Montgomery Bell in the Courts

Montgomery Bell was no stranger to the courts. He was sued frequently for failure to pay his debts in a timely manner. There has been much speculation about why this happened.

James M. Gifford, who wrote his Master's thesis in 1970 on "Montgomery Bell, Tennessee Ironmaster," recounted numerous lawsuits against Bell.[1] One possible explanation, according to Gifford, is that "he felt that, as a rich man, people were trying to take advantage of him." Gifford also concluded that "[t]he hard times of the Revolution and Bell's inherent Scotch-Irish frugality surely combined to promote this peculiar personal aversion to paying debts."[2]

The papers of Nannie S. Boyd, a collateral descendant of Bell, are stored at the Tennessee State Library and Archives. Mrs. Boyd wrote in the 1930s that she had "spent many hours scattered over a period of almost forty years piecing together the truth about Montgomery Bell."[3] She stated that Bell "was often sued, even for small amounts, sometimes for only a few dollars." She described this fact as "another eccentricity of a man who had many."[4]

A more objective explanation of why Bell was slow to pay his debts came from Ed Huddleston, the *Nashville Banner* reporter who wrote a series of articles about Bell in 1955. Huddleston attributed it to Bell's "contrariness" and added that Bell's hasty and vigorous development of his properties often left him "low on cash reserves."[5]

Another hypothesis was offered by Judy Isenhour in a January 1985 article in *Nashville Business Advantage* magazine. She observed that "[l]awsuits for payment of small debts were common" in the early 19th century and cited the lawsuits against Bell as an example. She said: "Like most of his peers, early Nashville business luminary Montgomery Bell tended to use the court system for an accounts receivable department, as well as an accounts payable department."[6]

An examination of the records at the State Library and Archives and several county archives adds context to this matter. In addition to being sued frequently, Bell also sued others to collect monies owed to him. This fact tends to support Isenhour's theory that businessmen used the courts to collect their debts.

In Williamson County, for example, there are records of six lawsuits filed against Bell.[7] However, there are also records of ten lawsuits that Bell filed against other persons or entities, usually for the collection of amounts owed to Bell.[8]

A larger number of lawsuits was filed against Bell in Dickson County, where he transacted most of his business. From 1804 (when he bought Cumberland Furnace) through 1828,[9] the records show a total of forty lawsuits filed against Bell. While this seems like a large number of cases, the yearly average during that period is about 1.5 cases — not an excessive number for the most successful businessman in Dickson County.

When Bell lost, he often appealed the trial court's decision and found himself in the Tennessee Supreme Court of Errors and Appeals, usually represented by notable Nashville attorney Francis B. Fogg. Bell won four and lost three of the cases appealed to the Tennessee Supreme Court.[10]

Montgomery Bell even made it to the United States Supreme Court on one occasion. In *Bell v. Morrison*, 26 U.S. 351 (1828), Bell sued in federal court to recover the value of iron castings sold to the Kentucky defendant. The Court's decision turned on the application of Kentucky's statute of limitations and the interpretation of that statute by Kentucky courts. Bell lost the case due primarily to his dilatoriness in filing the suit. Justice Joseph Story's opinion for the Court stated that "this opinion...is not unanimous, but of the majority of the Court."[11]

Bell's business behavior was sharp at times. But he was not alone among 19th century businessmen in being litigious, and he would not have accumulated a fortune had he not sought aggressively to protect his interests, in court when necessary.

CHAPTER FOURTEEN

Montgomery Bell: Life Outside Work

This book focuses primarily on Montgomery Bell's work activities because he was, in modern parlance, a workaholic. He loved what he did and spent most of his time making and selling iron and tending to his other business interests. He did not like high society and did not have many close friends.

Inevitable questions arise about other facets of his life. Where did he live? Did he have a family? Was he a religious man? How did he spend his spare time? Little information is available about these and other aspects of his daily life.

Homes

During his fifty-five years in middle Tennessee, Bell was a bit of a nomad.[1] He built several isolated homes in the woods close to his furnaces and forges. As James Gifford said in his Master's thesis, "[M]ost of [Bell's] life was spent in rude surroundings with the distinctly rough company of his ironworkers…. Most of his personal contacts were with his enslaved and other workers. Since his work meant so much to him, it is understandable that he would live near the furnaces and forges."[2] He ate the same food that his slaves ate, served on iron plates made in his furnaces and forges.

One home was located near the Cumberland Furnace in the small community by the same name. Another was built on a hilltop in the woods overlooking the Patterson Forge at the Narrows of the Harpeth. Bell's daughter and son-in-law and their children lived with Bell at this home near the Narrows.[3] Another of Bell's homes was built near his Valley Forge. Nothing remains of these homes, which Bell occupied on a rotating basis during his years in Tennessee.

Although little has been written about a home located in Whites Bend (now known as Bells Bend) along the Cumberland River in northwestern Davidson County, it is likely that Bell had such a home and lived there in the 1830s and 1840s. Bell had purchased almost 6,000 acres in Whites Bend in 1817.[4] On five separate days in 1835, he placed the same newspaper ad, stating that this land "will forthwith be laid off into lots to suit purchasers." In the ad, he said he was "residing on the premises, six miles west of Nashville." As explained in another chapter, the house still standing

Bricks found at the Bell home site at the Narrows. (Author photo)

in Bells Bend Park is likely the house Bell built and lived in for about fifteen years.

Those who needed to find Bell must have been confused about where he lived. A Notice in the *National Banner and Nashville Whig* on May 20, 1830, stated that "Montgomery Bell [was] living in White's Bend of Cumberland River". A Notice in the same newspaper on February 9, 1831, stated that "Montgomery Bell [was] living at the Narrows of Little Harpeth". (Both ads described stray horses that Bell had "taken up" and were for sale at a price stated in the ad.)

A few years before his death, Bell decided to upgrade his accommodations. In 1852, he purchased two tracts of land in Williamson County, south of Davidson County in the area that is now Brentwood. He bought 315 acres from David Reed for $14,000[5] and 240 acres from Charles T. Lewis for $4,097.[6] This land was located on Franklin Road near the Little Harpeth River and was good agricultural property.

Also on this property was a fine brick home known as Ashlawn, built in 1832 by Richard Christmas, a racehorse entrepreneur. The interior design of the house was very similar to Andrew Jackson's Hermitage, which likely appealed to Bell. Christmas and his wife and children all died in the 1840s, and the house passed through several owners before Bell bought the property in 1852.[7]

Apparently, though, Bell was not comfortable living in luxury. According to a history of Ashlawn prepared by a subsequent owner, Montgomery Bell "didn't treat the house well. His servants started open fires on the floors, which destroyed them."[8] "[F]oundry workmen quartered here added to the abuse."[9] Bell had never lived in a house that required substantial upkeep.

Bell enjoyed perfecting his agricultural skills more than maintaining the house. A short news item in Nashville's *Republican Banner* of June 11, 1853, described the crops being grown on Bell's farm:

> We were shown yesterday specimens of stalks of Rye, 6 feet in length; Oats 6 feet 6 inches; Timothy 6 feet; and Herdagrass 5 feet 6 inches. They were from the farm of Mr. Montgomery Bell, in Williamson county, and are certainly "a head and shoulders taller" than anything of this kind we have ever seen. The Timothy was taken from a 70 acre meadow, on which the grass stood, on an average 4 1/2 feet high. Does Williamson need any higher compliment upon her soil and productions than the mere statement of these facts?

Montgomery Bell was undoubtedly proud of his agricultural accomplishments. At age eighty-four, he had started a third career!

After three years in Williamson County, though, he decided that "fine country living" was not for him and moved back to his Valley Forge home in the woods. On November 1, 1854 (five months before his death), he sold to James Owen for $25,000 the two tracts he had bought in 1852.[10] In just three years, Bell realized a gain of almost $7,000 on the sale of this property. He had not lost his Midas touch.

Since Bell's sale of Ashlawn in 1854, the property has had a series of well-known owners. Henry and Martha Zellner bought Ashlawn in 1871 and lived there for almost thirty years. Their daughter Margaret married David Lipscomb, founder of the university that now bears his name. Andrew Mizell, prominent in the wholesale grocery business in Nashville, lived there with his family for thirty-seven years. In 1945, Mr. and Mrs. Stirton Oman, owners of the Oman Construction Company, bought and extensively remodeled Ashlawn and lived there for many years.[11] More recently, the home was the residence of Gwen Shamblin Lara, the Christian diet guru and founder of the Remnant Fellowship Church in Brentwood, who died in a tragic airplane crash in 2021.[12]

Family

Montgomery Bell never married, but he had two daughters. Evelina Deadrick Bell was born in 1808 when Montgomery was thirty-nine years old. Little is known about Evelina's mother, except that her name was Patsy Moss and she was white.[13]

Even though Evelina was born out of wedlock, Montgomery Bell was a good father to her. He sent her to the Nashville Female Academy, an elite girls school that had received its charter from the Tennessee legislature in 1817.[14] The school provided ten years of study and had a rigorous curriculum similar to the curriculum he later recommended for the school that bears his name.[15] Annual tuition at the Nashville Female Academy during the first six years was $200 ($7,000 in today's dollars), and during the last four years was $275.[16]

Evelina Bell, courtesy of Jay Swafford.

It is not known how many years Evelina attended the Nashville Female Academy. She was attending the school as early as 1821, and she received a diploma from the school in December 1825.[17] She was apparently a good student. A June 21,1824 news item in the *Nashville Whig* reported that Evelina was one of five students in the school's French class and that these students publicly "recited a chorus of Racine's sacred tragedy named Athalia, and read out, in English, several pages of the French Telemachus." The news article concluded by noting: "Their pronunciation, and readiness in translating into English what was offered to them in French, highly pleased a number of judges of French literature, who had been invited...." Montgomery Bell must have been very proud of his daughter.

Like many girls of that era, Evelina got married at an early age. She married her thirty-three-year-old cousin James L. Bell on November 9, 1824, when she was sixteen years old. The marriage was a fruitful one that produced thirteen children. After the death of James Bell in 1860, Evelina continued living in the area until her death in 1883 at the age of 74.

In 1838, when Bell was almost seventy years old, he fathered a daughter named Lucy, born to an enslaved woman named Patsy. According to the Swett-Smith family tree on *www.ancestry.com*, Patsy had been born in North Carolina to parents named Bob and Nicy. The Will of Ann Whitmell (the mother-in-law of Montgomery Bell's nephew John J. Bell), signed by her in August 1839, mentions an enslaved woman named Patsey (age 25) and an enslaved girl named Lucy (age seven months).[18] Based on their ages, it seems likely that Patsey was the mother of Lucy.

Details of Lucy Bell's life are scant. Census records show her living in Dickson and Cheatham Counties both before and after emancipation. According to the Swett-Smith family tree on Ancestry, seven children were born to Lucy Bell and Andrew Jackson Pardue between the years 1863 and 1881. She died in Ashland City in 1917 at age seventy-eight. The information on her Certificate of Death, supplied by her son Robert, lists Montgomery Bell as her father and Patsy Bell as her mother.

From early childhood, Bell was close to his nine siblings. Because the Revolution disrupted his formative years and prevented him from getting much formal education, he was undoubtedly grateful to his siblings for the home schooling he got from them.

At the age of twenty, he began an apprenticeship under his brother Zachariah in the hat business and learned the trade quickly. When his sister Elizabeth Bean unexpectedly lost her husband after their move to Kentucky in 1789, Montgomery responded to her cry for help.

He moved to Lexington, where he used the skills he had learned from his brother to start his own hatmaking business. He stayed in Lexington for about twelve years, living with his sister, and helped care for her six children.[19] In essence, he replaced their deceased father as the loving male figure in their lives. When he decided to move to Tennessee to go into the iron business about 1802, he turned his hatmaking business over to his sister's son, Patterson.[20]

In addition to entrusting his hat business to Patterson, Bell came to rely in later years on Patterson's son George Bain. George and his wife Kate Bain lived with Bell in Tennessee in the 1840s and 1850s, and George helped Bell manage his business.[21]

George went to Ohio and Illinois on Bell's behalf, looking for land to which Bell could send his enslaved workers after he decided to emancipate them.[22] Bain was unsuccessful in finding land because the state officials he met with did not want to have freed blacks relocated to their state. That led to Bell's decision to utilize the American Colonization Society. George Bain later negotiated with ACS officials on Bell's behalf and went to England to buy equipment that his emancipated slaves could use to establish an iron furnace and rolling mill in Liberia.[23]

Montgomery was especially close to his older brother Patterson, who remained in Pennsylvania his entire life. John J. Bell, one of Patterson's two children, moved to Tennessee in the early 19th century and married a woman named Nancy Whitmill of Dickson County. Census records show them and their eight children living in Middle Tennessee from at least 1820 until John's death in 1852. He was likely associated with his uncle Montgomery in the iron business.

James L. Bell, the son of Montgomery's brother James, was another Bell nephew who played a key role in his life. James played a *dual* role, though. Not only did he help his uncle manage his furnaces and forges, he also married Bell's daughter Evelina. For at least a few years, they all lived together in the house located at the Narrows of the Harpeth.

Montgomery Bell cared deeply for his daughter and son-in-law. They received a substantial part of his holdings by deed of gift in 1851.[24] The gift included almost 19,000 acres of land, including his home at the Narrows of the Harpeth, the Patterson Forge, and the Worley Furnace. James L. Bell was also one of the three executors named to probate his uncle's Will, and in addition to the 1851 deed of gift, he received under the Will the same bequest that the Will specified for all of Montgomery's nieces and nephews.

Another relative whose family played a role in Bell's life was his uncle Edward Leech, married to his mother's sister Sarah. Leech was a hatter in Philadelphia during the Revolutionary War and made hats for the Continental Army. Montgomery Bell and Edward Leech moved to Kentucky and later to Tennessee about the same time. They did business with each other on occasion, and in 1821 Bell conveyed to Leech 1,000 acres of land in Dickson County, Tennessee, in exchange for an inheritance Leech was due to receive in Pennsylvania.[25] The inheritance was large enough to enable Montgomery to purchase some of the land he bought while expanding his business.

In 1928 Nannie Boyd, a wealthy Tennessee resident, was gathering information about the life of Montgomery Bell, whom she greatly admired.[26] One of her sources was Edward Leech's great-grandson W.B. Leech, who wrote three letters to Mrs. Boyd containing extensive information about Bell. According to a letter of July 9, 1928, L.L. Leech (the father of W.B. Leech and the grandson of Edward Leech) "became very intimately associated with Montgomery Bell from 1840 up until Bell's death in 1855." According to a letter of November

20,1928, L.L. Leech "attended to a great deal of business for M. Bell, keeping his books, helped him arrange the shipment of slaves that was made to Liberia etc." L.L. Leech was present at the time [Bell] died and attended his burial the next day at the Narrows of Harpeth."

The terms of his Will reveal his deep devotion to the children of all his siblings. After making specific bequests for the use of his church and for the establishment of a school to be named for him, he left the rest of his extensive estate to his nieces and nephews. His Will noted that all his siblings were dead, but that eight of his nine siblings had children. The Will instructed his executors to sell all his property and divide the proceeds "into eight equal shares." Each of the eight shares would then be divided equally among the children (and in some cases, grandchildren) of each deceased brother and sister ("per stirpes", to use the language of the Will).

Bell was even-handed in the distribution of his wealth to the children of his siblings. He did not favor the children of one sibling over another. His devotion to his family and his desire to express gratitude for the important role they had played in his early life was real and touching.

First Presbyterian Church in Nashville. (Author photo)

Religious Affiliation

Montgomery Bell was raised in the Presbyterian Church. Like many Scots-Irish immigrants, his father, John Bell, was a staunch Presbyterian. The Bell family attended the Faggs Manor Presbyterian Church in Chester County, Pennsylvania. Montgomery's brother, Patterson Bell, moved as an adult to the neighboring county of Lancaster, where he joined the Middle Octorara Presbyterian Church. When John Bell died in 1796, Patterson was responsible for his funeral arrangements. John was buried in a small cemetery adjacent to the church that Patterson belonged to.

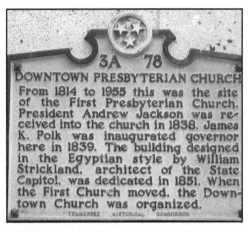

Plaque on the outside of the church. (Author photo)

While living in Middle Tennessee, Montgomery Bell attended the First Presbyterian Church in Nashville, which has a storied history.[27] It was formally organized in 1814, although its roots go back to the late 18th century. The founder was Rev. Gideon Blackburn, who established several Presbyterian

Rev. John Todd Edgar, courtesy of Log College Press.

churches in Tennessee, Kentucky, Indiana, and Ohio. Its first church building was completed in 1816 but destroyed by fire in 1832, and its second church building was completed in 1833 but again destroyed by fire in 1848.

The third church building, still standing, was designed by noted architect William Strickland, who also designed Tennessee's State Capitol. It was dedicated on Easter Sunday in 1851 and has graced downtown Nashville for almost two centuries. It was listed on the National Register of Historic Places in 1970.

Dr. John Todd Edgar became pastor in 1833 and remained so until his death in 1861. He and Montgomery Bell became friends, and Rev. Edgar undoubtedly influenced Bell's thinking about slavery and emancipation.

Although Bell attended this church for several years before becoming a member, the Sessional Records of the First Presbyterian Church show that Bell was formally admitted to church membership on September 26, 1846.[28] On that same day, Mrs. Adelicia Franklin (later known as Adelicia Acklen after her second marriage) was admitted to church membership. The paths of these two celebrated Tennesseans crossed briefly in church on that fall day in 1846. Adelicia Acklen, in 1867, gave the church a large bell, cast in New York and weighing more than 4,000 pounds — a bell which can still be heard in downtown Nashville today.[29]

The church had many prominent members in the first half of the 19th century. Rev. Blackburn, the church's founder, welcomed Rachel Jackson into membership. Her husband, Andrew Jackson, joined the church in 1838 after leaving the Presidency. Rev. Edgar presided at Andrew Jackson's funeral in 1845.[30] Jackson's friend, Judge John

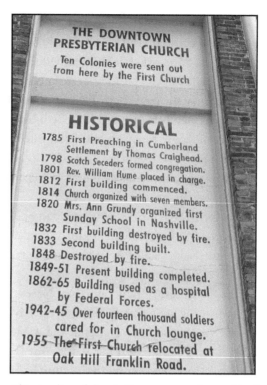

This timeline of church history seen on the outside of First Presbyterian Church. (Author photo)

Adelicia Acklen (Tennessee State Library and Archives)

Overton, who built Travellers Rest, a historic home in Nashville, was also a member of the church.

The first Sunday School in Nashville was begun in 1820 by Ann Phillips Grundy, wife of Felix Grundy, at various times a U. S. Congressman, Senator, and Attorney General. Both Felix and Ann Grundy were members.[31] Other prominent members included John Bell, United States Senator and 1860 Presidential candidate; Sara Childress Polk, wife of President James K. Polk; Howell E. Jackson, a U. S. Supreme Court Justice; Mrs. Monroe Harding, who gave her home as an orphanage; and Miss Martha O'Brien, who is memorialized by a settlement house in Nashville.[32]

In April 1855, Rev. Edgar presided at Montgomery Bell's funeral. Bell bequeathed $1,000 ($35,000 in today's dollars) to the church in his Will. This legacy was very helpful in addressing the church's financial woes during the Civil War.[33]

The First Presbyterian Church of Nashville played an important role during two of the nation's wars. During the Civil War, the Union Army used the church's auditorium for a hospital and stabled their horses in what is now the church dining room. During World War II, the church slept, showered, and fed servicemen who stayed in the church dining room.

In November 1954, the majority of the church's congregation voted to relocate to Oak Hill, the John Cheek estate on Franklin Road south of downtown Nashville.[34] A minority of the congregation decided to form the Downtown Presbyterian Church and stay in the original building in downtown Nashville, where they are an active congregation today.[35]

Horse Racing

Like Andrew Jackson and many other 19th century Tennesseans, Montgomery Bell enjoyed horse racing.[36] For most of the 19th century, Tennessee was the acknowledged "center of horse breeding and horse racing in the United States."[37]

As with everything he was involved in, he pursued the sport in a businesslike manner. He owned a horse named Eagle that sired other racehorses, and this, too, became a business for Bell.

In 1822 and 1823, he placed ads in local newspapers advertising the "services" of Eagle. According to ads that appeared in the *Nashville Whig* on April 10 and September 25, 1822, Eagle was "available at the stable of Mr. John Harding, six miles west of Nashville." The fee that Bell charged was $25, "paid before the mare is removed." The stable referred to in the ad was part of what became known as the Belle Meade Plantation, located on Harding Road in Nashville.

In June 1823, Bell placed an ad in the *Nashville Whig* on two occasions stating that Eagle would "stand the ensuing season at Mr. John Harding's, on Richland Creek, in Davidson county, on the same terms as last season." The ad went on to say, in Bell's florid style, that "Eagle is now twenty-eight years of age, and possesses all the life, spirit and action, of a horse in the prime of life." When Bell wrote this ad, he was fifty-four years old. Perhaps he was describing himself as well as Eagle!

However, just as he paced himself so that he would live to a ripe old age, he also paced Eagle. The ad concluded by stating that Eagle "is limited to thirty mares, and on no consideration will be let to more."

CHAPTER FIFTEEN

Montgomery Bell: Slave Owner and Emancipator

Montgomery Bell was a product of his times. Like thousands of 19th century Americans, he owned enslaved persons.[1]

The iron business was labor intensive. Bell needed a large number of workers to build and operate his facilities, and workers were in short supply in the rural areas in which these furnaces and forges were located. Enslaved persons constituted the largest portion of his work force.

As his life progressed, Bell came to understand the harshness of the institution of slavery. The transformation in Bell's thinking about slavery did not happen overnight. He first emancipated a group of his slaves in the 1830s, although this effort is shrouded in mystery. Near the end of his life, he emancipated three more large groups of his slaves and paid for their voyage to Liberia on ships chartered by the American Colonization Society. He also gave them money and equipment with which to utilize their ironmaking skills to start their own business in Liberia. His slaves were not forced to go to Liberia if they did not want to. It was their choice.

Slavery in Pennsylvania

It is not surprising that enslaved persons were a component of Bell's work force. After all, he had been raised in a Pennsylvania family that owned slaves. In the first census taken after ratification of the U.S. Constitution, his father John Bell was listed as owning eight enslaved persons.

Many Americans think that slavery was exclusively a Southern institution. However, most Northern states, including Pennsylvania, allowed slavery in the 18th and early 19th centuries.

In 1780, Pennsylvania passed an "Act for the Gradual Abolition of Slavery."[2] Under that law, every African American child (in the language of the statute, "every Negro or Mulatto child") born within the state *after* passage of the Act would become free upon reaching age twenty-eight. The law did *not* emancipate enslaved persons who were living in the state in 1780. If their owners *registered* them with the State, they would remain enslaved for the rest of their lives unless freed by their owners.

The Pennsylvania law thus emancipated *only* persons born into slavery *after* 1780, and such persons became free *only after* they turned twenty-eight years of age. The law did *not* prohibit the purchase and sale of registered slaves in Pennsylvania.

As the title of the Act made clear, the Pennsylvania law was a *gradual* abolition law. The number of registered slaves in Pennsylvania decreased over time. In 1790, there were 3,737 enslaved persons in the state. This number dropped to 1,706 by 1800 and to 795 by 1810. By 1840, there were still sixty-four enslaved persons in Pennsylvania. By 1850, there were none.

Other Northeastern states passed similar gradual abolition statutes, including Connecticut (1784), Rhode Island (1784), New York (1799), and New Jersey (1804).

The Use of Enslaved Persons at Iron Facilities

Montgomery Bell's use of enslaved persons at his furnaces and forges followed an employment practice typical at Southern iron facilities in the antebellum years.

Historian Charles B. Dew has written: "At most Southern blast furnaces slave labor played a large role in almost all phases of pig iron production. As founders, colliers, miners, teamsters, wood choppers, and general furnace hands, slaves constituted the bulk of the laboring force. An average charcoal blast furnace required some sixty or seventy slave workers."[3]

Historic preservation specialist Michael Thomas Gavin described the use of enslaved workers as "the only practical solution for the sustained development of any sizable [iron] enterprise" because "skilled native-born or immigrant workers remained extremely rare, so any regular output of pig iron had to be based on a solid underpinning of enslaved labor."[4]

In a 1959 article in *The Journal of Southern History*, historian S. Sydney Bradford enumerated the many jobs performed by the enslaved workers: "[O]n an ironworks plantation Negroes planted and harvested crops, cut and charcoaled wood, mined iron ore, drove wagons and manned boats, made shoes, ground flour, and worked as carpenters and blacksmiths."[5] Enslaved workers performed *agricultural* tasks to help feed the workers at the iron furnaces and forges.[6]

Slave owners were responsible for feeding and clothing the enslaved persons who worked at their iron facilities. According to a 1925 article in the *Tennessee Historical Magazine*, the slaves annually received two or three suits of clothes, a hat, three pairs of shoes, and a blanket. The teamsters were also given an overcoat. A slave's weekly ration of food included seven pounds of bacon, a peck of meal, and a quantity of molasses. Slaves would often barter with white residents in the area to obtain additional items such as melons, eggs, and other items, and many tended small garden plots to supplement their diets. In addition to clothing and food, the slave owner also supplied medical care and drugs through a physician employed to care for the health of the workers.[7]

Although enslaved persons were not paid regular wages, they did receive "cash or credit for work beyond that required of them."[8] They did extra work such as "driving wagons, chopping wood, and making baskets, tar, spikes, and rails…at night, on Sundays, and over the Christmas holidays." Their accounts were usually settled at the end of the year, when they received cash for the remainder of their unused credits.[9]

Montgomery Bell's Enslaved Workers

How did Montgomery Bell treat the enslaved workers at his furnaces and forges? According to Michael Thomas Gavin, a historic preservation specialist at Middle Tennessee State University (MTSU), Bell "invested an enormous amount of time instructing his slaves in the art and mystery of the iron trades."[10] Gavin wrote in his 2005 article in the *Tennessee Historical Quarterly*:

> Bell continually demonstrated great confidence in his African-American workforce and profitably employed large numbers of skilled and unskilled laborers. Although he hired additional men and women as needed from other slaveholders, Bell personally selected and carefully trained his own hands for every job at the works, including the specialized trades that required considerable technical knowledge…. [A] number of founders, engineers, forge-men, keepers, moulders, and blacksmiths could be counted among the veteran artisans staffing his various ironworks.[11]

According to Dickson County historian Robert E. Corlew, "Bell was said by some to have been kind to his slaves…. He was said to have given them large allowances of food and clothing and to have permitted them many liberties."[12]

Slavery was a harsh institution, though, even when the master was kind, and sometimes Bell's enslaved workers ran away. In a recent book, historian Bill Carey listed six ads placed by Bell in local newspapers seeking the public's help in locating specific slaves who had left his furnaces.[13] Bell was not the only slave owner who faced this problem. Carey's book devoted fifty-six pages to a list of runaway slave ads placed in local newspapers by Tennessee slave owners during a seventy-two-year period.[14]

In every discussion of how Bell treated his enslaved workers, the person who always receives special mention is James Worley, a slave who first worked with Bell in his hat business in Kentucky and then moved to Tennessee with Bell about 1802. The MTSU historic preservation specialist who wrote the above quoted article had this to say about Worley:

> For most of Bell's career, Worley acted as his trusted executive assistant, handling important business transactions and transporting large sums of cash over great distances. As the legendary ironmaster's agent, advisor, and confidant, Worley emerged as one of Tennessee's first prominent African-Americans. In 1844, after Bell completed the construction of the last of his blast furnaces (the remains of which still rest against a hillside along Old Furnace Road), he selected the name "Worley Furnace" in order to honor his faithful steward. This choice of an enslaved African American's name to designate an industrial facility may be unique in Tennessee history.[15]

Bell said that Worley "was never a dollar short" in all his dealings on Bell's behalf. He was offered a substantial sum of money for Worley, but replied on one occasion, "I would not take all of New Orleans for him."[16]

U.S. Constitutional Provisions Governing Slavery During Bell's Lifetime

The issue of slavery bedeviled Americans from the founding of our country and led to a horrific Civil War that killed more than 620,000 Americans. When the Founding Fathers gathered in Philadelphia in the summer of 1787 to write a new Constitution, though, they chose to omit any *direct* reference to slavery.

Three sections of the Constitution contained *indirect* acknowledgments of the existence of slavery in our young nation. Article I, Section 2 made a distinction between "free Persons" and "all other Persons" (i.e., enslaved persons) in determining the number of Representatives a State was entitled to have in the House of Representatives. An enslaved person would be counted as 3/5 of a person for purposes of determining representation.

Article I, Section 9 forbade Congress from passing any law prohibiting "the Migration or Importation of such persons as any of the States now existing shall think proper to admit" prior to the year 1808. The purpose of this provision was to *allow* Americans to continue bringing enslaved persons from Africa and elsewhere to the United States during the years 1787 to 1808. Although Congress passed legislation in 1807 outlawing the international slave trade, beginning January 1, 1808,[17] half a million enslaved Africans had been brought to this country before it became illegal to do so.[18] Even after passage of this law, the "historic record is rife with proof that slaves continued to pour into the country from Africa, with some estimates suggesting as many as ten thousand a year."[19]

Finally, Article IV, Section 2 provided that a "Person held to Service or Labour in one state" (i.e., an enslaved person) who escaped into another state had to "be delivered up on Claim of the Party to whom such Service or Labour may be due." This Constitutional provision was enforced by Congress through passage of the infamous Fugitive Slave Act of 1793, which was greatly strengthened in 1850.[20]

These three sections of the Constitution, of course, became null and void after ratification of the 13th and 14th Amendments, but they were the Law of the Land during the lifetime of Montgomery Bell.

Tennessee Laws Governing Emancipation during Bell's Lifetime

As he grew older, Bell changed his thinking about slavery. Beginning in the 1830s, he decided to emancipate most, if not all, of his slaves. After making this decision, he faced substantial obstacles created by the Tennessee legislature, which wanted to discourage emancipation because of a fear that freed African Americans would encourage slave uprisings.

Emancipation was not easy in Tennessee. A slave owner could not simply tell a slave that he was free to go. The Tennessee legislature passed laws strictly regulating the procedure by which a slave owner could emancipate his slaves if he decided to do so.[21]

An 1801 statute required a slave owner wishing to free a slave or slaves to file a petition with the County Court setting forth "the intention and motives for such emancipation."[22] The Court would grant the petition if 2/3 of the members of the Court found that emancipation "would be consistent with the interest and policy of the State" and if the slave owner "entered into bond with approved security in such sum as the Court thinks proper." Slave owners thought this procedure cumbersome and bureaucratic. The law created a disincentive to emancipation.

Sometimes a slave owner sought to free his slaves at the time of his death by including an emancipation provision in his Will. An 1829 law imposed a duty on the Executor of the deceased slave owner to petition the County Court to carry out the testator's intent.[23] If the Executor failed to carry out the testator's wishes, the slave could, acting through the slave's "next friend" (since slaves had no standing to go to court), file a bill in equity asking the court to order that the slave be set free (after posting a bond with good security).

The highly publicized 1831 slave rebellion in Virginia, instigated by Nat Turner, sent shock waves through the South, including Tennessee. In December of that year, the Tennessee legislature passed a law requiring that a slave who was emancipated by his owner must be "immediately removed" from Tennessee and that the condition of removal from Tennessee must be a part of the judgment of the court.[24]

This 1831 law also made it a crime for any "free person of color" to move to, or remain in, Tennessee for more than thirty days – a crime punishable by a jail term of one-to-two years. This section of the law was a ham-handed effort to rid the state of free African Americans, because they were believed to be instigators of trouble among slaves.[25]

By 1833, the proponents of the 1831 law had decided that it was unfair to those former slaves who had gained their freedom before the law was enacted. So, the legislature passed a law stating that if a slave had contracted for his freedom before December 1831, the emancipated person would not be required to leave Tennessee.[26]

The 1833 legislature also passed another law that reflected the true desire of most legislators regarding free blacks. The goal was to remove them not just from Tennessee, but from the United States. This law provided that the State would pay ten dollars to the American Colonization Society (ACS) for each free black removed from Tennessee by that organization (or its state auxiliary) to the coast of Africa.[27]

There are no records showing how much the State paid to the ACS pursuant to the 1833 law during the ten years that it was in effect. Whatever the amount, the legislature repealed this law in 1843.[28]

In 1834, the people of Tennessee voted to adopt a new state Constitution to replace the original 1796 Constitution. The members of the Constitutional Convention who drafted the 1834 Constitution were largely slave owners wanting to ensure that a future legislature would not take any action of the type being advocated by manumission societies.[29] Article II, Section 31 of the 1834 Constitution stated that "the General Assembly shall have no power to pass laws for the emancipation of slaves without the consent of their owner or owners."

Not surprisingly, many emancipated slaves wanted to remain in Tennessee, where they had friends and family. In 1842, the legislature again modified the harsh 1831 law by providing that a slave who was emancipated and living in Tennessee before 1836 could petition the County Court, setting forth the reasons why he wished to remain in Tennessee.[30] If the Court determined that the person filing the petition was "of good character," the Court could grant the petition, conditioned upon the applicant giving a bond of $500 (with two or more sureties) to ensure that the person would "keep the peace and be of good behavior towards all free white citizens" and "not become chargeable to the county." An applicant was limited to living in the county where the petition was filed and granted, and the applicant had to renew the "privilege" every five years.

By 1849, the Tennessee legislature had changed their mind again. They repealed the 1842 law and reinstated the harsh 1831 law requiring emancipated persons to leave the state.[31]

By 1854 (a year before Montgomery Bell's death), the legislature had reached the end of their road. They passed a law stating that all slaves acquiring a right to freedom, by contract or by the owner's Will, "shall be transported to the western coast of Africa."[32]

The costs of transporting a freed slave to Africa, of course, had to be paid by someone. Under the 1854 law, if the slave owner had raised a fund to pay these expenses or had agreed to pay the expenses himself, the money was to be paid into the Court. If there was no fund to pay the transportation expenses, the Court was required to place the freed slave in possession of the Clerk of Court, who would hire out the slave to raise money to pay the transportation expenses.

The 1854 law imposed a duty on the Governor of Tennessee to "make the necessary arrangements for conveying a freed slave to a seaport town of the United States, for transporting the slave to the western coast of Africa and for providing for his support for six months." When considered in the context of 21st century jurisprudence, there is no telling how many Constitutional provisions this 1854 law violated! But it does give a sense of the desperate lengths to which Tennessee lawmakers were willing to go to remove emancipated slaves from the state.

All these provisions of Tennessee law became inapplicable in 1865 after passage of the 13th Amendment abolishing slavery. But the laws discussed in this chapter were laws in effect during Montgomery Bell's lifetime — laws of which he was surely aware and with which he had to comply. They made it more difficult for him to free his slaves once he had decided that emancipation was the right course to take.

American Colonization Society

In the early 19th century, there was much discussion about how to address the slavery issue without tearing the country apart. One idea which emerged from those discussions was the idea of transporting slaves to the continent from which they or their ancestors had been brought to America, i.e., Africa.

On December 21, 1816, an organization was formed in Washington, D.C. known initially as The American Society for Colonizing Free People of Color of the United States and known later as the American Colonization Society (ACS). The first president of this new organization was Bushrod Washington, nephew of President George Washington and at that time an Associate Justice of the United States Supreme Court. He remained president until his death in 1829.[33] Subsequent ACS presidents included former U.S. President James Madison and three-time Presidential candidate Henry Clay.[34] Another prominent American who belonged to and supported the ACS was future President Abraham Lincoln.[35]

The first group of free blacks was sent to Africa in 1820, and the new colony of Liberia was established by the ACS on the western coast of Africa in 1822. The capitol of Liberia was named Monrovia, after then U.S. President James Monroe, another prominent supporter of the organization's efforts.[36]

In 1839, the Commonwealth of Liberia was organized under a governor appointed by the ACS. In 1847, Liberia declared its independence and adopted a constitution similar to the United States Constitution. It was the first African country to proclaim its independence and is Africa's first and oldest republic.[37]

In 1825, the ACS began publicizing its activities through a journal known as the *African Repository*, which provided an excellent record of the group's activities over a long period of years.[38] In 1837, the organization was incorporated in the State of Maryland under the name American Colonization Society.

In 1829, the ACS developed a plan for the creation of state societies, to be auxiliaries of the national group. In accordance with this plan, the Tennessee Colonization Society (TCS) was organized in December 1829, with the Rev. Philip Lindsley, president of the University of Nashville, as the group's first president.[39] Another key member of the TCS, was Francis B. Fogg, Montgomery Bell's long-time attorney. Another TCS supporter was Rev. John Todd Edgar, who in 1833 became pastor of Nashville's First Presbyterian Church, the church that Bell attended and eventually joined.

The formation of the TCS led to the passage of the 1833 law under which the State of Tennessee agreed to give the organization ten dollars for every free black person transported to Liberia from Tennessee.[40]

In 1850, the Tennessee legislature passed a bill incorporating the TCS.[41] The new law stated that the object of the organization was "to colonize with their own consent in Liberia, on the coast of Africa, the free people of color residing in this State...." It gave the TCS the authority to "take and receive any sum or sums of money, goods or chattels that should be given, sold, or bequeathed to them in any manner whatsoever." The obvious purpose was to encourage such gifts that would then be used to pay the expenses of transporting free blacks and emancipated slaves to Liberia.

The high-water mark for the colonization movement was in the late 1840s and the 1850s. At the national level, prominent politicians like Daniel Webster, Edward Everett, Stephen Douglas, Millard Fillmore, Henry Clay, and Abraham Lincoln attended ACS meetings and supported ACS efforts.[42] According to one historian who has studied ACS activities, "More slaveholders sent more bondpersons to Liberia between 1848 and 1860 than in the previous thirty years combined."[43]

Bell's Emancipation of His Slaves

Why did Montgomery Bell decide to emancipate his slaves? When did he make this important decision?

The answers to these two questions are not clear. Numerous sources shed light on the matter, though.

In the early 1830s, there was an ongoing effort to publicize the activities of the TCS, an effort that Bell was surely aware of. The TCS placed a Notice in the March 20, 1833 issue of the *National Banner and Nashville Daily Advertiser,* stating that a ship would leave New Orleans about April 1, taking "emigrants" (i.e., emancipated slaves) to Liberia. According to the Notice, emigrants desiring to travel to Liberia from Tennessee had to be at Nashville or Memphis by March 20, where they would be picked up and taken to New Orleans. The Notice further stated that the TCS or a "benevolent individual" would have to pay to the TCS Treasurer twenty-five dollars for every emigrant they wished to send to Liberia. Bell may have seen this Notice and started thinking about sending his slaves to Liberia. Whether or not he saw the Notice, historians are in general agreement that Bell took his first actions to begin the process of emancipation in the 1830s, although the details are far from clear.

Pastors undoubtedly played a role in Bell's decision to emancipate his slaves. In their 1986 history of Nashville's First Presbyterian Church, Wilbur F. Creighton, Jr. and Leland R. Johnson described an occasion in 1834 when "many American slaves" who had been emancipated by their owners met in the church dining room, where they were addressed by the Rev. John Todd Edgar before being placed on a ship headed to Liberia.[44] The book does not state that the freed slaves included slaves emancipated by Montgomery Bell, but it is possible that they did. The fact that Bell attended this church and its pastor played such a prominent role in this incident suggests that some of Bell's slaves had been freed and were among those who boarded the ship headed first to New Orleans and then to Liberia.[45]

In a 1978 feature article in the *Tennessean,* Louise Davis, a respected local historian, wrote about this incident:

> The sound of some 50 slaves' singing on the steps of old First Presbyterian Church at Fifth and Church Street that day in 1835 stopped Nashvillians in their tracks and must have stirred tight-lipped Montgomery Bell deeply. For these were his slaves – carefully selected and trained through years of exacting labor. And Bell himself had given them their freedom. He had led them to this church where he was a loyal member, and he had asked his pastor, the Rev. John Todd Edgar, to conduct a special service for them before they set forth on the long journey to Africa and independence. And when they had sung their last hymn and said their last prayer on the church steps, Bell walked down the hill with them to the river where they boarded the keelboat for New Orleans. There they would board the ship that Bell is said to have

chartered to take them to Liberia, the newly created country (about the size of the state of Ohio) on the west coast of Africa.[46]

The year in which this incident took place is not the same in the Church history as in Davis' article — 1834 vs. 1835. But other prominent historians have reached the conclusion that the incident at First Presbyterian Church *did* occur and that some of Bell's slaves were among those who boarded the ship for New Orleans, ultimately headed to Liberia.

In a book published on the eve of Nashville's 1980 Bicentennial, noted historian John Egerton wrote that "Montgomery Bell, a wealthy and eccentric manufacturer of iron products…freed fifty of his slaves in a ceremony at the Presbyterian Church…and walked with them down to the wharf, where they departed on a journey to Liberia."[47]

John F. Baker, Jr., a descendant of slaves that lived on a Robertson County, Tennessee tobacco plantation known as Wessyngton,[48] mentioned the incident in his 2009 book about his family's history:

> Clearly, Montgomery Bell, the iron baron of Dickson County, was the most outstanding of all the slaveholders to free blacks in Tennessee. Bell emancipated fifty slaves in 1835 and paid for their transportation to the newly created colony of Liberia on the west coast of Africa. Bell sent fifty more blacks to Liberia in 1853. Thirty-eight of them were members of one family. Bell brought a teacher from Philadelphia to teach his slaves to read and write, which was illegal in most states. In his lifetime he emancipated nearly 250 slaves and sent them to Africa. This would have cost him an estimated $100,000. Bell planned to emancipate some of his other slaves who did not want to leave the country to a free state, but he could not find a state that would permit it.[49]

Bobby L. Lovett, prominent local historian and long-time professor and dean at Tennessee State University[50], provided a different twist on the incident. He wrote that Bell was influenced by a speech given on October 14, 1833, in Nashville by abolitionist James G. Birney[51], a former slave owner who embraced colonization and later abolition of slavery. According to Lovett's book, Bell "freed and paid for the transport to Liberia of at least eighty-three of his slaves."[52]

One of the best discussions of this subject is found in the thoroughly researched 1970 Master's Thesis of MTSU graduate student James Maurice Gifford, who wrote that "as early as the 1830s Bell gave serious consideration to emancipating and colonizing some of his slaves."[53] Gifford gave credit to "a Methodist minister named Edwards"[54] for convincing Bell that he should emancipate his slaves. The 1831 and 1832 minutes of the Tennessee Conference of the Methodist Episcopal Church reveal that Wiley B. Edwards was a preacher who in the 1830s had responsibility for Methodist churches in the Forked Deer District of western Tennessee. Since one of the responsibilities of these Methodist itinerant preachers was to conduct camp meetings and revivals, it is possible that Bell met Rev. Edwards, who would surely have discussed emancipation with him.

Gifford was convinced that Bell's first effort to emancipate and colonize a group of his slaves occurred "sometime in the decade 1834-1844" and that Bell may have "chartered a small ship of his own to carry the [emancipated] slaves" to Liberia rather than utilizing a ship chartered by the ACS.[55]

We may never know for certain the details of these early efforts by Bell to free his slaves. The weight of the evidence is convincing, though, that Bell sent a group of his emancipated slaves to Liberia sometime in the 1830s.

By the 1850s, Bell had decided that he should work with the Colonization Society if he wished to free additional slaves. He had considered colonizing his slaves somewhere in the United States and had sent his great-nephew George Bain to Ohio and Illinois to look for a large tract of land for that purpose. Bain was rebuffed by the state officials with whom he met.[56] The sad reality was that most Northerners did not want emancipated Southern slaves moving to their states. In the words of Vanderbilt professor Richard J.M. Blackett: "America was not a place where the Negro could ever be free from racial animosity."[57]

Once he had made the decision to work with the ACS, Bell proceeded in the same methodical way that he ran his business. Gifford provided details of the steps that Bell took:

> Bell planned his next venture carefully. He had never known defeat and was determined to follow his conscience. George Bain spent several years helping Bell lay plans for the next trip and sort out the letters of aid and advice that came from the American Colonization Society and other interested parties. The final decision was a wise one. Bain was to travel to New York to talk with

officials of the Society; he then was to travel to England and buy what machinery was needed to set up a first class furnace and rolling mill. Finally, Bain was to travel with the Negroes to Africa and remain with them three years.[58]

Bell wanted his freed slaves to use the skills they had learned working at his iron furnaces and forges in their new home in Liberia, a country rich in iron ore.[59] Professor Blackett's 2010 article in the *Tennessee Historical Quarterly* described in detail the actions that followed as Bell sought to implement his goal.[60] Bell decided to send his emancipated slaves to Liberia in several groups. The ACS records contain accurate information about the trips which took Bell's slaves to Liberia in 1853 and 1854.

ACS records also contain three letters written by Montgomery Bell to William McLain of the ACS.[61] They provide fascinating insight into the process by which Bell went about the emancipation of his slaves.

In a letter written on December 7, 1853, Bell informed McLain that he had designated Samuel Henry Armstrong of Maury County as his "agent and attorney in fact" to accompany Bell's emancipated slaves to Savannah, Georgia, where they would board a ship chartered by the ACS for the trip to Liberia. In his letter, Bell described his emancipated slaves as "families of negroes of good character, of more than ordinary intelligence, and to whom I am much attached." His letter said they were taking their tools and other implements with them to Liberia. He advanced the sum of $2,500 (almost $100,000 in today's dollars) to his agent Armstrong to defray the expenses of the trip. His letter listed the slaves he was sending by name and age.

On December 21, 1853, Bell sent a second letter to McLain, thanking him for his efforts and informing him that he had "70 or 80 slaves besides whom I wish likewise sent to Liberia there to be free." Bell described these slaves as "mechanics, miners, colliers, moulders, and fully competent to build a furnace for making iron and carrying it on themselves." He obviously had a high degree of confidence in the slaves he was emancipating and sending to Liberia.

The first trip was aboard the ship known as *General Pierce* (named for then-President Franklin Pierce, who had been a Brigadier General in the Mexican-American War). This ship had been chartered by the ACS and sailed from Savannah, Georgia to Liberia in December 1853, carrying eighty-five emancipated slaves, thirty-eight of whom had been freed by Montgomery Bell. The names and ages of these formerly enslaved persons are found in the February

1854 issue of the *African Repository*. Bell's group was headed by Thomas and Louisa Scott, both in their fifties, and included many of their children and grandchildren. Twenty-four of the thirty-eight persons in this group were under the age of twenty.[62] According to Professor Blackett's article, "there were no reports of deaths or complaints about overcrowding" on this trip.[63]

The success of the first voyage persuaded Bell to send additional groups of his emancipated slaves to Liberia. Emancipation occupied Bell's thoughts during the winter of 1853-54. He worked closely with his pastor, Rev. John Edgar, during this period. ACS records contain two letters that Rev. Edgar wrote to William McLain of the ACS.

In a February 18, 1854 letter, Rev. Edgar told McLain that Bell was planning to send "as many as he can, designing eventually…to send most of his servants, still amounting to considerably upwards of one hundred." He said Bell hoped the ACS would urge the government of Liberia to set aside a territory containing iron ore so that Bell's emancipated slaves could pursue "the business to which they have been accustomed in this country and for which they are well qualified." Rev. Edgar also told McLain in this letter that Bell was "unwilling that his people, whom he designs to send to Liberia, should embark" from New Orleans because of "the usually prevailing epidemics at N. Orleans." He suggested Norfolk, Baltimore, Savannah, or Charleston as safer ports of departure to Liberia.

Map showing the location of Liberia. (Wikipedia)

In a March 7, 1854 letter, Rev. Edgar told McLain that Bell was "now

Map of West Africa in 1839 showing the location of Liberia. (Wikimedia Commons)

in his 86th year and is becoming very infirm." Rev. Edgar expressed to McLain his hope about Bell: "Should he be spared another year or two, I think he will send all or most of his people, now amounting to nearly two hundred."

On May 3, 1854, Bell wrote directly to McLain, confirming that he would send fifty emancipated slaves to Liberia on ACS ships. He described them as "all of good character" and said, "there are no better hands." He singled out Elijah Worley (a son of James Worley) as "an engineer fully competent to build a furnace and carry it on." This time, he sent $2,200 (about $75,000 in today's dollars) with his agent Sam Armstrong to defray the expenses of the trip.

Two ships were chartered by the ACS in the spring of 1854. Twenty-eight of Bell's slaves were transported on the ship *Sophia Walker*, and twenty-one were transported on the brig *Harp*. Their names were listed in the July 1854 issue of the *African Repository*.[64] The September 1854 issue of the *African Repository* mentioned the amount that Col. Montgomery Bell contributed "toward the passage and support" of his emancipated slaves that traveled to Liberia on these two ships.[65] Like the earlier group, the majority of these two groups were under the age of twenty. Tennessee was second only to Virginia in the total number of emancipated slaves sent to Liberia in 1854 on ACS ships.[66]

In late June 1854, William McLain spoke to the ACS Executive Committee with pride about Bell's emancipation efforts in 1853 and 1854. ACS records contain McLain's summary of Bell's actions and plans for emancipation of the rest of his slaves:

> Montgomery Bell Esq. of Tenn., having sent to Liberia thirty-eight of his iron men in the General Pierce last December, had sent fifty more in the Sophia Walker last month, and ... he intends to send another large company about the 1st December next, and the remainder of his slaves as soon as he can complete the arrangements; making in all about two hundred and fifty citizens of Liberia; that he is so anxious to have his people comfortably settled in the iron ore district, that he is intending to commission his nephew, George C. Bain, Esq., who thoroughly understands his plans and designs, to visit Liberia, and assist his people in selecting the best location, and making all the necessary arrangements for their most successfully entering on the business of making iron; that Mr. Bain is now in this city [Washington], making inquiries and arrangements; that he proposes going to Liberia by way of England, where he intends to

procure machinery and everything necessary to enable the people to commence the manufacture of iron to the very best advantage.

Mr. Bell has received a very encouraging letter from Thomas Scott, the leader of the company who sailed in December, saying that he has found fine beds of iron [in the] interior of Linow about twenty-five miles. The company who sailed in the Sophia Walker will stop at Bassa to acclimate, and make investigations [in the] interior of that settlement. They will thus be enabled to make a survey of the whole ground, and select the place which is nearest the coast, easiest of access, richest in ore, and most suitable, all things considered for laying the foundations of the long desired interior settlement.[67]

Bell's plan for emancipation of his slaves through their relocation to iron-rich Liberia reflects the same careful forethought he used when siting his iron furnaces in Tennessee.

Following the completion of the 1854 voyages that took Bell's emancipated slaves to Liberia, Samuel Armstrong wrote a June 30 letter to William McLain confirming that they had made it safely. In this letter, Armstrong also told McLain that he had just completed a visit with Montgomery Bell to give him a full report about the trip. Armstrong said Bell "was glad to find that we had got his people off in so good health."[68] Bell told Armstrong that he was "doing all he could to dispose of his iron works and farm so as he can send 100 [slaves] this winter." Bell said he was "under a solemn promise to a great many of them to send them this winter."

Newspapers publicized Bell's decision to emancipate his slaves and send them to Liberia. A December 13, 1853 article in *The Tennessean* stated that eighty "emigrants" traveled by train from Nashville to Savannah, where they embarked on a ship which would take them to Liberia. The group of eighty included thirty who had been freed by William E. Kennedy of Maury County, twelve who had been freed under the will of Rev. Thomas Douglass of Williamson County, and thirty-eight who had been freed by Col. Montgomery Bell[69] of Davidson County. The article stated that this was "the largest company that ever emigrated from Tennessee" and that they "were well furnished with mechanical tools and agricultural implements and an abundant supply of comfortable clothing and other necessaries of life." According to the article, Col. Bell "paid all the expenses of his [emancipated slaves] from Nashville to Liberia."

Similar articles appeared in several Pennsylvania newspapers, which had an interest because Bell was a Pennsylvania native and still had family ties in the state. A January 28, 1854 article in *The Sunbury [PA] Gazette* described Bell's emancipated slaves as "the iron men of Tennessee" and said they included "miners, colliers, moulders, and are fully competent to build a furnace for making iron and carrying it on themselves."

This same article mentioned that Bell "has a large number more, of whom he wants to send about eighty as soon as the Society can take them and is willing to pay one half the expenses of transportation and support." A January 27, 1854 article in the *Nashville Union and American* quoted William McLain as saying that "a distinguished gentleman has avowed his readiness to contribute $2,400 to enable the Society to send eighty of the people of Montgomery Bell, Esq. of Nashville, Tennessee, to Liberia in our next vessel."[70] The "distinguished gentleman" was William Appleton, a Massachusetts businessman and politician who was "noted for benevolence toward public causes" and had been present at the annual ACS meeting in Washington in January 1854.[71] The records of the ACS Executive Committee contain a January 18, 1854 letter from Appleton, pledging $2,400 to enable Montgomery Bell "to carry out his benevolent intentions."[72]

After the two groups of Bell's emancipated slaves had made the journey to Liberia in May and June 1854, an article appeared in *The Tennessean* on August 1, 1854, describing Bell's plans to emancipate additional slaves. This article described the role that Bell's nephew George Bain was playing by going to England and "procuring such machinery, and other necessaries, as will be of use to the negroes in commencing their works." This article said that "it is the intention of Mr. Bell to spare no expense in order to give his negroes a fair start." This article concluded by stating: "We hope [Bell] may live to see his plans successful, and his negroes prosperous citizens of Liberia."

In the summer of 1854, the ACS announced that its next ship would sail from Savannah to Liberia in December 1854. Bain informed the ACS that Bell "would be ready to send out 100 [emancipated slaves]" on that ship. Due to a shortage of funds, the ACS postponed that trip to May 1855.

In the first months of 1855, Bell's nephew George Bain wrote two letters to McLain. His February 12 letter said Bell planned to send additional emancipated slaves on the next ACS trip to Liberia and added that Bain would accompany the slaves on the trip to "carry out [Bell's] former designs, viz., constructing iron works." In a March 6 letter, Bain requested McLain to send to Bell "all letters from the people he sent over" to Liberia. Bell had a continuing interest in the welfare of the slaves he had emancipated.

Sadly, Bell did not live until the next ACS trip. He died on April 1, 1855. It seems clear that Bell had made a firm decision to emancipate all his slaves, but his death prevented him from achieving his goal.[73]

The fate of Bell's emancipated slaves in Liberia is not known. In 1854, one of them sent him a "bar of iron" made in Liberia — evidence that his emancipated slaves had achieved some success in establishing an iron furnace there. As Professor Blackett wrote: "There is no way of knowing what role the Middle Tennesseans played in developing what by the twentieth century would become one of the mainstays of Liberia's economy."

What was the overall impact of colonization? According to Eric Burin, the historian who has studied the movement most thoroughly, 562 slave owners emancipated and sent 6,043 of their slaves to Liberia during the years between 1820 and 1860.[74] Another 4,095 free blacks went to Liberia during the same period of time.[75]

Was the colonization movement a success? In a larger sense, most would agree that it was not.[76] But "the decisions of Kennedy and Bell to manumit and transport their slaves were the colonization movement's greatest successes in the decade before the war."[77]

Bell tried his best to use this method of emancipating his slaves and giving them an opportunity to use the skills he had taught them to make a living and achieve success in a land free from racial animosity. He had been persuaded that colonization was "the one legitimate and practical means of emancipation."[78] Only his death in 1855 prevented him from completing his mission.

Ed Huddleston, the *Nashville Banner* reporter who wrote a series of twelve articles about Bell in 1955, was impressed that Bell overcame the many obstacles placed in the way of a Tennessee slave owner who decided to emancipate his slaves:

> To his eternal credit, Montgomery Bell surmounted these obstacles. Rarely in his life did he hesitate to kick the teeth down the throat of convention. The difficulties of manumission magnify his courage, his will, his generosity.[79]

CHAPTER SIXTEEN

Montgomery Bell's Estate

Montgomery Bell died quietly at his Valley Forge home on April 1, 1855, at the age of eighty-six. Despite his prominence in life, there were no lengthy obituaries describing his many accomplishments.

Nashville's *Republican Banner* of April 3, 1855, carried a simple but dignified Notice:

> **DIED. On the 1st inst., at Valley Forge,**
> **Dickson County, Tennessee, MONTGOMERY**
> **BELL, in the 87th year of his age.**
> **His friends are respectfully invited**
> **to attend his burial, at the Narrows of**
> **Harpeth, Davidson County, on Tuesday**
> **the 3d of April, at 11 o'clock.**
> **Service by Rev. Dr. Edgar.**

Bell Cemetery (Author photo)

The scenic Harpeth River between the Tunnel and the Haines farm. (Author photo)

We do not know how many people attended his funeral. One that was present was L.L. Leech, Bell's cousin, who lived in Dickson County and had assisted Bell with his business affairs.[1] The eulogy was delivered by his long-time friend Rev. John Todd Edgar, pastor of the First Presbyterian Church in Nashville. He was buried in a small cemetery within sight of the tunnel he had built about 1819, next to his granddaughter Eveline, who had died as a young child. His granddaughter Mary was buried next to them three years later.

Francis Fogg (Tennessee State Library and Archives)

Montgomery Bell signed his Will on July 1, 1852, while living in Williamson County. It had been drawn up by his long-time attorney Francis Fogg, but there is no doubt that Bell dictated the language and content of the Will. His signing of the Will was witnessed by Fogg and Nathaniel Baxter, at that time a Circuit Court Judge.

Bell appointed three persons to serve as his Executors. All were men he trusted to use proper care in disposing of his considerable assets. First was his nephew/son-in-law James L. Bell, to whom he had already given a significant portion of his iron properties in 1851. The other two were prominent local businessmen. W.E. Watkins was active in the Methodist Church and the Democratic Party. O.P. McRoberts owned substantial real estate and served as agent for the owners of lead and coal mines.[2]

Bell's Will was recorded with the Davidson County Court on December 11, 1855.[3]

Shortly after his death, his Executors began the process on carrying out the wishes he expressed in his Will. They placed a Notice in the *Nashville Union and American* on April 14, 1855, notifying the public that they were serving as Bell's Executors and encouraging persons having claims against Bell to present them promptly. On April 25 and 26, they compiled an inventory of the assets Bell owned at the time of his death. The total value of these assets (not including his slaves) was $72,426.20, which in today's dollars would be approximately $2.5 million.

The Executors later compiled a list of the 135 enslaved persons Bell owned at the time of his death. Fifty-two of these slaves were leased to his nephew/son-in-law James L. Bell pursuant to a lease that expired August 14, 1858. The remaining eighty-three slaves, most of whom were children, were living at Valley Forge. This list contained the names and ages of the slaves.[4]

On February 19, 1856, Bell's Executors sold these slaves at a public auction held at Valley Forge. In his Will, Bell had admonished his Executors to sell his slaves "to good masters who will treat them kindly and not remove them beyond the limits of this state" and not to separate families. Presumably, his intentions were carried out.

According to a newspaper article announcing the results of the sale, approximately half of the enslaved persons were under the age of twenty. The sale netted $106,105 for Bell's estate, approximately $3.7 million in today's dollars.[5]

On March 12, 1856, the Executors placed a Notice in the *Nashville Union and American* headlined "Executor's Sale – Ten Thousand Acres of Land in Dickson County, Tennessee."[6] The properties mentioned in this ad included the iron properties Bell still owned at the time of his death.

The Executors sold 654 acres to Robert Oakley in April 1856[7] and 392.5 acres to Robert McNeilly in September 1856.[8] Both these tracts lay on Jones Creek.

The Executors had difficulty selling the Jackson Furnace properties and had to place an ad in Nashville newspapers on several occasions in the fall of 1856.[9] They finally sold 1,845.5 acres to a group of five persons in late November 1856.[10]

By the spring of 1857, the Executors were still trying to sell the so-called "second Tunnell excavated by the late Montgomery Bell at the Narrows."[11] This was the property Bell had excluded in his deed of gift to his nephew/son-in-law in 1851. The description of the property in the newspaper ad is titillating: "This property is well worth the examination and attention of capitalists, or persons wishing to manufacture. It is an excellent chance for speculation." A second ad stated that this property would be sold at public auction at the Davidson County Courthouse on May 5, 1857.[12] The results of such a sale are not evident in the public record.

The Executors had no trouble implementing the first two provisions of Bell's Will: $20,000 was placed in the care of Planters Bank for the creation of Montgomery Bell Academy, and $1,000 was conveyed to the First Presbyterian Church of Nashville to help defray its debt.

The implementation of the third provision of Bell's Will required considerable research by the Executors. Bell had specified that the "rest residue remainder of [his] estate both real and personal" be sold by his Executors and that the proceeds be divided into eight shares. Each share would then be distributed to the children and grandchildren of his eight deceased siblings. (The ninth sibling Zachariah never married and had no children.) The distribution to Bell's nieces and nephews was to be "per stirpes," meaning that the share set aside for each sibling's children would be divided equally among the children of that sibling (or the grandchildren where a sibling's child had died).

All nine of Bell's brothers and sisters had died many years before Bell's own death in 1855. Making a complete list of his siblings' children (and grandchildren) required a time-consuming investigation in the pre-internet age. Two Special Commissioners (S.L. Finley and H.M.R. Fogg) were appointed by the Executors to "ascertain and report the names and places of residence of the legatees and next of kin of Montgomery Bell."

The two Commissioners filed a nine-page Report with the Court, setting forth in detail the heirs of each of Bell's brothers and sisters and their places of residence where known.[13] Finley and Fogg, the two Commissioners, were both lawyers and persuaded many of the heirs to hire one of them to represent their interests in the legal proceedings.

The total amount of Bell's Estate distributed to these nieces and nephews was $40,000, about $1.4 million in today's dollars. The largest amount that any individual received was $5,000. The smallest amount was $104.16.

Bell had played no favorites in his Will. Each sibling's heirs received the same portion of Bell's Estate. The amount that each individual heir received was determined solely according to the number of children that each sibling had sired. His nieces and nephews must have been very grateful to Uncle Montgomery for what was clearly a windfall for each of them.

It may seem strange that Montgomery Bell chose to leave so much of his fortune to the descendants of his siblings rather than to his own grandchildren. There is no obvious explanation for this decision. Like everything else in his life, Bell did things the way he thought appropriate.

CHAPTER SEVENTEEN

Last Will and Testament of Montgomery Bell

In the name of God, Amen.

I Montgomery Bell now residing in Williamson County Tennessee, do hereby make and publish this my last Will and Testament.

First. I hereby give, bequeath and devise to the University of Nashville a Corporation formerly existing under the name of Cumberland College in Davidson County, and their successors forever the sum of twenty thousand dollars in trust to and for the following uses and purposes and for none other, to wit, That the Trustees of said University of Nashville invest the said sum of twenty thousand dollars as follows, in State bonds or in good notes secured by mortgage on real estate of double the value, the interest to be paid semiannually, which interest is to be appropriated for the support of an Academy or school to be called the Montgomery Bell Academy forever for the education of children not less than ten or more than fourteen years old who are not able to support and educate themselves and whose parents are not able to do so. The children are to be educated in the common branches of an English Education reading, writing, arithmetic, geography, and such other branches, including mathematics and the ancient or modern languages as may be established by a plan to be set forth and adopted by the Trustees of said University. The scholars to be male children, and to continue until they arrive at the age of eighteen years and to be selected from time to time by the Trustees and designated by them, whereof I would prefer ten from Davidson, five children from Williamson, five from Dickson and five from Montgomery or about in that proportion from those counties in our State of Tennessee. The said Academy to be established in the County of Davidson where said University may deem it most suitable and to be under their supervision and control, and the said University of Nashville if the Trustees thereof shall think it necessary, may apply to the General Assembly for an act to incorporate said Academy according to the plan or system to be devised by said University having regard to my objects hereinbefore stated, the education of poor children. I hereby direct my executors to pay over to said University the said sum of twenty thousand dollars within one year after my decease to be held by said Corporation and the successors for the purposes and trusts before mentioned. The money to be paid out of the money due me for the Whites Bend tract of land.

2nd. I give and bequeath to John M. Hill and Dr. John Edgar one thousand dollars which I wish appropriated for the payment of the debts due from or otherwise for the benefit of the First Presbyterian Church in Nashville, which is also to be paid out of the money due me for the Whites Bend tract of land.

3dly. All the rest, residue and remainder of my estate both real and personal consisting of lands negroes and debts due to me and all other property of every description I give, devise and bequeath to my Executors William E. Watkins, John McRoberts and James Bell and the survivors or survivor of them and the heirs of the survivor or survivors in trust for the following purposes, to pay in the first place all my debts, secondly a reasonable compensation for the services of my two executors Watkins and McRoberts to be fixed by the County or Chancery Court, my nephew James Bell will not require any compensation as I have given him by deed of gift a good deal of property and he is also entitled to a portion by the provisions of this will. Thirdly, my said executors, or the survivors or survivor, or the heirs of the survivor are authorized to sell at public or private sale all my property both real and personal for cash or on credit at their discretion taking good security from the purchasers, to collect all my debts, and to execute any deed or deeds that may be necessary and the proceeds thereof, except as provided in foregoing items in this will, are to be divided into eight equal shares being the number of my deceased brothers and sisters who left any child or children. One equal share I give and bequeath to the children and grandchildren of each of my brothers and sisters which shall be living at the time of my death, the grandchildren to stand in the place of their parent. All my brothers and sisters are dead and my belief is that there were eight who died leaving children or a child or grandchildren and my will is that the children and grandchildren of each of my brothers and sisters which children and grandchildren shall be living at my death shall have the part or share that their father or mother would have if living and were my legatees, such children and grandchildren to stand in the place of their parent, and to represent their parent, the division and distribution to be per stirpes and not per capita. My object is to allow my grand nephews and grand nieces living at my death who would be excluded by the Statutes of Distribution from any share in my personal estate to stand in the place of their fathers or mothers and for the distribution to be made according to the number of my brothers and sisters who have children or grandchildren living at my death. My executors or the survivors or survivor are authorized to have any of my negroes valued by a disinterested person or persons according to their discretion and to deliver to my legatees or any of them their part in negroes at valuation instead of selling the negroes. I entreat and desire my executors to sell my negroes to good masters who will treat them kindly and not remove them beyond the limits of this State, and that families may not be separated if possible to prevent it, and these objects are to be attained although the price may not be so great and the negroes not sell for as much as by pursuing the usual course of sale.

I hereby constitute and appoint my friends William E. Watkins, John McRoberts and my nephew James Bell my executors and trustees and desire that they may not be required to give security as executors or trustees as I have confidence in their integrity.

In witness whereof I have hereunto set my hand and published this as my Will revoking all other Wills before made, this 1st July 1852.

M. Bell

Signed and published in presence of
F.B. Fogg
Nathaniel Baxter

CHAPTER EIGHTEEN

Montgomery Bell State Park

O ver the years, the name Montgomery Bell has been attached to several facilities and institutions. For the people of Tennessee and beyond, the most significant is Montgomery Bell State Park.

Located on U.S. Highway 70 in Dickson County, the park has a fascinating history. It originated as a part of Franklin Roosevelt's New Deal.

Before the 1930s, Tennessee did not have a state park system. In 1925, the Tennessee General Assembly created the State Park and Forestry Commission and gave it the power to acquire land for state parks and forests.[1] During its twelve years of existence, though, the Commission accomplished little. The only area acquired by the Commission that later became a state park was Pickett State Forest, deeded to the State in 1933 by the Stearns Coal and Lumber Company.[2]

The impetus for the creation of state parks in Tennessee came from federal agencies during the New Deal years (1933-1939). The federal agency that made the greatest contribution to the development of Tennessee's state parks was the Tennessee Valley Authority (TVA), which developed seven of Tennessee's parks before turning over management of these parks to the State.[3]

The other federal agency that played a major role in developing Tennessee parks was the National Park Service (NPS). During the early years of the New Deal, NPS worked with another federal agency known as the Resettlement Administration, which identified sub-marginal agricultural lands and aided

The entrance to Montgomery Bell State Park. (Author photo)

in finding new homes for the occupants. The NPS acquired these lands, and the Civilian Conservation Corps (CCC) provided workers to reforest these depleted lands and to construct recreation facilities on them, where appropriate.[4]

As one historian has said, "The program was a mixture of reclamation, conservation, reforestation, and recreation under planned development."[5] From the beginning, the intent of the federal agencies was to turn the areas over to the State once the development was completed.

Marker dedicated to the Civilian Conservation Corps whose members helped build Montgomery Bell State Park in the 1930s-40s. (Author photo)

The four Tennessee parks created with NPS assistance were Montgomery Bell, Fall Creek Falls, Shelby Forest, and Steele Creek. While they were being developed, the NPS called them Recreational Demonstration Areas.[6] According to a history of the CCC, "The work involved in recreational demonstration areas included conservation of water, soil, forests, and wildlife resources, and creation of public recreational facilities such as roads, trails, dams, cabins, park structures, swimming pools, and picnicking and camping facilities."[7]

The area that is now Montgomery Bell State Park was brought to the attention of the NPS by several prominent Dickson County citizens, including Dr. George B. Slayden, Dickson physician; R.T. Reeder, agent for the Texas Company; T.H. Richardson, Dickson County Agricultural Agent; A.J. Byrn, agent for the Federal Land Bank; and the members of the Dickson County Lions Club.[8] In 1934, they undertook to convince the NPS that the proposed area met the federal criteria of having both sub-marginal land that was exhausted for agricultural purposes and also land with outstanding natural features that made it suitable for a recreational park.[9]

Their efforts were successful. In 1935, the Resettlement Administration and the NPS began developing the Montgomery Bell Recreational Demonstration Area. The work was performed by the CCC.[10]

The initial work was performed by CCC Company 1474 in 1935. The bulk of the work was performed by CCC Company 4497, an African American group of workers,[11] who built two lakes (Lake Acorn and Lake Woodhaven), two group camps, a park office, and a ranger residence. Company 4497 continued its work until 1940. CCC Company 3464 took over and completed the construction of the park in 1941-42.[12] On May 25, 1943, the federal government conveyed all the land included in the Montgomery Bell Recreational Demonstration Area to the State of Tennessee to be used as a state park.[13]

A statue known as Iron Mike has been erected at the Park's visitor center to recognize the dedication and hard work of the CCC in creating this park and many other significant park areas in Tennessee and throughout the country.[14] The CCC is generally regarded as one of the most successful New Deal programs, which resulted in the establishment of 711 state parks throughout the country.[15]

The park is located about thirty miles west of Nashville. It contains 3,782 acres and is Dickson County's top tourist attraction. According to the park's website (*www.tnstateparks/parks/ montgomery-bell.com*), it has a 117-room lodge and conference center, a restaurant, an 18-hole golf course, cabin rentals, RV and tent camping sites, two lakes for swimming, boating, and fishing, picnic spaces with tables and grills, nineteen miles of hiking trails, and twenty miles of mountain bike trails.

The park also has two features of historical significance.

Statue of Iron Mike. (Author photo)

Trailhead sign for Montgomery Bell Trail. (Author photo)

The Cumberland Presbyterian Church was founded in 1810 by three Presbyterian ministers (Samuel McAdow, Finis Ewing, and Samuel King) in McAdow's cabin, which was located within the area that is now the park. They established a new branch of the Presbyterian Church principally because they did not agree with the Church's rigid educational standards for the clergy that had made it very difficult for frontier communities to obtain enough ministers to meet their needs. A replica of McAdow's cabin and a nearby chapel have been built on land

Cumberland Presbyterian Church located in Montgomery Bell State Park. (Author photo)

Sign marking the site of Laurel Furnace inside the park. (Author photo)

located within the park, although this land is still owned by the Cumberland Presbyterian Church. The chapel conducts Sunday services in the summer.[16]

Also found in the park are the remains of the Laurel Iron Furnace, constructed in 1817 by one of Montgomery Bell's main competitors, Richard C. Napier. This furnace continued operation until the Civil War; the ore pits and slag heaps are visible throughout the park, especially on the Ore Pit Trail.[17] Bell purchased pig iron bars made at Napier's Laurel Furnace for refining at Bell's Patterson Forge at the Narrows of the Harpeth.[18] The relationship between Laurel Furnace and Bell's Patterson Forge was a factor in the decision to name the park for Montgomery Bell.[19]

CHAPTER NINETEEN

Montgomery Bell Bridges

Tennessee State Route (SR) 49 is an east-west highway that stretches 104 miles from Robertson County in the east to Stewart County in the west, winding its way through the hills of northern Middle Tennessee.[1] It crosses the Cumberland River and the Harpeth River in Cheatham County near Ashland City.

SR 49 was included in the planned State Highway System designed in 1923 by the Tennessee Department of Highways and Public Works (the predecessor of the current Department of Transportation). Construction of the roads in this planned highway system began in 1925.[2]

At the time SR 49 was being built in the 1920s, there was no bridge across the Cumberland River at Ashland City. Travelers had to take a private toll ferry — a major impediment to travel in upper middle Tennessee.[3]

In 1927, the Tennessee legislature created the Special Bridge Program (SBP) under which the Department of Highways would construct seventeen state-operated toll bridges with matching federal funds made available through the 1926 Federal-Aid Highway Act. This was the only time the State of Tennessee has used tolls to fund transportation facilities.[4] Pursuant to the SBP, the 1929 General Assembly authorized funds for the erection of a toll bridge across the Cumberland River at Ashland City.[5]

Senate Joint Resolution 28, signed by Governor Henry Horton on March 28, 1929, officially named the bridge the Montgomery Bell Bridge.[6] The Resolution described Bell as "one of the pioneer citizens of the section to be opened up by this bridge" and said he "operated many iron works in the early days, and did many other things for the development of that section of the county." The Resolution lamented that his "name and fame has almost faded from memory" and said that naming the bridge for him was a way "to honor and preserve his memory."

Work on the bridge began in May 1930 and was completed in about a year, at a cost of $327,825.25. The two-lane bridge was 1,931.70 feet long.[7] At the time the bridge was being built, construction of SR 49 also proceeded on both sides of the Cumberland River.[8]

SR 49 and the Montgomery Bell Bridge would eventually link five rural county seat towns — Springfield, Ashland City, Charlotte, Erin, and Dover. It was also the only bridge over the Cumberland between Clarksville and Nashville.[9]

Another problem had to be solved, though. Four miles west of the new Montgomery Bell Bridge over the Cumberland River, SR 49 came to the Harpeth River, which in 1931 had no bridge over it. This posed an inconvenience to travelers and reduced the number of vehicles that would pay tolls to cross the Cumberland on the new Montgomery Bell Bridge.[10]

In late 1931, the State obtained federal funds to help pay for construction of a bridge across the Harpeth.[11] A new two-lane bridge over the Harpeth was completed in 1933 but was not named for anyone at the time it was built.

Since at least 1957, though, U.S. Geological Survey maps of the area have referred to this Harpeth River bridge as the Montgomery Bell Bridge.[12] So there were **two** Montgomery Bell Bridges within four miles of each other!

The American Automobile Association reported in 1934 that the "Ashland City-Charlotte Bridge" (i.e., the Montgomery Bell Bridge) over the Cumberland was open twenty-four hours a day and charged a toll of fifty cents — a steep amount in 1934. The tolls were controversial, especially for local citizens who crossed the bridge regularly, and were eliminated by the Tennessee legislature in 1939.[13]

Montgomery Bell Bridge over the Harpeth River on State Route 49. (Author photo)

Both bridges have since been replaced due to their age. The bridge over the Cumberland River was replaced in 1998 by a four-lane bridge that was renamed Veterans Memorial Bridge — a name suggested by the American Legion.[14] The bridge over the Harpeth River was replaced in 2014 by a two-lane bridge with shoulders,[15] but it is still known as the Montgomery Bell Bridge. Beneath this bridge on the shore of the Harpeth is a lovely U.S. Army Corps of Engineers campground and picnic area.

Veterans Memorial Bridge (Author photo)

CHAPTER TWENTY

Montgomery Bell Academy

Montgomery Bell's proudest legacy is the school which bears his name — Montgomery Bell Academy (MBA). It was created in 1867 as a direct result of $20,000 bequeathed by Bell for this purpose. The bequest was the first item mentioned in his Will, which had been drawn up by his lawyer in 1852, three years before his death. In today's dollars, $20,000 is the equivalent of about $700,000.[1]

The bequest was made to the Trustees of the University of Nashville, a school with a very long history. Six years after the founding of Nashville by James Robertson and his band of intrepid pioneers — when Tennessee was still a part of North Carolina — the General Assembly of North Carolina passed an Act authorizing the establishment of a school to be known as Davidson Academy and setting aside 240 acres for the use of that academy.[2] Rev. Thomas B. Craighead, a Presbyterian minister, was chosen to serve as the first president of the school, which opened in the fall of 1786.[3] Statehood was ten years in the future for Tennessee.

The iconic logo of Montgeromy Bell Academy. (Author photo)

In 1806, the United States Congress passed an Act granting land to the State of Tennessee to be used for educational purposes.[4] The Trustees of Davidson Academy petitioned the Tennessee legislature to charter Cumberland College in order to

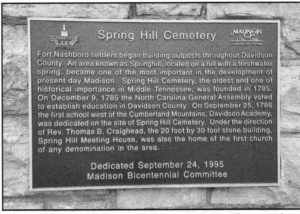

Spring Hill Cemetery, site of the original Davidson Academy. (Author photo)

be able to take advantage of this federal legislation. The Charter of Cumberland College was approved by the legislature on September 11, 1806, and it became the successor to Davidson Academy. The Charter authorized Cumberland College to grant Bachelor of Arts and Master of Arts degrees.[5] Craighead, the principal of Davidson Academy, served for three years as president of the college.

The college closed in 1816 because of financial difficulties. The Trustees launched a fund-raising drive and sought a new president to guide the college. In 1824, they secured the

Philip Lindsley (Tennessee State Library and Archives)

services of Philip Lindsley to serve as president of Cumberland College. A graduate of Princeton University (known then as the College of New Jersey), he was an extraordinary choice and served as president until 1850.[6]

At Lindsley's instigation, the Trustees of Cumberland College sought a name change for their university. An 1826 Act of the Tennessee General Assembly changed the name to the University of Nashville.[7] The prestige of the University of Nashville was enhanced the next year when the General Assembly named Andrew Jackson (soon to be President of the United States) and William Carroll (Tennessee's six-term Governor) as Trustees.[8]

Philip Lindsley was concerned with *higher education*, though, not preparatory school education. During his twenty-five years as president, the University of Nashville did not have a preparatory school department, even though Davidson Academy had been a preparatory school and Cumberland College had had a preparatory department.[9]

Despite Lindsley's outstanding qualifications as president, the University was constantly plagued by a lack of funds.

John Berrien Lindsley (Wikimedia Commons)

Out of frustration, Lindsley resigned in 1850 to take a more secure position at a seminary in Indiana.[10]

Philip Lindsley's son, John Berrien Lindsley, succeeded his father as president. The Trustees decided to close the Literary Department of the University temporarily in 1850, but John Lindsley immediately organized a Medical School at the University.[11] The Literary Department re-opened briefly in 1854, and in 1855 Lindsley was given the title of Chancellor.[12]

In 1855, the Trustees of the University of Nashville approved a merger with the Western Military Institute, which had been granted a charter by the Tennessee legislature in 1854.[13] With the prospect of war on the horizon, Chancellor Lindsley became a strong advocate of military education. The merger helped to revive the University of Nashville temporarily.[14]

The Civil War began six years after the merger and disrupted activities at the University of Nashville in a major way until it ended in 1865. By 1867, the Trustees were ready to re-open the school, and they voted to establish a preparatory department under the name Montgomery Bell Academy thanks to a bequest from the old ironmaster.[15]

Montgomery Bell had died in 1855, and his Will was probated in the years following his death.[16] The level of detail in the Will concerning the school is remarkable. For a man with little formal education, Bell knew exactly what he wanted the school to be and how he wanted his money used.

The Will specified that the sum of $20,000 from his estate was to be invested by the Trustees of the University of Nashville "in state bonds or in good notes secured by mortgage on real estate of double the value, the interest to be paid semi-annually." Bell the businessman knew how to invest money in a manner that would securely maximize the return on that investment, and he wanted the Trustees to invest his money in that manner.

His Will specified that the interest on the invested money was to be used "for the support of an Academy or school to be called the Montgomery Bell Academy forever." Bell was not shy about attaching his name to the school created with his bequest.

The Will stated that the interest was to be used "for the education of children not less than ten or more than fourteen years old who are not able to support and educate themselves and whose parents are not able to do so."[17] According to the Will, these "scholars" had to be "male children", and the subsidy of their education would "continue until they arrive at the age of eighteen years."

MBA today is essentially what Bell envisioned in 1852. The school has six grades (7th through 12th grades) in which the age of the students ranges from 12 to 18 years of age. It is a school for boys only.

Bell's Will specified the type of education he wanted these boys to receive: "The children are to be educated in the common branches of an English Education: reading, writing, arithmetic, geography, and such other branches including mathematics and the ancient or modern languages as may be established by a plan to be set forth and adopted by the Trustees of said University." Bell had confidence that the Trustees would adopt an appropriate curriculum, but his Will provided a blueprint for them to follow.

Bell had done business primarily in four Tennessee counties – Davidson, Dickson, Montgomery, and Williamson. While the Will did not require that the students who received financial assistance from his bequest be from these counties, Bell expressed a preference that the students be selected by the Trustees in approximately the following ratio – ten from Davidson County and five from each of the other three counties. The Will specified that the Academy be established in Davidson County at a location deemed most suitable by the Trustees of the University of Nashville.

Under the careful management of Dempsey Weaver, cashier of Planters Bank, Bell's $20,000 bequest had been invested in Tennessee bonds and had grown to $46,000 (more than $1.6 million in today's dollars).[18] MBA began classes on September 9, 1867. The course of study at that time was seven years — three years of grammar school and four years of high school. For those students who could pay, tuition was $60 for grammar school and $80 for high school. At the beginning of the school year, there were twenty-six students, but that number had grown to seventy-four by the end of the school year.[19]

Montgomery Bell chose to make his bequest to the University of Nashville at least in part because of his confidence in Francis Fogg, Bell's long-time attorney. Fogg served on the Board of Trustees of the University of Nashville for more than fifty years — longer than any other Trustee.[20] Fogg was the first president of the Nashville Board of Education and one of the two persons for whom the Hume-Fogg High School in downtown Nashville is named.

Francis Fogg plaque outside Hume-Fogg School. (Author photo)

In 2017, MBA celebrated its 150th anniversary. The school's history has been chronicled in three thoroughly researched books.

The first, entitled *History of Montgomery Bell Academy*, was written in 1954 by James C. Rule, at that time the Principal of MBA's high school department and for many years a beloved mathematics teacher and tennis coach. A copy of Rule's book is found in MBA's archives.

The second, entitled *Gentleman, Scholar, Athlete: The History of Montgomery Bell Academy*, was written by Ridley Wills II, a celebrated Nashville historian and 1952 MBA graduate who chaired MBA's Board of Trustees from

The Bell Tower at Montgomery Bell Academy. (Author photo)

The campus of Montgomery Bell Academy. (Author photo)

1988 to 1997. Published in 2005, Wills' book is available through MBA and Amazon.

The third, entitled *From the Hill to the Horizon: Montgomery Bell Academy 1867-2017*, was released by the school at the time of the events surrounding the celebration of the school's 150th anniversary.[21] It is also available through MBA and Amazon.

In the 21st century, the school sits quietly on a hill on Harding Road, a main east-west thoroughfare named for the Harding family, who owned Belle Meade Plantation,[22] and to whom Bell sold iron products from his furnaces and forges. The campus has been located on that hill for more than a century since the school purchased thirty-two acres from a Nashville businessman named Garland Tinsley in 1914. Appropriately, the street that runs beside the school is Montgomery Bell Avenue. The student newspaper is *The Bell Ringer*, and the yearbook is *The Bell*.

Montgomery Bell would be very pleased that the *official* name of the school, in the records of the Tennessee Secretary of State, is Montgomery Bell Academy of the University of Nashville — a fitting reminder of the bequest that allowed the founding of the school in 1867.

CHAPTER TWENTY-ONE

Bells Bend

In 1817, while Montgomery Bell was living in Dickson County, he and Jenkins Whitesides jointly purchased 5,932.75 acres in Davidson County from the Estate of William Tait for $23,731. The deed described this enormous tract as "the land commonly called Whites Bend," on the north side of the Cumberland River, below the mouth of Whites Creek, and including the mouth of Sul-

phur Creek.[1] Because it is located at a bend in the Cumberland River, the land is essentially a large peninsula.

On early 19th century maps, the area was known as Whites Bend because it was part of a Revolutionary War land grant made to the father of James White, an early settler in Davidson County.[2] Bell built a sawmill and gristmill on the property, known as Bell's Mill. Later 19th century maps began to refer to the entire peninsula as Bells Bend rather than Whites Bend.[3] Bell sold the

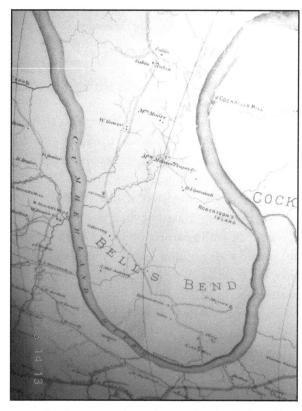

1871 map depicting Bells Bend, west of Nashville, by William Foster.

THE HISTORY OF BELL'S MILL

"... the Steam Saw and Grist Mill known as Bell's Steam Mill on the South side of said Bend on the Cumberland river... " – Excerpt from 1850s property deed

Bell's Mill, located at the south tip of Bells Bend of the Cumberland River west of Nashville, was associated with Montgomery Bell, one of Tennessee's first industrialists and the owner of a vast network of iron works in Middle Tennessee prior to the Civil War. The extent to which he was involved with the gristmill and sawmill in Bells Bend is not clear, but he owned the property between 1817 and 1850.

The complex was still referred to as Bell's Mill during the Civil War. In late 1864, this section of the Cumberland River was the site of an extended engagement between Confederate artillery emplaced on the bluff across from the mill area and Union gunboats and supply vessels traveling to and from federally-occupied Nashville.

The mill complex may not have operated much beyond 1850. An 1871 map labels the site "Bell's Old Mill" (Figure 8). Later maps do not show the mill site.

No reference was found to the Bells Bend mill complex prior to the 1850s, so it is not clear when it was built. However, Bell and a partner purchased the property in 1817, which is also the year that his partner opened a steam flouring mill in Nashville, the first in the city.

In 1834 there were six steam-powered mills in Tennessee, with four of these located in and around Nashville on major rivers. Steam mills required a source of water for the boiler, and in the early period these operations were limited to areas accessible by boat or train to allow for transport of the heavy mill equipment.

Many questions remain about the Bell's Mill complex and its role in the history of Middle Tennessee in the antebellum period. A more extensive search of original records related to Montgomery Bell and Tennessee industry may reveal additional details about the site, which seems to have been overshadowed in the historical record by Bell's more well-known enterprises.

Museum sign showing the history of Bell's Mill. (Author photo)

property to two brothers, James and George Anderson, in 1850 for $85,000 — more than three times the purchase price in 1817.[4] The land was later subdivided and sold by the Andersons.[5]

In early December 1864, about ten years after Montgomery Bell's death, a Civil War skirmish took place in the Cumberland River at Bells Bend. Confederate troops assumed positions on the south side of the river in the vicinity of what is now Brookmeade Park in west Nashville — across the river from Bells Bend. The Confederate artillery fired on Union ships intermittently for almost two weeks as part of their blockade of the river. When the Battle of Nashville began in earnest on December 15, 1864, the Confederate troops abandoned their position on the riverbank to join General John Bell Hood's troops in other parts of Nashville. The two-week skirmish came to be known as the Battle of Bell's Mill.[6]

The property on which Bell's Mill was located is now owned by Harpeth Valley Utility District (HVUD), which in 2011 commissioned an archaeological survey of the mill site. The survey was performed by TRC Environmental Corporation, which prepared a very thorough report documenting its findings.[7]

According to the TRC report, "a scatter of stone, brick, and metal debris" associated with the mill was found "in a wooded area of the property near the southern tip of Bells Bend." The report said it is likely there was "an associated river landing in the vicinity of the mill complex."[8] Several of the artifacts found by TRC investigators are now on display at the office of Bells Bend Park, located within a mile of the HVUD property.

Although much of Davidson County has seen significant development over the years, Bells Bend has remained pastoral and largely undeveloped. In the 19th century, Hydes Ferry Pike connected Bells Bend to Nashville. State Route 12 – the road from Nashville to Ashland City — now parallels the old Hydes Ferry Pike. It runs through the community of Scottsboro, named for Tom Scott, whose general store was located at the intersection of Sulphur Creek, Old Hickory Boulevard, and Hydes Ferry Pike.[9]

The property once owned by Montgomery Bell has been home to many families who have lived there for generations, including the Cleeses, Gowers, Andersons, Wittenmeiers, Buchanans, Barnes, Graves, Wests, Hulans, and Rogers.[10] The farms owned by these families have supplied crops, livestock, and dairy products to Nashville and surrounding areas for many years. Beginning in the 19th century, Clees Ferry was used to take these goods to market in Nashville.

One well known 19th century resident of Bells Bend was David Lipscomb, one of the founders of the Church of Christ and the Nashville Bible School.[11] He and his brother William purchased 643 acres from Tolbert Fanning in 1857 for $16,275.[12] This was part of the property once owned by Montgomery Bell.

David Lipscomb "established bachelor's quarters on the farm." He built a log home, a corn mill, a sawmill, and several outbuildings on his property.[13] After his marriage in 1862, he took his bride to Bells Bend, which remained their primary residence until they moved to a farm on Granny White Pike in 1884.[14] He and his wife "began cultivating the land in Bells Bend with much success. It became a model of efficiency and productivity."[15]

Living in Bells Bend created practical problems for Lipscomb, though, since he had to commute to Nashville to perform his Church work. He and Mark Cockrell established a ferry that enabled him to cross the Cumberland River at his farm.[16] The Lipscombs continued to own their Bells Bend property even after their move to Granny White Pike in 1884, but finally sold it in 1895.[17]

In the late 20th and early 21st centuries, Bells Bend has been the subject of several controversial land use proposals. Eastman Kodak purchased 808 acres in Bells Bend around 1970 to build a chemical plant, but eventually decided not to build it.[18]

In 1989, Metropolitan Nashville's government decided to locate a solid waste landfill on the Eastman property. The community adamantly opposed this land use, and the proposal was eventually rejected by the Tennessee Department of Environment and Conservation.[19] The Metropolitan Government purchased the property and in 2007 established Bells Bend Park on 808 acres. The park has several hiking trails and features regular nature programs.

Also located within the Park boundaries is a house that was built about 1840 and is now referred to as the "John Bell house." Since the house is located about a mile from the site of Bell's Mill, it is probable that Montgomery Bell constructed this house and lived in it during the 1840s. Montgomery's nephew John J. Bell may also have lived in the house for some period of time.[20]

The huge tracts of undeveloped land in Bells Bend continue to attract the interest of developers. In 2005, a proposed development known as Bells Landing would have included a cluster of 1,200 residential units mixed with retail spaces at the end of a five-mile,

The entrance to Bells Bend Park. (Author photo)

The home of John Bell, now located in Bells Bend Park. (Author photo)

two-lane road, built on 835 acres.[21] This proposal was not approved by the Planning Commission.[22]

Another even larger development was proposed in 2008 by Jack May, a member of a prominent Nashville family. Dubbed May Town Center, this mega-development on 1,400 acres was envisioned as an alternate downtown, with 600,000 square feet of office and retail space, more than 8,000 condominiums, nine corporate campuses, and a skyscraper. In June 2009, the May Town Center proposal was rejected by the Planning Commission, and the Metropolitan Council member who sponsored the bill withdrew his support for the proposal.[23]

For the foreseeable future, Bells Bend will remain a quiet pastoral community. It is impossible to know which side of these controversies would have received Montgomery Bell's support, but one thing is certain. Bell knew a good piece of property when he saw it!

CHAPTER TWENTY-TWO

Rhodes College

Rhodes College is a well respected private liberal arts college in Memphis, Tennessee, with a current enrollment of 2,000 students. Most Tennesseans and most Rhodes College graduates are not aware that Montgomery Bell was one of the original benefactors whose generosity helped the college get its start.

The roots of the college lie deep in Tennessee history. In 1806, the legislature began establishing Academies in each of Tennessee's counties, presided over by Trustees named by the General Assembly. This was the forerunner of the state's public education system.

The Rural Academy was created in Montgomery County.[1] Five years later, the name of the school was changed to Mount Pleasant Academy.[2] In 1825, the name was changed again to Clarksville Academy.[3]

The Masonic Order of Montgomery County was a strong supporter of Clarksville Academy,[4] which "increased steadily in reputation and prosperity."[5] The Trustees of the Academy decided to develop it into a college. To accomplish this change, they "realized that it would be necessary to find somewhere strong financial backing."[6]

The Trustees turned to the wealthy iron barons of Middle Tennessee. First on the donor list was Montgomery Bell. Other prominent ironmasters who made gifts were Anthony Van Leer, Samuel Stacker, Robert Baxter, William Stewart, Daniel Hillman, William Dick, and Marinus Stacker.[7] The amount that each contributed is not known, but the total amount was sufficient to get the college started.

The Trustees of the Academy were authorized by the legislature to transfer the Academy's property to the Masonic Grand Lodge of Tennessee,[8] and "the 'collegiate department' of the Academy opened on January 1, 1849, with a faculty of six and an enrollment of 105."[9] Within the first year, though, the Masonic Lodge of Tennessee withdrew its support from the college because the various local Masonic lodges each wanted a small college to be located within each of their borders rather than one large college in Clarksville. In 1851, the property was conveyed to a new legal entity created by the Tennessee legislature known as the Montgomery Masonic College, whose Trustees would be selected by the Montgomery County Masonic Lodge.[10]

Because the college needed additional financial support, the president of the college, William M. Stewart,[11] turned to the Presbyterian Church. The Presbyterian Synod of Nashville agreed to sponsor the school, and the Tennessee legislature renamed it Stewart College in 1856.[12] The college was closed during the Civil War, but by 1870 it had re-opened and there were 101 students in attendance.[13]

The Presbyterian Synod decided to change the name of the college to broaden its appeal, and in 1879 it officially became Southwestern Presbyterian College.[14] Among the faculty members in the 1880s was Joseph Wilson, father of future U.S. President Woodrow Wilson.[15] Enrollment rose to 181 students by 1917, but the influenza pandemic of 1918 reduced the number to fifty by the end of World War I.[16]

In 1924, the City of Memphis enticed the Trustees to move the college from Clarksville, because Memphis had never before had a four-year liberal arts college. The name was shortened to Southwestern, and the new campus of 124 acres supported an enrollment of 406 when the college re-opened in 1925.[17] In 1945, the name was changed again to Southwestern at Memphis, in order to distinguish it from other American universities with Southwestern as a part of their names.[18]

Peyton N. Rhodes, a physics professor at Southwestern since 1926, became president of the college in 1949 and remained in that position until 1966. In 1984, the Trustees voted to change the name of the

Halliburton Tower at Rhodes College. (Author photo)

Marble slab on the side of Halliburton Tower at Rhodes College. (Author photo)

college to Rhodes College, honoring the long-time president whose tenure had seen the construction of so many new buildings.[19]

While the college was still located in Clarksville, a marble slab was inscribed to honor the original donors whose gifts had made the creation of the college possible in 1849. When a high-rise tower was built on the campus in Memphis in 1962 to honor Richard Halliburton,[20] the slab was built into the side of that Tower. Although the location of the slab makes it difficult for passers-by to read, these are the words on the slab:

THIS MARBLE SLAB
placed here by the Trustees of this College
is dedicated as a monument of the
generous beneficence of
MONTGOMERY BELL
ANTHONY W. VANLEER
SAMUEL STACKER
ROBERT BAXTER
WILLIAM M. STEWART
DANIEL HILLMAN
WILLIAM DICK &
MARINUS STACKER
In a noble desire to promote and
encourage public instruction they
contributed largely to the erection of
this edifice and this record of their
liberality is intended to testify to the
gratitude and applause of the patrons
and friends of this institution.
1850.[21]

CHAPTER TWENTY-THREE

Montgomery Bell's Legacy

Montgomery Bell's legacy casts a long shadow that extends into present-day. Montgomery Bell State Park has hosted visitors from throughout the country for more than eighty years. Two Montgomery Bell Bridges have carried motorists across the Cumberland and Harpeth Rivers in Cheatham County for more than ninety years. Montgomery Bell Academy has educated students from Middle Tennessee for more than 150 years.

The name Bell has been affixed to several geographic areas associated with Montgomery Bell. Foremost is Bells Bend — the peninsula on the Cumberland River in western Davidson County where he owned 6,000 acres from 1817 to 1850 and operated a sawmill and gristmill, as well as living there part-time.

Two unincorporated communities were also named for him. Bellsburg lies along State Route 49 in Dickson County, thirteen miles east of Charlotte and seven miles west of Ashland City.[1] Montgomery Bell platted the area

Sign welcoming visitors to Bellsburg, Tennessee. (Author photo)

Mt. Zion AME Church. (Author photo)

Cemetery beside Mt. Zion Church. (Author photo)

and named it Bellsville.[2] A post office was established in the community in 1849, and it was renamed Bellsburg in 1893.[3] The post office was closed in 1905. More than seventy-five descendants of Bell's enslaved workforce are buried in a small cemetery adjacent to the Mount Zion African Methodist Episcopal Church in Bellsburg.

Bell Town sign on US Hwy 70 in Cheatham County. (Author photo)

The second unincorporated community named for Bell is Bell Town, located in Cheatham County on U.S. Highway 70, less than a mile from the Dickson County line. It was settled after the Civil War by formerly enslaved persons that had worked at Bell's furnaces and forges. There has never been a Post Office named Bell Town, but there is a road sign on Highway 70 denoting the general location of the community.[4]

Montgomery Bell's *human* legacy is found in his many descendants. During the research for this book, I had the pleasure of speaking with many of them. They are universally proud to be descended from such a prominent historical figure.

His daughter Evelina and her husband James L. Bell (Montgomery's nephew) had thirteen children, nine of whom grew to adulthood and produced children of their own. Following is a list of the children born to Evelina and James over a period of twenty-six years:[5]

1) Montgomery Bell (1825-1825)
2) Nicholas Montgomery Bell (1826-1882)
3) Mary Jane Bell Stockard (1829-1864)
4) Ann Perry Bell Hogan (1831-1929)
5) Thomas Finley Bell (1833-1863)
6) James Patterson Bell (1836- ?)
7) Rebecca Bell Brown (1838- after 1880)
8) Mary E. Bell (1840-1853)
9) Alexander Hamilton Bell (1841-1908)
10) Caroline Bell Douglas (1843-1874)
11) Mary Patterson Bell (1845-1858)
12) John Boyd Bell (1848-1889)
13) Eveline Bell (1850-1851)

Many Bell descendants living in Middle Tennessee are from Alexander Hamilton Bell's branch of the family tree. This group of Bell descendants has been informally organized by Jay Preston Swafford (a Robertson County resident), Amanda Bell Williams (a Cheatham County resident), and the late Marie Bell Allbert (who was a Dickson County resident) to celebrate the birthday of Thomas Roscoe Bell. Since his death in 1977, they continue to gather for a pot-luck dinner every September at a church picnic shelter in Cheatham County, preserving the memory of their illustrious ancestor.

Because of his longstanding interest in family history and his adept use of the Ancestry website, Swafford sports the

Gravesite of Alexander Hamilton Bell. (Author photo)

Bell descendants gather at the annual family potluck dinner. (Author photo)

Craggie Hope United Methodist Church, where Bell descendants gather each year. (Author photo)

title of "Bell family researcher." With the help of many other Bell descendants, he has put together a website (*www.montgomerybellfamily. homestead.com*) that includes much informative background information about their patriarch. Swafford is also the custodian of the family

Jay Swafford holding the Bell family Bible. (Author photo)

Bible that Montgomery Bell purchased about a year before his death. The Bible bears Montgomery's signature and has been passed down from generation to generation, beginning with his daughter Evelina.

Montgomery Bell is buried in a small family cemetery on property belonging to Wesley Haines, Bell's great-great-great-great-great-grandson. Haines' property is located on Leatherwood Road in Cheatham County, within sight of the Narrows of the Harpeth. The cemetery is surrounded by a stone wall and is nicely maintained by the Haines family. Also buried in the cemetery are two of Bell's grandchildren (Mary and Eveline), who died in childhood.

Less than half a mile from the Haines property is Chestnut Grove Cemetery, another

Montgomery Bell monument on the Haines property. (Author photo)

small family cemetery in which Alexander Hamilton Bell and several of his family members are buried. At the time of his death in 1908, Alexander Bell owned the property where the cemetery is located. It is situated in a grove of evergreen trees, surrounded by a wooden fence, and is well maintained. The property borders the Harpeth River, just downstream from the Narrows.

Another Montgomery Bell grandson who has descendants in Middle Tennessee is John Boyd Bell. One of these descendants is Lauren Gregory, the great-great-great-great-great-granddaughter of Montgomery Bell. Her husband, Daniel Gregory, maintains the Find-A-Grave memorial page concerning Montgomery Bell. Several of her ancestors are buried in the Scott Cemetery, a small cemetery located on Cedar Hill Road, which leads to the Narrows of the Harpeth from Highway 70.

The oldest of Evelina's children who lived to adulthood was Nicholas Montgomery Bell, known throughout his life as Montgomery. One of his sons, William Perkins Bell, moved to Denton, Texas (near Dallas) in the late 19th century, and succeeding generations of his family have resided there ever since. According to Nancy Bell Cortes, great-granddaughter of William Perkins Bell, her father, Billy Bell, was an avid family historian who made several trips to

Tennessee to learn more about his great-great-great-grandfather Montgomery Bell. Sadly, Billy Bell died in 2018 without making provision for the deposit of his research materials in a library or archive.

Ann Perry Bell lived the longest life of Evelina's thirteen children. After marrying George Hogan and living in Nashville most of her life, she died in 1929 at the age of ninety-eight in San Diego, California, at the home of one of her sons. Her obituary in a Nashville newspaper mentioned that her grandson, Dr. Percy H. Woodall, was a prominent osteopathic physician in Birmingham, Alabama. In 1902, Dr. Woodall authored a textbook used in osteopathic medical schools entitled *A Manual of Osteopathic Gynecology.*[6]

Montgomery Bell's daughter, Lucy Bell, had seven children with Andrew Jackson Pardue:[7]

1) Ann Bell (1863 -?)
2) Robert Bruce Bell (1867-1935)
3) William Bell (1869 -?)
4) Albert Bell (1871-1918)
5) Walter Bell (1873-1935)
6) Gertrude Bell Jackson (1878-1945)
7) Bessie Bell Swett (1881-1976)

The youngest of Lucy's children, Bessie Bell, married Robert Lee Simpkins Swett. Over a period of thirty years, Bessie and Robert Swett had thirteen children and started a family dynasty that has lasted to this day. Bessie lived to the ripe old age of ninety-four, dying in Nashville in 1976.

In 1954 Walter Swett, the fourth child of Bessie and Robert, founded Swett's Restaurant, a Nashville landmark that is still serving customers seventy years later. The success of this beloved restaurant demonstrates that Walter and his children inherited the business acumen of Walter's great-grandfather, Montgomery Bell.

Walter Swett, courtesy of David Swett.

Swett's Restaurant in Nashville, Tennessee. (Author photo)

An appropriate postscript to the Swett family story is that one of Walter's grandchildren, Michael Swett, a 2006 graduate of Montgomery Bell Academy, has been teaching mathematics at his alma mater since 2019. His great-great-great-grandfather would approve.

Acknowledgments

Many people have assisted me during my two years of research for this book. I begin by thanking the two persons to whom this book is dedicated – Rick Hollis and Jay Swafford. Their enthusiasm about Montgomery Bell is infectious and inspired me throughout my work on the book.

A native and former mayor of Charlotte, Tennessee, Rick knows more about Dickson County history than I will ever learn. He took me on field trips to the sites of Bell's furnaces and forges, which would have been difficult to locate without his assistance. He previewed several chapters of this book and made many suggestions for additions and changes.

A great-great-great-grandson of Montgomery Bell, Jay has helped create a website containing much useful information about Bell's long life. He put me in touch with many Bell descendants and was kind enough to invite me to the annual gathering of many of those descendants in 2022 and 2023. He previewed several chapters of this book and had valuable input.

I made three trips to Chester County, Pennsylvania, a county with a rich history. I was assisted by Stacy Hutcheson at the Chester County Archives and Margaret Baillie at the Chester County History Center. Donna McCool, a local history buff who lives in Cochranville, spent an afternoon driving me around Chester County and introduced me to Barry Girvin at the Middle Octorara Presbyterian Church and to Eric Buzby, the owner of the house on Gum Tree Road where Montgomery Bell lived as a child. Joshua Ehrman, of the Pennsylvania State Association of Boroughs, helped me understand Pennsylvania's complicated system of local governments.

I made two trips to Kentucky, where I was helped by Sarah Hubbard and other librarians at the Lexington Public Library and by Rusty Heckeman at the Kentucky State Archives in Frankfort. Richard Lucas, president of the Jessamine County Historical Society, provided useful information about the property that Bell owned in that county. Also helpful were librarians at the

Kentucky Historical Society in Frankfort and the Harrodsburg Historical Society.

Although I did not visit the Maryland State Archives in Annapolis, I received assistance over the phone from Danielle Smith and Claire Lattin, who later sent me documents pertaining to Bell's brother-in-law William Bean, who moved with Bell's sister Elizabeth from Maryland to Kentucky in 1789.

Most of my research was done in Tennessee. All research about prominent Tennesseans begins at the Tennessee State Library and Archives and its beautiful new facility in downtown Nashville, where I spent many memorable hours and was always treated with courtesy and respect by the wonderful staff.

I also visited the archives of the counties in which Bell did business and was received with patience by all the following individuals:

Pam Edwards in Dickson County
Sarah Fry in Montgomery County
Walter Pitt in Cheatham County
Jim Long in Stewart County
Rhonda Taylor and Gary Waddey in Hickman County
Lisa Lundstrom in Williamson County

In each of those counties, I also spent time at the office of the Register of Deeds to obtain copies of the deeds to which Montgomery Bell was a party.

I especially enjoyed my time in Dickson County, which I came to love as much as Montgomery Bell did. While there, I met with Alan Ragan, Dickson County historian; Zach Kinslow, executive director of the Clement Railroad Hotel Museum; and Serina Gilbert, board chair of the Promise Land Heritage Association. Other Dickson Countians who were of assistance include local attorney Jerry Smith, who helped me get in touch with Rick Hollis, and Ed England, who joined me for my first meeting with Rick Hollis. Brian Huffines, who lives near Bell's Valley Forge site, was gracious in allowing access to the property.

In Davidson County, I received help from the following persons at the Nashville Public Library: Darnetha Myers, Sarah Arntz, Grace Hulme, and Raymond Kinzounza. I also visited the Beaman Library at Lipscomb University to look at the Papers of Henry Clay, copies of which are maintained there, and the Central Library at Vanderbilt University.

LinnAnn Welch, head ranger at Nashville's Bells Bend Park, was especially generous with her time and gave me a private tour of the house Bell built in Bells Bend in the 1840's. Residents and former residents of Bells Bend who provided information about the area where Bell lived in the 1840's and early 1850's include Lena Buck, Jerry Graves, Mary Louise Buchanan, and Kitty Spry.

Others from the Nashville area who helped on specific subjects include Bill Caruso and Clinton Holloway of the First Presbyterian Church; Gratia Strother, archivist of the Tennessee-Western Kentucky Conference of the United Methodist Church; and Brad Roberts of the Harpeth Valley Utility District, who gave me a tour of the site on the Cumberland River where Bell's gristmill and sawmill were located.

Natalie Bell, who has relatives in the Bell Town area of Cheatham County, was helpful in providing information about the history of that community. Gwen McReynolds of Jackson, Tennessee made me aware of facts about the founding of the Cumberland Presbyterian Church in the area which is now Montgomery Bell State Park.

Two of the rangers at Montgomery Bell State Park, Eric Runkle and Tim Wheatley, opened the park's files to me so that I could learn more about the park's history. Tammy Sellers, of the Tennessee Department of Transportation, helped me find background information about the Montgomery Bell Bridges. Angela Klausner allowed me to spend several hours perusing documents in the Archives of Montgomery Bell Academy, during which I found interesting information about the founding and history of the school. Linda Bonnin and William Short of Rhodes College assisted me in learning more about the slab which graces the side of Halliburton Tower.

I wish to especially thank professors Richard Blackett of Vanderbilt University and Eric Burin of the University of North Dakota for previewing the chapter on slavery and emancipation and making helpful suggestions. These are areas in which their expertise is extensive.

A few persons deserve special mention. A long-time history teacher at MBA, Clay Bailey, has been enormously helpful by previewing several chapters of my book and by serving as a sounding board for me in deciding how to organize and present the story of Bell's life. Clay has the distinction of being the first person with whom I discussed the need for a biography of Bell. My high school classmate Frank Stevens is the only person who previewed all the chapters of this book as it was being written, and I appreciate his suggestions for improvements. Bill Howell, another high school classmate, helped me think through how best to present certain aspects of Bell's life. My law partners at Tune, Entrekin and White have been supportive of my work on the book.

During the course of my research, I have enjoyed talking and visiting with many of Bell's descendants. I will not attempt to name them all. But I want to give special thanks to Wesley Haines, who owns the property on which Montgomery Bell is buried and who does a fine job of maintaining the cemetery. Wes also showed me the location of Bell's home on a ridge at the Narrows of the Harpeth.

I also want to thank Michael Swett for taking me to his family's restaurant for a Sunday lunch, during which I met his father David Swett and other members of the Swett family. Swett's Restaurant is clearly the hub of the north Nashville community in which it is located.

As I sought a publisher for this book, I consulted several of my author friends who helped me understand the publishing world. They include Tyler Boyd, Bob Brandt, Bill Carey, Bill Haltom, Suzanne Robertson, and Ashley Wiltshire. Special thanks go to Tyler, who suggested that I submit my book proposal to Acclaim Press, a company that has been wonderful to work with.

Finally, after completing the text, I asked four persons to read the finished product, with an eye toward making comments for use on the book cover— Clay Bailey, Bob Buchanan, Paul Clements, and Judge Hamilton Gayden. All agreed readily, and their comments are appreciated.

Endnotes

Introduction

[1] Two biographies by celebrated Presidential historians draw heavily on the diaries kept by the subjects of those biographies. David McCullough, *John Adams* (Simon & Shuster, Inc., New York, 2001); Jon Meacham, *Destiny and Power: The American Odyssey of George Herbert Walker Bush* (Random House, New York, 2016).

[2] Stephen E. Ambrose, *Undaunted Courage: Meriwether Lewis, Thomas Jefferson, and the Opening of the American West* (Simon & Schuster, New York, 1996).

[3] John Livingston, *Portraits of Eminent Americans Now Living, with Biographical and Historical Memoirs of their Lives and Actions*, Volume IV (Cornish, Lamport & Co., New York, 1854), at 275-279.

[4] "Montgomery Bell" (*Nashville Daily American*, May 6, 1883).

[5] "Montgomery Bell" (*The Nashville American*, June 21, 1901).

[6] Mrs. Boyd's grandfather, Edward Leach, married Sarah Patterson, the sister of Montgomery Bell's mother.

[7] Christine Sadler, "Montgomery Bell, Founder of School for Boys, Turned River Through Cliff to Serve Foundry" (*Nashville Banner*, May 18, 1932).

[8] Huddleston's articles were published in the *Nashville Banner* on successive days between May 9 and May 21, 1955.

[9] Louise Davis, "The Iron Master and His Slaves" (*Tennessean*, March 12, 1978).

[10] Graham's articles were published in the *South Cheatham Advocate* on a weekly basis between November 25, 2000 and January 20, 2001.

[11] Michael Holt died in 2013. His research materials have not been deposited at any library or archive and are not available to the public.

[12] Rick Hollis, "Iron Master Montgomery Bell" (Dickson County, Tennessee 1803-2003, Dickson County Bicentennial Commission, 2003).

[13] Robert E. Corlew, *A History of Dickson County, Tennessee* (Southern Historical Press, Inc., Greenville, S.C., 1956).

[14] George E. Jackson, *Cumberland Furnace: A Frontier Industrial Village* (Donning Co. Publishers, 1994).

Chapter 1 – Who Was Montgomery Bell?

[1] Rick Hollis, "Iron Master Montgomery Bell" (Dickson County, Tennessee 1803-2003, Dickson County Bicentennial Commission, 2003), at 34.

[2] Ed Huddleston, "Montgomery Bell, Founder of MBA, 'Man of Mystery'" (*Nashville Banner*, May 9, 1955).

[3] Ed Huddleston, "Furnaces Offered for Sale after Hard Times Period" (*Nashville Banner*, May 12, 1955).

[4] Ed Huddleston, "Fate of Freed Slaves Sent to Liberia Still Mystery" (*Nashville Banner*, May 17, 1955).

[5] Louise Davis, "The Iron Master and His Slaves" (*Tennessean*, March 12, 1978).

[6] "Montgomery Bell" (*Nashville Daily American*, May 6, 1883).

[7] The New York publisher was Cornish, Lamport & Co. The four volumes are still available in many libraries and through used booksellers. In addition to being a practicing attorney in New York City, John Livingston was "the first great American legal entrepreneur." His *Law Register* was "one of the earliest attempts to provide a national law directory" – the forerunner of *Martindale-Hubbell*. He published the *Monthly Law Magazine*, which summarized significant commercial cases from throughout the country. He was also a leading seller of legal books, like modern com-

panies such as Thomson Reuters Corporation. M. H. Hoeflich, "John Livingston & the Business of Law in Nineteenth-Century America," *The American Journal of Legal History* (Vol. 44, No. 4, Oct. 2000), at 347-368.

8   Livingston, Volume IV, at 275.
9   Livingston, Volume IV, at 279.
10 Robert E. Dalton, "Montgomery Bell and the Narrows of Harpeth", *Tennessee Historical Quarterly, XXXV (*Spring 1976*)*, at 3.

Chapter 2 – Chester County, Pennsylvania

1   King Charles II owed a debt to William Penn's father that he was unable to pay in gold, but the King had plenty of land in the New World that could be used to pay his debts. So, on March 4, 1681, King Charles signed a charter granting all the land between the colonies of Maryland and New York, west of the Delaware River, to William Penn to pay the debt he owed to Penn's by-then deceased father. Douglas R. Harper, *West Chester to 1865: That Elegant & Notorious Place* (Chester County Historical Society, West Chester, PA, 1999), at 16.
2   Charles II served as King of England from 1660 to 1685. The next King of England to take the name Charles is King Charles III, who became King in 2022 upon the death of his mother, Queen Elizabeth II.
3   Harper, at 17. These three counties were established by Penn on December 4, 1682. He was 38 years old at the time.
4   EXplorePAhistory.com, "Chester County Historical Marker."
5   Pennsylvania's system of local government differs markedly from that of Tennessee and the majority of states. A Township is essentially a subdivision of a County. Every Pennsylvania county has several Townships within its borders. Each Township has its own governing body and is responsible for providing services such as police, firefighting, water, sewer, refuse collection, and road maintenance. Pennsylvania Governor's Center for Local Government Services, *Township Commissioner's Handbook* (5th ed., 2018, Harrisburg), at 3; Wikipedia entry, "Township (United States)." Chester County currently has fifty-seven Townships within its borders. Wikipedia entry, "Chester County, Pennsylvania."
6   EXplorePAhistory.com, "Chester County Historical Marker." One of the three men who operated the Coventry forge was Mordecai Lincoln, the great-great-grandfather of President Abraham Lincoln. Arthur Cecil Bining, *Pennsylvania Iron Manufacture in the Eighteenth Century* (Pennsylvania Historical Society, Vol. IV, Harrisburg, 1938), at 51; Louis A. Warren, "The Lincolns of Berks County," *Historical Review of Berks County* (April 1949).
7   EXplorePAhistory.com, "Chester County Historical Marker."
8   Wikipedia entry, "Chester County, Pennsylvania."
9   Carolyn T. Adams, Encyclopedia of Greater Philadelphia, "Chester County, Pennsylvania."
10 Adams, Encyclopedia of Greater Philadelphia, "Chester County, Pennsylvania."
11 William C. Kashatus, *Just Over the Line: Chester County and the Underground Railroad* (Chester County Historical Society in cooperation with Penn State University Press, 2002), at 7-8.
12 Wikipedia entry, "Mason-Dixon Line."
13 Kashatus, at 69-71.
14 Kashatus, at 42, 80.
15 Wikipedia entry, "Lincoln University (Pennsylvania)."

Chapter 3 – Montgomery Bell: Child of the American Revolution

1   Tennessee Encyclopedia, "Montgomery Bell", written by Robert E. Corlew.
2   Wiki Tree entry, "John Bell II (1705-1796)".
3   The township was named for Launcelot Fallowfield, an early English settler who purchased this property in western Chester County from William Penn. C. W. Heathcote, Sr., *A History of Chester County, Pennsylvania* (National Historical Association, Inc., Harrisburg, 1932), at 191.
4   The years of birth and death of Montgomery's parents and siblings are drawn from several family tree lists on *www.ancestry.com*, as well as from information provided by Jay Swafford, the Bell family researcher.

5   According to Heathcote's history of Chester County, John Bell was one of the three largest land-owners in the county. Heathcote, at 192.

6   West Fallowfield Township Road Docket, 1775, Volume B, page 130.

7   Conversations with Chester County residents Rick Lyon and Rick McMinn in 2023.

8   George E. Jackson, *Cumberland Furnace: A Frontier Industrial Village* (Donning Co. Publishers, 1994), at 20.

9   Jackson, at 21. The *Westminster Magazine* was an 18th century British magazine published from 1773 to 1785. John Bell, Jr.'s sketch of Washington's life appeared in Volume 8 at pages 413-416 (the August 1780 issue), during the midst of the Revolutionary War. It discussed Washington's service in the British army during the French and Indian War, as well as his service as Commander of the Continental Army fighting the British. Since the *Westminster Magazine* was widely read in Great Britain, English readers gained new insight into the man the British troops were fighting.

10   According to a recent history of Chester County, Patterson Bell's 8th Battalion "played a key role for the Americans" at the Battle of Brandywine. Douglas R. Harper, *West Chester to 1865: That Elegant and Notorious Place* (Chester County Historical Society, West Chester, PA, 1999), at 105.

11   Jackson, at 20.

12   Ed Huddleston, "Furnaces of Ironmaster Developed Unusual Names" (*Nashville Banner*, May 10, 1955).

13   Montgomery's brother William Bell also attended the College of Philadelphia but was expelled after two years "for bad behavior," according to a February 2, 1975 letter from James L. Hogan to Marwood Darlington of the Chester County Historical Society. Hogan was a Bell descendant.

14   Much of the information about Patterson Bell was provided by Donna W. McCool, a long-time resident of Chester County. Bell's service on the Supreme Executive Council is mentioned in Harper's recent history of Chester County, which recounts Bell's seizure of one traitor's estate in which the "total lost estate was worth 300 pounds in furniture, horses, cows, sheep, and hogs, all of which 'was seized and sold for the use of the New Created State [i.e., Pennsylvania].' " Harper, at 120.

15   *Faith and Works of Middle Octorara since 1727*, at 471.

16   John Bell's Will is on file in the Chester County Archives.

17   J. Smith Futhey and Gilbert Cope, *History of Chester County, Pennsylvania, with Genealogical and Biographical Sketches* (Louis H. Everts, Philadelphia, 1881), at 251.

18   John Livingston, *Portraits of Eminent Americans Now Living, with Biographical and Historical Memoirs of their Lives and Actions*, Volume IV (Cornish, Lamport & Co., New York, 1854), at 276; Heathcote, at 192.

19   Wikipedia entry, "Tanning (leather)."

20   Ron Chernow, *Grant* (Penguin Books, New York, 2017), at 8.

21   Tennessee Encyclopedia, "Montgomery Bell"; Livingston, at 276.

22   Livingston, at 276.

23   Livingston, at 276.

Chapter 4 – Fayette County, Kentucky

1   Lowell H. Harrison and James C. Klotter, *A New History of Kentucky* (The University Press of Kentucky, Lexington, 1997), at 18.

2   Harrison and Klotter, at 25.

3   Harrison and Klotter, at 25-29.

4   Harrison and Klotter, at 29.

5   Harrison and Klotter, at 41-45.

6   Harrison and Klotter, at 48.

7   Harrison and Klotter, at 53.

8   Harrison and Klotter, at 58-64.

9   Harrison and Klotter, at 58-61.

10   Harrison and Klotter, at 60-64.

11   Isaac Shelby initially settled in Tennessee, but moved to Kentucky after the Revolutionary War ended. Following his final term as Kentucky governor, President James Monroe appointed Shelby

and Andrew Jackson to serve as commissioners to negotiate a treaty with the Chickasaw Indians for the transfer of their rights in lands in western Kentucky and western Tennessee. The Western Purchase (also known as the Chickasaw Cession), signed on January 7, 1819, resulted in the transfer to the United States of the Chickasaws' interest in all lands in Kentucky and Tennessee west of the Tennessee River. The purchase price was $20,000 per year for fifteen years, which amounted to 4.5 cents per acre. Shelby County, Tennessee, formed later in 1819, was named for Isaac Shelby. Tennessee Encyclopedia of History and Culture (Tennessee Historical Society, Nashville, 1998), "Shelby County" and "Isaac Shelby", at 844-845; Phillip Langsdon, *Tennessee: A Political History* (Hillsboro Press, Franklin, TN, 2000), at 55-56.

[12] Harrison and Klotter, at 65-68.

[13] Harrison and Klotter, at 99.

[14] Foster Ockerman, Jr., *A New History of Lexington, Kentucky* (The History Press, Charleston, SC, 2021), at 10.

[15] Wikipedia entry, "Fayette County, Kentucky". Fayette County was the first county in the United States to be named for General Lafayette. Mrs. William Everett Bach, "Fayette County, Kentucky Records", *The Register of the Kentucky Historical Society*, Vol. 47, No. 160 (July 1949), at 250.

[16] Harrison and Klotter, at 99; Ockerman, at 17-18. Lexington, Kentucky was the first town in the United States to be named after the scene of this famous battle. Bach, at 250.

[17] Ockerman, at 18.

[18] Ockerman, at 21-22.

[19] Ockerman, at 23-24.

[20] Charles R. Staples, *The History of Pioneer Lexington: 1779-1806* (The University of Kentucky Press, Lexington, 1939), with a Foreword to the 1996 edition by Thomas D. Clark, at viii and 10.

[21] Staples (Clark Foreword), at viii.

[22] Ockerman, at 28-29.

[23] Ockerman, at 29.

[24] Ockerman, at 31.

[25] James C. Klotter and Freda C. Klotter, *A Concise History of Kentucky* (The University Press of Kentucky, Lexington, 2008), at 48.

[26] Ockerman, at 54.

[27] Klotter and Klotter, at 93.

[28] Ockerman, at 55.

[29] Ockerman, at 134-138.

Chapter 5 – Montgomery Bell: Hatter

[1] George E. Jackson, *Cumberland Furnace: A Frontier Industrial Village* (Donning Co. Publishers, 1994), at 21; John Livingston, *Portraits of Eminent Americans Now Living, with Biographical and Historical Memoirs and Actions*, Volume IV (Cornish, Lamport & Co., New York, 1854), at 276.

[2] Livingston, at 276.

[3] Livingston, at 276.

[4] Jackson, at 21; Livingston, at 276.

[5] R. Turner Wilcox, *The Mode in Hats and Headdress* (Dover Publications, Mineola, New York, 2008), at 147.

[6] Wilcox, at 145-146, 188.

[7] Wilcox, at 198.

[8] Wilcox, at 211.

[9] Hilda Amphlett, *Hats: A History of Fashion in Headwear* (Dover Publications, Mineola, New York, 2003), at 123.

[10] Hudson Bay Company (HBC) website (*www.hbcheritage.com*).

[11] HBC website.

[12] Amusing Planet website (*www.amusingplanet.com*).

[13] Amusing Planet website.

[14] North Carolina Encyclopedia website (*www.ncpedia.org*), "Hatting".

[15] The French-Canadian Genealogist website (*www.tfcg.com*), "The Hatter".

[16] Tennessee Encyclopedia website (*www.tennesseeencyclopedia.net*) "Montgomery Bell", written by Robert E. Corlew; Jackson, at 21.

[17] *The Kentucky Gazette* was the leading newspaper in Lexington in the 1790's.

[18] Mrs. William Everett Bach, "Fayette County, Kentucky Records", *The Register of the Kentucky Historical Society*, Vol. 47, No. 160 (July 1949), at 250. Remnants of the burned records were recovered and restored, to the extent possible, and are maintained at the Fayette County Clerk's office in a book labeled "Burnt Deeds." In the index to the Burnt Deeds book, there is evidence that Montgomery Bell purchased property from John Smith and Thomas Garland in what later became Jessamine County.

[19] Fayette County District Court Deed Book C, page 91. A veteran of the American Revolution, Nathaniel Rochester was a large land speculator in several states, including New York, where the city of Rochester was later named for him. James F. Hopkins, Editor, *The Papers of Henry Clay: The Rising Statesman: 1797-1814*, Vol. 1, (University of Kentucky Press, Lexington, 1959), at 120 n.2.

[20] Jessamine County is located south of Fayette County. The county seat is Nicholasville.

[21] Tennessee Encyclopedia website, "Montgomery Bell"; Jackson, at 21.

[22] Bell paid 250 pounds to Benjamin S. Cox in 1798 for part of a lot at the corner of Main and Cross Streets. Fayette County District Court Deed Book B, page 150. The Trustees of the Town of Lexington sold Bell two lots (Nos. 47 and 91) in 1798 and 1799 respectively for 1 shilling and 4 shillings, respectively. Fayette County District Court Deed Book B, page 186, and Fayette County District Court Deed Book C, page 75. Lot 91, located on Mulberry Street, was five acres in size.

[23] He sold a lot to Nicholas Bright for $500, a five-acre lot to John W. Hunt for $200, and a lot to James Rose for 105 pounds. These deeds are recorded in Fayette County District Court Deed Book C, pages 125, 126, and 489, respectively.

[24] Fayette County Deed Book D, page 205. Trotter and Scott paid $900 for the lot.

[25] The lease was recorded in Fayette County District Court Deed Book C, page 612. Cook Publications, based in Evansville, Indiana, has done an excellent job of summarizing early Fayette County (including some Jessamine County) deeds and other records. The citations in these footnotes often refer to that publication. Michael L. Cook and Bettie A. Cummings Cook, *Fayette County, Kentucky Records*, Volume 2 (Cook Publications, Evansville, 1985), at 257-258.

[26] Cook, at 282; Fayette County District Court Deed Book D, page 184.

[27] Jessamine County Deed Book A, page 470. Kay paid $1,050 for 150 acres.

[28] Jessamine County Deed Book A, page 471. Gatewood paid $400 for 190.5 acres.

[29] Jessamine County Deed Book A, page 473. Samuel paid $798 for 114 acres.

[30] Jessamine County Deed Book A, page 544. Jeffreys paid $917 for 131 acres. Even though the property was located in Jessamine County, this deed was also recorded in Fayette County Circuit Court Deed Book A, page 177.

[31] Jessamine County Deed Book B, page 379. Clay paid $1,000 for 164 acres. This transaction is mentioned in the Papers of Henry Clay, Vol. 1, at 119. Clay noted in his Papers that Bell "had recently moved to Nashville, Tennessee."

[32] Even though the property was located in Jessamine County, this deed was recorded in Fayette County Circuit Court Deed Book A, page 192. Jordan paid 5 shillings for 175 acres.

[33] Jessamine County Deed Book B, page 276. Harrison paid $1,000 for 174 acres.

[34] Jessamine County Deed Book A, page 522. Jordan paid $875 for 125 acres.

[35] Jessamine County Deed Book A, page 545. Brown paid $15,000 for this valuable tract of 228.75 acres.

[36] Billy Jackson Bower, *Mills, Murders and More in Early Days of Jessamine County, Kentucky* (Jessamine County Historical Society, Nicholasville, Kentucky, 1998), at 26-28.

[37] Jackson, at 21.

[38] J. Winston Coleman, Jr., *Lexington's First City Directory: Published by Joseph Charless for the Year 1806* (Winburn Press, Lexington, KY, 1953), at 4. The name of Bell's nephew is spelled "Bean" or "Bain" in different places. A Notice to potential creditors of her late husband was placed in the *Kentucky Gazette* on January 15, 1791, by Elizabeth Bean, who refers to her husband as William Bean. Since she spelled her name "Bean" in the ad, that appears to be the correct spelling. It is

not clear why her son spelled his name "Bain." Patterson Bain became a successful businessman in Lexington, building a hotel as well as continuing to operate the hat business. Robert Peter, *History of Fayette County, Kentucky* (Chicago, O. L. Baskin & Co., 1882), at 28. He also served as a Private in Trotter's Cavalry during the War of 1812. Peter, at 421. His mother, Elizabeth Bean (Bell's sister), died in Lexington in 1809.

[39] Charles R. Staples, *The History of Pioneer Lexington: 1779-1806* (The University of Kentucky Press, Lexington, 1939), at 265.

[40] Staples, at 148. Banks' ability to notarize documents was undoubtedly one reason that Bell chose to give Banks his Power of Attorney.

[41] Staples, at 162.

[42] Staples, at 176-177.

[43] Staples, at 186-187.

[44] Peter, at 28.

[45] Kentucky historic marker, located on the plaza outside the Lexington Public Library.

[46] Staples, at 179.

[47] James F. Hopkins, Editor, *The Papers of Henry Clay: The Rising Statesman: 1797-1814*, Vol. 1, (University of Kentucky Press, Lexington, 1959), at 120.

[48] Hopkins, Vol. 1, at 129. The clients for whom Clay obtained judgments against Bell were Arthur T. Taul, Jonathan Taul, and Jesse Coter.

[49] Hopkins, Vol. 1, at 146.

[50] James F. Hopkins, Editor, *The Papers of Henry Clay: The Rising Statesman: 1815-1820*, Vol. 2, (University of Kentucky Press, Lexington, 1961), at 210 n.1; *Wagnon v. Clay*, 8 Ky. 257 (1817).

[51] Billy Jackson Bower, *A History of the Ash Grove Pike, Catnip Hill Pike and Other Byways of Jessamine County, Kentucky* (Jessamine County Historical Society, Nicholasville, Kentucky, 2002), at 6; Transylvania University website, *www.transy.edu*. The author gratefully acknowledges the assistance of Richard Lucas, president of the Jessamine County Historical Society, in making him aware of local historian Billy Jackson Bower, who has written several books about the history of Jessamine County.

Chapter 6 - Iron

[1] George E. Jackson, *Cumberland Furnace: A Frontier Industrial Village* (The Donning Company Publishers, Virginia Beach, VA, 1994), at 11.

[2] Royal Society of Chemistry website: *www.rsc.org/periodic-table/history* (hereafter cited as "Royal Society website").

[3] Royal Society website.

[4] Arthur Cecil Bining, *Pennsylvania Iron Manufacture in the Eighteenth Century* (Pennsylvania Historical Society, Vol. IV, Harrisburg, 1938), at 13,67.

[5] Royal Society website.

[6] Anne Kelly Knowles, *Mastering Iron* (University of Chicago Press, Chicago, 2013), at 1.

[7] Royal Society website.

[8] Royal Society website.

[9] James M. Swank, *History of the Manufacture of Iron in All Ages* (Alpha Editions 2019, reprinting of 2nd Edition, Philadelphia, 1892), at 11-12, 15-17.

[10] Swank, at 21-25.

[11] Swank, at 34-45.

[12] Swank, at 52.

[13] Swank, at 62.

[14] Swank, at 101; Bining, at 13.

[15] Swank, at 103; Bining, at 14.

[16] Swank, at 103-105; Bining, at 14-16.

[17] Swank, at 108-110; Bining, at 16; Gerald G. Eggert, *The Iron Industry in Pennsylvania* (Pennsylvania Historical Association, History Studies No. 25, 2012), at 15.

[18] Swank, at 112-117; Bining, at 16.

[19] Swank, at 163-167; Bining, at 50-51; Eggert, at 19.

20 Jackson, at 11.
21 Swank, at 231-232; Bining, at 7.
22 Swank, at 172.
23 Swank, at 167.
24 The Borough of Pottstown was originally known as Pottsgrove. The name was changed to Pottstown when it was incorporated as a Borough in 1815. Wikipedia entry, "Pottstown, Pennsylvania."
25 Swank, at 174-175; Bining, at 51.
26 Swank, at 175.
27 Swank, at 182-183; Bining, at 56-57; Susan Dieffenbach, *Cornwall Iron Furnace* (Stackpole Books, Mechanicsburg, PA, 2003), at 5, 19.
28 Swank, at 175; Bining, at 51.
29 Swank, at 198.
30 Jackson, at 11.
31 Knowles, at 75; Bining, 71.
32 Knowles, at 75.
33 Bining, at 30.
34 Eggert, at 3.
35 National Park Service Handbook No. 124, *Hopewell Furnace* (1983), at 53 (hereafter cited as "Hopewell Furnace").
36 Eggert, at 3; Bining, at 74.
37 Eggert, at 3-4.
38 Eggert, at 3.
39 Hopewell Furnace, at 53; Bining, at 73-74; Dieffenbach, at 13.
40 Eggert, at 5; Bining, at 75.
41 Dieffenbach, at 11.
42 Bining, at 75; Dieffenbach, at 11.
43 Buena Coleman Daniel, *The Iron Industry in Dickson County, Tennessee* (M.A. thesis, Austin Peay State University, 1970), at 30-31.
44 Knowles, at 76; Bining, at 69-70; Daniel, at 36-37.
45 Daniel, at 37; Robert E. Corlew, *A History of Dickson County, Tennessee* (Southern Historical Press, Inc., Greenville, S.C., 1956), at 25.
46 Daniel, at 31-32. Brown hematite ore is also known as limonite.
47 Bining, at 80.
48 Ernest F. Burchard, *The Brown Iron Ores of West-Middle Tennessee* (U. S. Geological Survey Bulletin 795-D, Washington, 1927), at 67.
49 Daniel, at 42.
50 Hopewell Furnace, at 48.
51 Daniel, at 45; Dieffenbach, at 12-13.
52 Daniel, at 42; Eggert, at 2.
53 Bining, at 77-83.
54 Daniel, at 42-43.
55 Bining, at 77; Eggert, at 6-11.
56 Daniel, at 44; Corlew, at 25.
57 Bining, at 79; Hopewell Furnace, at 48.
58 Bining, at 78; Eggert, at 8.
59 Bining, at 82, 95; Eggert, at 8; Swank, at 89.
60 Bining, at 82; Eggert, at 8-11.
61 Corlew, at 25.
62 Bining, at 80; Dieffenbach, at 14.
63 Hopewell Furnace, at 15.
64 Bining, at 80; Dieffenbach, at 15; Hopewell Furnace, at 15.
65 Bining, at 81; Hopewell Furnace, at 49-50.
66 Eggert, at 12; Dieffenbach, at 15; Hopewell Furnace, at 16-17.
67 Eggert, at 12-14; Swank, at 92-93.

68 Bining, at 85.
69 Bining, at 85.
70 Bining, at 88-89; Eggert, at 14; Swank, at 93.
71 Lucia Stanton, *"Those Who Labor for My Happiness": Slavery at Thomas Jefferson's Monticello* (University of Virginia Press, Charlottesville, 2012), at 9-11.
72 Bining, at 39-40; Hopewell Furnace, at 40.
73 Bining, at 60-61.
74 Bining, at 44; Knowles, at 118,189.
75 Bining, at 110-115; Daniel, at 49-51.

Chapter 7 – Dickson County, Tennessee

1   Robert E. Corlew, *A History of Dickson County, Tennessee* (Southern Historical Press, Inc., Greenville, S.C., 1956), at 13; Paul H. Bergeron, Stephen V. Ash, and Jeanette Keith, *Tennesseans and Their History* (The University of Tennessee Press, Knoxville, 1999), at 21.
2   Wikipedia entry, "Province of North Carolina."
3   Corlew, at 13; Bergeron, Ash, and Keith, at 29-30; Walter T. Durham, *Before Tennessee: The Southwest Territory* (Rocky Mount Historical Association, Piney Flats, TN, 1990), at 17.
4   Durham, at 17; Bergeron, Ash, and Keith, at 30-33. In the early days of Tennessee, the flatboat was the most common mode of river travel. A large riverboat measured 20 by 100 feet, was steered by a board fastened to a pole at the rear of the boat, and was steadied by sweeps called "broadhorns" on each side of the boat. A roof generally extended over a portion of the hull, and there were crude bunks for sleeping and a stone hearth for cooking. Bergeron, Ash, and Keith, at 37. An entry in the Tennessee Encyclopedia, entitled "River Transportation" and written by Michael Allen, distinguishes keelboats from flatboats. Keelboats could travel upstream and were propelled by "wind, rowing, poling, or hand-winching … through the Herculean efforts of their crews." Flatboats were "flat-bottomed, box-shaped craft" steered "with a stern oar and three additional oars, one each on the port, starboard, and bow," traveled only downstream, and were dismantled at the end of the journey and sold for lumber.
5   Durham, at 18; Bergeron, Ash, and Keith, at 33.
6   Durham, at 18.
7   Durham, at 8; Bergeron, Ash, and Keith, at 34. Davidson County was the fourth county created by the North Carolina general assembly in the area that is now Tennessee. The counties of Washington, Sullivan, and Greene had been created previously in the eastern part of the area which is now Tennessee.
8   Durham, at 18; Bergeron, Ash, and Keith, at 34.
9   Durham, at 19-20; Bergeron, Ash, and Keith, at 34.
10 Durham, at 20; Bergeron, Ash, and Keith, at 34. The name Mero District was a misspelled tribute to the Spanish governor in New Orleans, Don Estevan Miro, with whom they were trying to curry favor at the time. Bergeron, Ash, and Keith, at 36.
11 Durham, at 27; Bergeron, Ash, and Keith, at 47.
12 Durham, at 1-3, 31; Bergeron, Ash, and Keith, at 48.
13 Durham, at 32. The Northwest Territory included lands north of the Ohio River and east of the Mississippi River. The states of Ohio, Indiana, Illinois, Michigan, Wisconsin, and most of Minnesota were eventually created from the Northwest Territory.
14 Durham, at 33; Bergeron, Ash, and Keith, at 49.
15 Durham, at 42-44; Bergeron, Ash, and Keith, at 50.
16 Durham, at 53; Bergeron, Ash, and Keith, at 59.
17 Durham, at 98-99.
18 The Territorial legislature was first elected in 1793 and first met in 1794. Phillip Langsdon, *Tennessee: A Political History* (Hillsboro Press, Franklin, TN, 2000), at 20.
19 Durham, at 197.
20 Durham, at 209; Bergeron, Ash, and Keith, at 63; Robert V. Remini, *The Life of Andrew Jackson* (Harper & Row Publishers, Inc., New York, 1988), at 28-29. According to Remini, the 77,263 persons who lived in the Southwest Territory in 1795 included 65,776 free white persons, 10,613 enslaved persons, and 973 free Negroes.

[21] Durham, at 252-258; Bergeron, Ash, and Keith, at 64-66.

[22] The word "Tennessee" was a uniquely American name, unlike the names of several of the then existing states, such as Virginia and the Carolinas. There was a Cherokee town named Tannassee on the banks of the Tannassee River near Knoxville. Langsdon, at 23.

[23] Durham, 263; Bergeron, Ash, and Keith, at 68.

[24] Durham, at 270; Bergeron, Ash, and Keith, at 68-69.

[25] Ch. 66, Tennessee Public Acts of 1803.

[26] Corlew, at 19; Sherry J. Kilgore, *The Heritage of Dickson County, Tennessee, 1803-2006* (Walsworth Publishing Co. 2007), Article 3, at 3.

[27] Corlew, at 19.

[28] Corlew, at 20-21; Ch. 39, Tennessee Public Acts of 1804.

[29] Corlew, at 21.

[30] Corlew, at 21.

[31] Dickson County Deed Book A, page 324.

[32] Ch. 56, Tennessee Public Acts of 1807.

[33] Corlew, at 21; Kilgore, at 3.

[34] Corlew, at 226.

[35] Corlew, at 29; Robert E. Corlew, *Tennessee: A Short History* (2nd Ed., University of Tennessee Press, Knoxville, 1981), at 227-228 (hereafter cited as "Corlew II"),

[36] Corlew II, at 229.

[37] Corlew II, at 230-231; Corlew, at 60-61; Buena Coleman Daniel, "The Iron Industry in Dickson County, Tennessee" (M.A. thesis, Austin Peay State University, 1970), at 30.

[38] Daniel, at 30.

[39] Daniel, at 1.

[40] Daniel, at 36.

[41] Daniel, at 1.

[42] Daniel, at 6.

[43] Daniel, at iv.

[44] Corlew, at 60-61.

[45] Gerard Troost, *Third Geological Report to the Twenty-First General Assembly of the State of Tennessee* (Nashville, 1835), at 28-29.

[46] Wikipedia entry, "Dickson County, Tennessee."

[47] Wikipedia entry, "Frank G. Clement."

[48] Vaughn and Mary Elizabeth Fults, *Bellsburg* (1976), at 29.

Chapter 8 – Montgomery Bell: Ironmaster

[1] Dickson County Deed Book C, page 304.

[2] Tennessee Encyclopedia, "Montgomery Bell", written by Robert E. Corlew.

[3] Dickson County Deed Book A, page 28. The purchase price was $1,820 for 520 acres.

[4] Dickson County Deed Book C, page 306. The purchase price was $400 for 100 acres.

[5] Dickson County Deed Book D, page 57. The purchase price was $268 for 260 acres.

[6] Dickson County Deed Book C, page 305. The purchase price was $400 for 120 acres.

[7] Dickson County Deed Book A, page 459. The purchase price was $1,920 for 960 acres.

[8] Dickson County Deed Book C, page 301. The purchase price was $600 for 114 acres.

[9] Dickson County Deed Book c, page 301. The purchase price was $640 for 640 acres.

[10] Dickson County Deed Book C, page 303. The purchase price was $420 for 640 acres.

[11] Dickson County Deed Book C, page 301. The purchase price was $170 for 255 acres.

[12] Dickson County Deed Book C, page 303. The purchase price was $600 for 640 acres.

[13] Dickson County Deed Book D, page 26.

[14] George E. Jackson, *Cumberland Furnace: A Frontier Industrial Village* (Donning Co. Publishers, 1994), at 23.

[15] Bell's pattern of recording deeds was not consistent. Sometimes he recorded a deed soon after the transaction was completed. Sometimes he did not record the deed until years after the transaction. It is conceivable that there are some deeds which were never recorded.

[16] Samuel D. Smith, Charles P. Stripling, and James M. Brannon, *A Cultural Resource Survey of Tennessee's Western Highland Rim Iron Industry, 1790s-1930s* (Tennessee Department of Conservation, Division of Archeology, Research Series No. 8, 1988), at 68.

[17] James M. Gifford, *Montgomery Bell, Tennessee Ironmaster* (M.A. thesis, Middle Tennessee State University, 1970), at 14-15.

[18] Gifford, at 15; Robert E. Corlew, *A History of Dickson County, Tennessee* (Southern Historical Press, Inc., Greenville, S.C., 1956), at 24.

[19] Jackson, at 23; Buena Coleman Daniel, "The Iron Industry in Dickson County, Tennessee" (M.A. thesis, Austin Peay State University, 1970), at 8.

[20] *Sketches and Anecdotes of the Family of Brown* (The American Historical Magazine, Vol. VII, No. 2, April 1902), at 148.

[21] *Sketches and Anecdotes of the Family of Brown*, at 148.

[22] Montgomery County Deeds, Book B, page 738.

[23] Tennessee Encyclopedia, "Montgomery Bell".

[24] Montgomery County Deed Book I, page 14. The purchase price was $4,000 for 445 acres.

[25] Montgomery County Deed Book I, pages 693 and 694. The purchase price was $2,000 for 400 acres.

[26] Montgomery County Deed Book I, page 1076.

[27] Smith, Stripling, and Brannon, at 92.

[28] This property is now located in Cheatham County, which was created by the Tennessee legislature in 1856, the year after Bell's death.

[29] Dickson County Deed Book C, page 306. The purchase price was $2,300 for 705 acres.

[30] Dickson County Deed Book C, page 529. The purchase price was $2,000 for 182 acres.

[31] Gifford, at 19.

[32] Smith, Stripling, and Brannon, at 69.

[33] Daniel, at 63.

[34] Jackson, at 24.

[35] Jackson, at 24.

[36] *The Clarion and Tennessee State Gazette* (May 4, 1819).

[37] *The Nashville Gazette* (September 23, 1825). The same ad had appeared in the *Nashville Whig* on August 6 and September 17, 1825, as well as in the *Pittsburgh Weekly Gazette* on August 19, 1825.

[38] The spelling in the ad, as it appears in this book, is the same as the original which appeared in the newspaper. Although the spelling of several words, such as "scite," differ from the modern spelling of these words, the spelling used by even the best educated persons in the 19th century was often quite bad by modern standards.

[39] Dickson County Deed Book D, page 140.

[40] Michael Thomas Gavin, "From Bands of Iron to Promise Land: The African-American Contribution to Middle Tennessee's Antebellum Iron Industry", *Tennessee Historical Quarterly*, Vol. LXIV, No. 1 (Spring 2005), at 30.

[41] Dickson County Deed Book D, page 404. The purchase price was $1,800 for 350 acres.

[42] Dickson County Deed Book D, page 405. The purchase price was $300 for 3,200 acres.

[43] Dickson County Deed Book E, page 24. The purchase price was $1,000 for 315 acres.

[44] Dickson County Deed Book F, pages 100 and 111. The purchase price was $1,500 for 200 acres.

[45] Dickson County Deed Book F, page 65. The purchase price was $300 for 340 acres.

[46] Dickson County Deed Book F, page 221.

[47] Dickson County Deed Book G, pages 83-84.

[48] Gifford, at 20; Livingston, at 278.

[49] Dickson County Deed Book D, page 420.

[50] Dickson County Deed Book F, page 220.

[51] Dickson County Deed Book F, page 112. The purchase price was $40 for 20 acres.

[52] Dickson County Deed Book D, page 212. The purchase price was $5,000 for 160 acres.

[53] Dickson County Deed Book J, page 230.

[54] Jackson, at 24-25; Gifford, at 20; John Livingston, *Portraits of Eminent Americans Now Living, with Biographical and Historical Memoirs of their Lives and Actions*, Volume IV (Cornish, Lamport & Co., New York, 1854), at 278.

[55] Smith, Stripling, and Brannon, at 70-71.

[56] Hickman County Deed Book O, page 37.

[57] W. Jerome D. Spence and David L. Spence, *A History of Hickman County, Tennessee* (Gospel Advocate Publishing Company, Nashville, 1900), at 63.

[58] Spence, at 64.

[59] Daniel, at 1.

[60] Daniel, at 46.

[61] Daniel, at 53; Gifford, at 21-22.

[62] Gifford, at 22.

[63] Nannie Boyd, "Montgomery Bell – Iron Master and Liberator" (unpublished manuscript in Tennessee State Library and Archives), at 21.

[64] Gifford, at 22.

[65] Gifford, at 23.

[66] This incident was reported in the local newspaper. *Clarksville Jeffersonian* (May 7, 1851).

[67] Davidson County Deed Book 15, page 332; Dickson County Deed Book J, page 363.

[68] Dickson County Deed Book L, page 384.

[69] Dickson County Deed Book L, page 142. The purchase price was $884 for 654 acres.

[70] Dickson County Deed Book L, page 517. The purchase price was $1,505 for 392.5 acres.

[71] Dickson County Deed Book L, page 512.

Chapter 9 – Cumberland Furnace

[1] Buena Coleman Daniel, "The Iron Industry in Dickson County, Tennessee" (M.A. thesis, Austin Peay State University, 1970), at 5. Historians disagree about the year in which Robertson built Cumberland Furnace, but the most widely accepted year is 1793. Daniel, at 12-13.

[2] George E. Jackson, *Cumberland Furnace: A Frontier Industrial Village* (Donning Co. Publishers, 1994), at 14-16.

[3] Robert E. Corlew, *Tennessee: A Short History* (University of Tennessee Press, 2nd Edition, 1990), at 155; Russell Scott Koonts, "'An Angel has Fallen': The Glasgow Land Frauds and the Establishment of the North Carolina Supreme Court" (M.A. thesis, North Carolina State University, 1995).

[4] Tennessee Encyclopedia of History and Culture, "Cumberland Furnace" (Tennessee Historical Society). The print version of this Encyclopedia was published by the Tennessee Historical Society in 1998, and the online version was launched in 2002.

[5] Tennessee Encyclopedia, "Cumberland Furnace"; Jackson, at 14-15; Daniel, at 14.

[6] Daniel, at 14; J. B Killebrew, *Iron and Coal of Tennessee* (Nashville, 1881), at 108.

[7] Daniel, at 14.

[8] Daniel, at 14.

[9] Jackson, at 19.

[10] James M. Gifford, *Montgomery Bell, Tennessee Ironmaster* (M.A. thesis, Middle Tennessee State University, 1970), at 5. According to a Notice placed in *The Tennessee Gazette* on June 8, 1803, the "partnership of Adam Shepherd & Co. in business of the Cumberland furnace" had been dissolved. This Notice was signed by Adam Sheipherd, James Robertson, and John Jones on May 24, 1803. Shepherd and Jones were Robertson's partners in the operation of the Cumberland Furnace.

[11] Daniel, at 14-15.

[12] Jackson, at 21; Daniel, at 16; Dickson County Deed Records, Book C, at 304.

[13] *Dickson County History* (The Goodspeed Publishing Co., Chicago and Nashville, 1887), at 2.

[14] Jackson, at 23.

[15] National Archives and Records Administration, Washington: Miscellaneous Letters Received by the Secretary of the Navy, 1801-1884 (MPub M124, NAID 710854, microfilm roll 32, page 76).

[16] Jackson, at 23; Tennessee Encyclopedia, "Cumberland Furnace."

[17] Jackson, at 23; Tennessee Encyclopedia, "Cumberland Furnace."

[18] Sherry J. Kilgore, *The Heritage of Dickson County, Tennessee, 1803-2006* (Walsworth Publishing Co., 2007), Article 3, at 3.

[19] Jackson, at 24.

[20] Jackson, at 28; Tennessee Encyclopedia, "Cumberland Furnace."

[21] Jackson, at 28; Tennessee Encyclopedia, "Cumberland Furnace."

[22] Daniel, at 21.

[23] Jackson, at 28.

[24] Jackson, at 28.

[25] Jackson, at 29.

[26] Jackson, at 30-32; Tennessee Encyclopedia, "Cumberland Furnace."

[27] Leroy P. Graf and Ralph W. Haskins, Editors, *The Papers of Andrew Johnson, Volume 6, 1862-1864* (The University of Tennessee Press, Knoxville, 1983), at 404-405.

[28] Jackson, at 34-37; Tennessee Encyclopedia, "Cumberland Furnace."

[29] Killebrew, at 108.

[30] Killebrew, at 108.

[31] Killebrew, at 108.

[32] Killebrew, at 110.

[33] Killebrew, at 111.

[34] Jackson, at 35-36.

[35] Jackson, at 38; Tennessee Encyclopedia, "Cumberland Furnace."

[36] Jackson, at 38-40; Tennessee Encyclopedia, "Cumberland Furnace."

[37] Jackson, at 42-44.

[38] The president of the Warner Iron Company was Joseph Warner, son of James Warner, who had been active in the iron business before his death in 1895. Don H. Doyle, *Nashville in the New South: 1880-1930* (The University of Tennessee Press, Knoxville, 1985), at 49. Joseph had two brothers, Percy Warner and Edwin Warner, for whom parks are named in Nashville. Leland R. Johnson, *The Parks of Nashville* (Metropolitan Nashville and Davidson County Board of Parks and Recreation, Nashville, 1986), at 256-258. In 1913 Joseph Warner built a home he named Overbrook on Harding Road in Nashville. He lived in that house for ten years before selling it to the St. Cecelia Congregation of the Dominican Sisters in 1923. The building has housed a Catholic elementary school called Overbrook School since 1936. It is located directly across the street from Montgomery Bell Academy, the school named for the former owner of Cumberland Furnace. Wikipedia entry, "Overbrook" (Nashville, Tennessee).

[39] Jackson, at 45; Tennessee Encyclopedia, "Cumberland Furnace."

[40] Jackson, at 45-47.

[41] *J.J. Kimbro & Son v. Joseph Warner & Warner Iron Co.*, Dickson County Chancery Court Minute Book 5 (1930- 1941), at 273-274.

[42] *www.ancestry.com* (Joseph M. Warner); *J. J. Kimbro & Son v. Joseph Warner & Warner Iron Co.*, Dickson County Chancery Court Minute Book 5 (1930-1941), at 455.

[43] *J.J. Kimbro & Son v. Joseph Warner & Warner Iron Co.*, Dickson County Chancery Court Minute Book 5 (1930-1941), at 495-507. This order was later modified to establish a plan by which Cumberland Iron Company would purchase Cumberland Furnace. *J. J. Kimbro & Son v. Joseph Warner & Warner Iron Co.*, Dickson County Chancery Court Minute Book 5 (1930-1941), at 556-567.

[44] Jackson, at 47; Tennessee Encyclopedia, "Cumberland Furnace."

[45] Daniel, at 5, 8.

[46] Jackson, at 48; Tennessee Encyclopedia, "Cumberland Furnace."

[47] Gail Hammerquist, "National Register of Historic Places Nomination Form: Drouillard House", National Park Service (March 1977).

[48] The mansion is now owned by a company known as Onsite, which uses the mansion and several adjacent buildings for emotional wellness workshops and programs. *www.onsiteworkshops.com.*

[49] In 2023, the Tennessee General Assembly adopted House Joint Resolution 233, recognizing the accomplishments of Serina Gilbert, board chair of the Promise Land Heritage Association, and the historic significance of the community of Promise Land.

Chapter 10 – The Tunnel

1 Robie S. Lange, "National Historic Landmark Nomination: Montgomery Bell Tunnel", National Park Service (Oct. 1993), at 4-5.

2 Robert E. Dalton, "Montgomery Bell and the Narrows of Harpeth", *Tennessee Historical Quarterly,* Vol. *XXXV (*Spring 1976*)*, at 6-7.

3 Davidson County Deed Book K, page 222. One historian has stated that Bell bought the land at the Narrows of the Harpeth from Johnathan Johnston in 1818. Dalton, at 7. The author of this book could find no record of such a purchase. However, Bell may have bought additional property from Johnston at the Narrows of the Harpeth and not recorded the deed.

4 Gosta E. Sandstrom, *Tunnels* (New York 1963), at 64-67.

5 Sandstrom, at 82-83; Dalton, at 7.

6 Lange, at 7. This seemingly primitive method of building a tunnel was used in America for another 40 years, until the development of the power drill for cutting rock. At about the same time, the use of black powder explosive was abandoned in favor of nitroglycerin, the forerunner of dynamite and similar explosives for rock blasting. Archibald Black, *The Story of Tunnels* (Whittlesey House, 1937), at 41.

7 Dalton, at 8; Sarah Foster Kelley, *West Nashville...Its People and Environs* (Self-published, Nashville, 1987), at 143.

8 House Journal, 1822, at 37.

9 House Journal, 1822, at 99.

10 House Journal, 1822, at 147.

11 Dalton, at 16.

12 A transcript of Jackson's letter to Calhoun is contained in the archives of Montgomery Bell Academy. Jackson told Calhoun that Bell had previously had a contract with the Navy Department in 1812 or 1813 and that the cannon balls he supplied "were considered of a superior quality." Jackson told Calhoun that Bell's site at the Narrows of the Harpeth "is well calculated for the erection of armory."

13 Lange, at 8; Ch. 49, Tennessee Public Acts of 1823, adopted by the Tennessee General Assembly in November 1823.

14 Ch. 49, Tennessee Public Acts of 1823.

15 Dalton, at 14-22. Robert Dalton's article contains a lengthy discussion of the federal government's evaluation of the Narrows of the Harpeth as a potential site for an armory. As it turned out, Congress did not choose a site for the armory until 1862, when it was finally established at Rock Island, Illinois.

16 Dalton, at 22.

17 Dalton, at 22; 1829 Memorial of Montgomery Bell to the General Assembly of the State of Tennessee (copy in the Montgomery Bell file at the Tennessee State Library and Archives).

18 Davidson County Deed Book Y, page 14.

19 Davidson County Deed Book Y, page 16.

20 Dalton, at 22.

21 1831 Petition of Montgomery Bell to the General Assembly of the State of Tennessee (copy in the Montgomery Bell file at the Tennessee State Library and Archives).

22 Dalton at 23; Ch. 82, Tennessee Public Acts of 1833.

23 Davidson County Deed Book Y, page 19.

24 Davidson County Deed Book 11, page 338.

25 Dalton, at 24-25.

26 Buena Coleman Daniel, *The Iron Industry in Dickson County, Tennessee* (M.A. thesis, Austin Peay State University, 1970), at 19.

27 Albert F. Ganier, *Brief History of Montgomery Bell Park* (unpublished paper, 1968).

28 Dalton, at 23.

29 Dickson County Deed Book L, page 384.

30 Cheatham County Deed Book 75, page 273.

31 Cheatham County Deed Book 196, page 380.

32 Lange, at 9.

[33] Cheatham County Deed Book 395, page 637.

[34] Andy Sher, "Park Addition Adds Buffer to Bell Tunnel," *Nashville Banner* (Dec. 25, 1996).

[35] Lange, at 8; Dalton, at 25. This house was destroyed by fire in the early 20th century.

[36] Dalton, at 26. The cemetery is located on property currently owned by Wesley Haines, who is a descendant of Montgomery Bell.

[37] *The History of Tunneling in the United States* (Society for Mining, Metallurgy & Exploration, 2017).

Chapter 11 – Montgomery Bell: Land Developer

[1] Bobbie Kalman, *The Gristmill* (Crabtree Publishing Co., New York, 1993).

[2] In January 1800, Bell sold a lot on the corner of Main and Cross Streets to Nicholas Bright for $500. Fayette County District Court Deed Book C, page 125. He sold another lot to John W. Hunt for $200. Fayette County District Court Deed Book C, page 126. In 1802, he sold a lot on Water Street to George Trotter and Alexander Scott for $900. Fayette County District Court Deed Book D, page 205. These three deeds are described in Michael L. Cook and Bettie A. Cummings Cook, Volume 2, *Fayette County Kentucky Records* (Cook Publications, Evansville, 1985), at 174, 175, and 284.

[3] Fayette County District Court Deed Book C, page 91.

[4] Cook, at 257-258; Fayette County District Court Deed Book C, page 612.

[5] Dickson County Deed Book C, page 445. The purchase price was $4,000 for 640 acres.

[6] Dickson County Deed Book C, page 447. The purchase price was $200 for 100 acres.

[7] Dickson County Deed Book D, page 121. The purchase price was $7,000 for 875 acres.

[8] Dickson County Deed Book D, page 341. The purchase price was $100 for 100 acres.

[9] Dickson County Deed Book D, page 678. The purchase price was $500 for 100 acres.

[10] Dickson County Deed Book E, page 318. The purchase price was $2,000 for 813 acres and two town lots.

[11] Wikitree entries, "Christopher Robertson" and "James Robertson".

[12] Dickson County Deed Book C, page 417. The purchase price for this property was $5,000.

[13] Dickson County Deed Book D, page 656. The purchase price for this property was $7,000.

[14] Dickson County Deed Book F, page 59. The purchase price for this lot with a house on it was $200.

[15] Dickson County Deed Book F, page 59. The purchase price for these two lots was $54.

[16] Dickson County Deed Book F, page 60. The purchase price for these improved lots was $502.

[17] Dickson County Deed Book F, page 155. The purchase price for this lot was $64.

[18] Dickson County Deed Book F, page 155. The purchase price for this lot was $25.

[19] Dickson County Deed Book G, page 187. The purchase price for this lot was $132.

[20] Dickson County Deed Book K, pages 52 and 53. The purchase price for these two lots was $36.

[21] Dickson County Deed Book J, page 444. The purchase price for these four lots was $145.

[22] Dickson County Deed Book J, page 445. The purchase price for these six lots was $270.

[23] Dickson County Deed Book J, page 460. The $20 per acre figure is mathematically correct.

[24] Dickson County Deed Book J, page 466.

[25] Montgomery County Deed Book I, page 14 and page 17; Montgomery County Deed Book H, page 668.

[26] Montgomery County Deed Book I, page 14.

[27] Montgomery County Minute Book 2, page 312.

[28] Montgomery County Deed Book M, page 115. The purchase price was $4,370 for 3,923.25 acres.

[29] Montgomery County Deed Book P, page 44.

[30] Montgomery County Deed Book N, page 370.

[31] Montgomery County Deed Book P, page 43.

[32] Montgomery County Deed Book R, page 282.

[33] Montgomery County Deed Book R, page 578. The purchase price was $500 for 160 acres.

[34] Montgomery County Deed Book R, page 592. The purchase price was $1,000 for 300 acres.

[35] Montgomery County Deed Book R, page 577. The purchase price was $100 for 160 acres.

[36] Montgomery County Deed Book R, page 347.

[37] Davidson County Deed Book M, page 194. The purchase price for this lot was $2,910.

[38] Davidson County Deed Book M, page 197. The purchase price for this lot was $3,500.

[39] Davidson County Deed Book M, page 198. The purchase price for this lot was $7,000.

[40] John Trotwood Moore, *Tennessee: The Volunteer State 1769-1923*, Vol. II (The S. J. Clarke Publishing Co., Nashville, 1923), at 85-86.

[41] The first plat of downtown Nashville was prepared in 1784 by Thomas Molloy and can be found at *https://nashvillehistory.blogspot.com/*.

[42] Davidson County Deed Book N, page 15. The purchase price for this lot was $16,630.

[43] Davidson County Deed Book N, page 378. The purchase price was $15,000 for these 6 acres.

[44] Davidson County Deed Book N, page 476.

[45] Davidson County Deed Book O, page 317. The purchase price was $2,500 for 7 1/3 acres.

[46] He sold his portion of Lot No. 10 (containing the brick house) to Hazael Hewitt in July 1819 for $2,814.75. Davidson County Deed Book N, page 438. He sold the lot he had acquired from William Carroll in 1817 to Henry M. Rutledge in April 1820 for $11,000. Davidson County Deed Book N, page 478. He sold 8 lots to William Carroll in February 1821 for $3,000. Davidson County Deed Book O, page 468.

[47] He bought the 796 acres from Alfred Balch in February 1822 for $3,000. Davidson County Deed Book Q, page 820. He sold this tract in October 1831 to Thomas W. Shearon for $2,000. Davidson County Deed Book U, page 305.

[48] Davidson County Deed Book M, page 199.

[49] Later maps began referring to this area as Bells Bend rather than Whites Bend because of Montgomery Bell's ownership of the property and the mills he built on the property. LinnAnn Welch, "The Cultural Significance of Bells Bend", *Tennessee Conservationist* (Sept.-Oct. 2021), at 7.

[50] Davidson County Deed Book 14, page 44; Sarah Foster Kelley, *West Nashville...Its People and Environs* (Self-published, Nashville, 1987), at 93.

Chapter 12 – Montgomery Bell: Spa Owner

[1] Mai Flourney Van Deren Van Arsdall, "The Springs at Harrodsburg" (*The Register of the Kentucky Historical Society,* Vol. 61, No. 4, Oct. 1963), at 300.

[2] Wikipedia entry, "Harrodsburg, Kentucky".

[3] Van Arsdall, at 302-303.

[4] Bobbi Dawn Rightmyer, *A History of Harrodsburg: Saratoga of the South* (History Press, Charleston, S.C., 2022), at 21.

[5] Van Arsdall, at 304.

[6] Van Arsdall, at 305.

[7] Van Arsdall, at 305.

[8] Rightmyer, at 18.

[9] Van Arsdall, at 309; Rightmyer, at 25.

[10] Van Arsdall, at 310-311; Rightmyer, at 25.

[11] Van Arsdall, at 312; Rightmyer, at 27.

[12] J. Roderick Heller, III, *Democracy's Lawyer: Felix Grundy of the Old Southwest* (Louisiana State University Press, Baton Rouge, 2010), at 74-75. After Grundy's move to Tennessee, his career soared to meteoric heights. In addition to becoming the best criminal defense lawyer in the state, he was elected to two terms in the U. S. House of Representatives and two terms in the U. S. Senate. He was a close political associate of Andrew Jackson and James K. Polk and was appointed U. S. Attorney General by President Martin Van Buren.

[13] Van Arsdall, at 312; Rightmyer, at 28.

[14] Van Arsdall, at 313. British money was used extensively at that time in the United States as a medium of exchange.

[15] Van Arsdall, at 314; Rightmyer, at 29.

[16] Mercer County Court Records, Deed Book 7, Page 219. Bell acquired a moiety interest in 227 acres. Van Arsdal and Jennings had previously conveyed one acre to Rev. Head in appreciation for his assistance in discovering and promoting the Springs. Rightmyer, at 32-33.

[17] Mercer County Court Records, Deed Book 7, Page 407. Van Arsdall, at 317; Rightmyer, at 34.

[18] Van Arsdall, at 317-318.

[19] Van Arsdall, at 318-319; Rightmyer, at 34-35.

[20] Van Arsdall, at 319.

[21] Rightmyer, at 35.

[22] Van Arsdall, at 321.

[23] Van Arsdall, at 321-322.

[24] Van Arsdall, at 322; Rightmyer, at 38.

[25] Van Arsdall, at 324; Rightmyer, at 39.

[26] Van Arsdall, 325-326.

[27] Van Arsdall, at 326; Rightmyer, at 42.

[28] Van Arsdall, at 327; Rightmyer, at 42.

[29] Van Arsdall, at 328; Rightmyer, at 42-50.

[30] Rightmyer, at 50-53.

[31] Jeremy Agnew, *Healing Waters: A History of Victorian Spas* (McFarland & Co., Inc., Jefferson, N.C., 2019), at 167.

Chapter 13 – Montgomery Bell in the Courts

[1] James M. Gifford, *Montgomery Bell, Tennessee Ironmaster* (M.A. thesis, Middle Tennessee State University, 1970), at 49-54.

[2] Gifford, at 52.

[3] Nannie S. Boyd, *Montgomery Bell – Iron Master and Liberator* (Montgomery Bell Papers, Tennessee State Library and Archives), at 8.

[4] Boyd, at 42.

[5] Ed Huddleston, "1819 Panic Caught Banks, Ironmaster Sought To Sell" (*Nashville Banner*, May 14, 1955).

[6] Judy Isenhour, "When Nashville Was 'Lawsuit City'" (*Nashville Business Advantage* magazine, Vol. 7, No. 9, January 1985), at 37.

[7] The suits against Bell were filed by John Catron (future U. S. Supreme Court Justice), John Wright, Nashville Bank, Robert Farquarson, Robert Smiley, and William Banks.

[8] The suits were filed by Bell against Anthony Butler, Hiram Wells, John Catron, Nathaniel A. McNairy, Nichol and others, Samuel Weakley, Nashville Bank, Thomas Hickman, Thomas Whiteside, and Tennessee and Alabama Railroad.

[9] Records of suits after 1828 are not readily available at the Tennessee State Library and Archives.

[10] These are the seven cases decided by the Tennessee Supreme Court of Errors and Appeals involving Bell:

   a. *M'Daniel v. Bell et al.*, 4 Tenn. 258 (1817).

   b. *Bell v. The Bank of Nashville*, 7 Tenn. 269 (1823).

   c. *Smiley v. Bell*, 8 Tenn. 378 (1828).

   d. *Bell v. Bullion*, 10 Tenn. 479 (1831).

   e. *Bell v. Johnson et al.*, 12 Tenn. 194 (1833).

   f. *Tate's Executors v. Bell*, 12 Tenn. 202 (1833).

   g. *McNairy v. Bell*, 14 Tenn. 302 (1834).

[11] 26 U. S. at 375. The Opinion did not state what the division of votes on the Court was.

Chapter 14 – Montgomery Bell: Life Outside Work

[1] The U. S. Census records provide some insight into where Bell lived. The 1820 Census lists him as a resident of Dickson County, probably because of his home at Cumberland Furnace. The 1830 Census lists him in both Dickson and Davidson Counties. The 1840 and 1850 Censuses list him as a resident of Davidson County. Bell's home at the Narrows of the Harpeth was in Davidson County until 1856 (when Cheatham County was created), so the listing in Davidson County is attributable to either his home at the Narrows or to his home in Bells Bend.

[2] James M. Gifford, *Montgomery Bell, Tennessee Ironmaster* (M.A. thesis, Middle Tennessee State University, 1970), at 48, 60-61.

[3] An article entitled "The Long Ago" appeared in a Nashville newspaper *The Daily American* on August 17, 1882, and quoted Bell's daughter Evelina describing her life at the Narrows property in 1830.

4   Davidson County Deed Book M, page 199.

5   Williamson County Deed Book U, page 431.

6   Williamson County Deed Book V, page 70.

7   Virginia McDaniel Bowman, *Historic Williamson County: Old Homes and Sites* (Blue & Gray Press, Nashville, 1971), at 50-51.

8   Francis A. Oman, *Ashlawn*.

9   Bowman, at 51.

10 Williamson County Deed Book W, page 373.

11 Bowman, at 51.

12 Wikipedia entry, "Gwen Shamblin Lara".

13 The name of Evelina's mother is found on several family tree sites on *www.ancestry.com*.

14 Ch. 1, Tennessee Public Acts of 1817.

15 The curriculum is set forth in a news item in the *Nashville Whig* on December 20, 1824.

16 History of the Nashville Female Academy, in a folder at the Tennessee State Library and Archives.

17 A copy of her diploma is found in the Bell-Hogan folder at the Tennessee State Library and Archives.

18 Laura Willis, *Dickson County, Tennessee Will Book, Volume 1 (1838-1847)*, at 79-80. A copy of this book is in the Dickson County Archives.

19 Robert E. Corlew, *A History of Dickson County, Tennessee* (Southern Historical Press, Inc., Greenville, S.C., 1956), at 23.

20 Patterson Bain was one of seven hatters listed in Lexington's First City Directory for the Year 1806, originally published by Joseph Charless and republished by J. Winston Coleman, Jr. in 1953 (Winburn Press, Lexington, 1953). The spelling of Bain's name is a mystery. His parents William and Elizabeth Bean spelled the family name differently – Bean v. Bain – as evidenced by a Notice placed in the *Kentucky Gazette* on January 15, 1791 by Elizabeth Bean.

21 Nannie Boyd, "Montgomery Bell – Iron Master and Liberator" (unpublished manuscript in Tennessee State Library and Archives), at 28.

22 Boyd, at 29.

23 Boyd, at 44.

24 Davidson County Deed Book 15, page 332; Dickson County Deed Book J, page 363.

25 Dickson County Deed Book C, page 394.

26 The letters from W. B. Leech to Nannie Bord are dated July 9, August 2, and November 20, 1928. Copies are in the Montgomery Bell folder at the Tennessee State Library and Archives.

27 The details of the church's history are taken from two sources: pages xx-xxiii of a book entitled *The First Presbyterian Church of Nashville: A Documentary History*, edited by Wilbur F. Creighton, Jr. and Leland R. Johnson (Nashville, 1986), and James A. Hoobler, "Karnack on the Cumberland" (*Tennessee Historical Quarterly*, Vol. 35, No. 3, Fall 1976), at 251-262.

28 First Presbyterian Church of Nashville, Session Minutes, Vol. 1, at 178.

29 Hoobler, at 260.

30 Damaris Witherspoon Steele, *First Church: A History of Nashville First Presbyterian Church, Vol. 1 (1785-1900)*, at 54-55; Hoobler, at 253-254.

31 J. Roderick Heller, III, *Democracy's Lawyer: Felix Grundy of the Old Southwest* (Louisiana State University Press, Baton Rouge, 2010), at 117, 119.

32 Hoobler, at 254-255.

33 Steele, at 103.

34 The estate was named Oak Hill by Van Leer Kirkman after he purchased the property from Col. John Overton in 1887 and, using his wife's money, Kirkman built a "palatial residence" there. Following the Civil War, Kirkman and his sister Mary Florence Kirkman Drouillard had owned and operated the Cumberland Furnace for several years until he sold his interest to his sister and her husband in 1870. The Oak Hill estate has another tie to the Cumberland Furnace. From 1925 to 1929, the property was owned by Rogers Caldwell, whose company operated the furnace before its closure in 1942. Caldwell sold the property to Frank L. Cheek, a son of Joel Owsley Cheek, the founder of Cheek-Neal Coffee Company. William C. Caruso, *Out Franklin Road: The*

Oak Hill Home of Nashville's First Presbyterian Church (First Presbyterian Church of Nashville, 2023), chapters 3 and 4.

[35] Hoobler, at 256-257.

[36] Tennessee Encyclopedia entry, "Montgomery Bell", written by Robert E. Corlew.

[37] Tennessee Encyclopedia entry, "Early Horseracing Tracks", written by Tara Mitchell Mielnik.

Chapter 15 – Montgomery Bell: Slave Owner and Emancipator

[1] U.S. Census records show the number of enslaved persons owned by Montgomery Bell in each year for which the census records are available at the Tennessee State Library and Archives:

1820 – 83
1830 – 70
1840 – 67
1850 – 322

The 1850 Census record shows the ages of Bell's slaves. The majority were children under the age of 20, who had been born to parents that were owned by Bell. It is clear that the increase in the number of slaves owned by Bell from 1840 to 1850 was due largely to the fact that his female slaves were giving birth to children.

[2] The information about Pennsylvania's Gradual Abolition Act is taken from the following websites:
https://www.mountvernon.org/library/digitalhistory/digital-encyclopedia/article/gradual-abolition-act-of-1780
https://www.battlefields.org/learn/primary-sources/pennsylvania-act-gradual-abolition-slavery-1780
http://www.phmc.state.pa.us/portal/communities/documents/1776-1865/abolition-slavery.html

[3] Charles B. Dew, "Disciplining Slave Ironworkers in the Antebellum South: Coercion, Conciliation, and Accommodation" (*American Historical Review* 79, 1974), at 396-397.

[4] Michael Thomas Gavin, "From Bonds of Iron to Promise Land: The African-American Contribution to Middle Tennessee's Antebellum Iron Industry" (*Tennessee Historical Quarterly*, Vol. LXIV, No. 1, Spring 2005), at 26.

[5] S. Sydney Bradford, "The Negro Ironworker in Ante Bellum Virginia" (*The Journal of Southern History*, Vol. XXV, No. 2, May 1959), at 197-198.

[6] James M. Gifford, *Montgomery Bell, Tennessee Ironmaster* (M.A. thesis, Middle Tennessee State University, 1970), at 30. Since the completion of his graduate education, Gifford has served as CEO of the Jesse Stuart Foundation in Ashland, Kentucky for almost forty years.

[7] Anonymous, "Furnaces and Forges" (*Tennessee Historical Magazine*, Vol. IX, No. 3, October 1925), at 191.

[8] John Bezis-Selfa, "A Tale of Two Ironworks: Slavery, Free Labor, Work, and Resistance in the Early Republic" (*William and Mary Quarterly*, Third Series, Vol. LVI, No. 4, October 1999), at 690.

[9] Bradford, at 199-200.

[10] Gavin, at 35.

[11] Gavin, at 28.

[12] Robert E. Corlew, *A History of Dickson County, Tennessee* (Southern Historical Press, Inc., Greenville, S.C., 1956), at 26.

[13] Bill Carey, *Runaways, Coffles, and Fancy Girls: A History of Slavery in Tennessee* (Clearbrook Press, Nashville, 2018), at 239, 242, 243, 269, 270, 272.

[14] Carey, at 237-293.

[15] Gavin, at 28.

[16] Corlew, at 71.

[17] Chapter 22 of the Acts of the Ninth Congress, 1807.

[18] Wikipedia entry, "Slavery in the United States".

[19] Ben Raines, *The Last Slave Ship* (Simon & Shuster, New York, 2022), at 14.

[20] Chapter 7 of the Acts of the Second Congress, 1793; Chapter 60 of the Acts of the Thirty-First Congress, 1850.

[21] An excellent discussion of Tennessee's laws governing the procedure that had to be followed in order to emancipate a slave is found in a 1932 article: James W. Patton, "The Progress of Emancipation in Tennessee, 1796-1860" (*The Journal of Negro History*, Vol. XVII, No. 1, January 1932), at 74-78.

22 Ch. 27, Tennessee Public Acts of 1801.

23 Ch. 29, Tennessee Public Acts of 1829.

24 Ch. 102, Tennessee Public Acts of 1831.

25 Richard J. M. Blackett, "Montgomery Bell, William E. Kennedy, and Middle Tennessee and Liberia" (*Tennessee Historical Quarterly*, Vol. 69, No. 4, Winter 2010), at 296.

26 Ch. 81, Tennessee Public Acts of 1833.

27 Ch. 64, Tennessee Public Acts of 1833. This Act stated that the amount paid by the State could not exceed $500 per year, thus limiting to 50 persons per year the number of free blacks that the State would pay to have removed to Africa.

28 Ch. 15, Tennessee Public Acts of 1843.

29 During the 1834 Constitutional Convention, a three-man committee appointed by the president of the Convention issued a report which concluded that "colonization of slaves...was the best way to provide for the eventual abolition of slavery." Paul H. Bergeron, Stephen V. Ash, and Jeanette Keith, *Tennesseans and Their History* (The University of Tennessee Press, Knoxville, 1999), at 93-94.

30 Ch. 191, Tennessee Public Acts of 1842.

31 Ch. 107, Tennessee Public Acts of 1849.

32 Ch. 50, Tennessee Public Acts of 1854.

33 Wikipedia entry, "Bushrod Washington".

34 Wikipedia entry, "American Colonization Society".

35 Wikipedia entries, "Liberia" and "American Colonization Society"; Nikole Hannah-Jones, "Democracy", *The 1619 Project* (One World, New York, 2021), at 22-23.

36 Wikipedia entries, "Liberia" and "American Colonization Society".

37 Wikipedia entry, "Liberia".

38 According to the January 1855 issue of the *African Repository* (Vol. 31, No. 1, at 1), the first issue of the *African Repository* was published in March 1825. Regular monthly issues appeared until February 1839, when it began to be published semi-monthly. In March 1842, monthly publication of the *Repository* began again and continued thereafter.

39 Patton, at 99.

40 Ch. 64, Tennessee Public Acts of 1833.

41 Ch. 130, Tennessee Public Acts of 1850.

42 Eric Burin, *Slavery and the Peculiar Solution: A History of the American Colonization Society* (University Press of Florida, Gainesville, 2005), at 28.

43 Burin, at 29.

44 Wilbur F. Creighton, Jr. and Leland R. Johnson, *The First Presbyterian Church of Nashville: A Documentary History* (Nashville, 1986), at xxii.

45 Rev. John Todd Edgar was a vice-president of the American Colonization Society. According to ACS records, he was one of only three men from Tennessee to serve as an ACS vice-president. *African Repository*, February 1855 issue (Vol. 31, No. 2, at 41-42).

46 Louise Davis, "The Iron Master and His Slaves" (*The Tennessean*, March 12, 1978).

47 John Egerton, *Nashville: The Faces of Two Centuries 1780-1980* (Plus Media Inc., Nashville, 1979), at 84.

48 One Tennessee history has characterized the Wessyngton plantation as "truly immense," with 5,100 improved acres and 274 slaves. Bergeron, Ash, and Keith, at 111.

49 Baker, at 87.

50 A recent issue of the *Tennessee Historical Quarterly* contains a fond remembrance of Bobby Lovett written by Linda T. Wynn, Assistant Director for State Programs of the Tennessee Historical Commission. The article, which appears at pages 98-101 of the Spring 2023 issue, is entitled *Remembering Bobby Lee Lovett, PhD: Noted Historian, Professor of History, and Former Dean of Tennessee State University's College of Arts and Sciences, 1943-2022.*

51 Despite having previously been a slave owner on an Alabama plantation, James G. Birney was the 1840 and 1844 Presidential candidate of the Liberty Party, which favored abolition. Like Montgomery Bell, his views about slavery evolved over time. Wikipedia entry, "James G. Birney". Birney's presence as a third-party candidate in the very close Presidential contest of 1844 may

have tipped the scales in favor of the winner, James K. Polk of Tennessee. Peter S. Canellos, *The Great Dissenter: The Story of John Marshall Harlan, America's Judicial Hero* (Simon & Schuster, New York, 2021), at 58.

[52] Bobby L. Lovett, *The African-American History of Nashville, Tennessee 1780-1930* (University of Arkansas Press, Fayetteville, Arkansas, 1999), at 19.

[53] Gifford, at 35.

[54] Gifford, at 37.

[55] Gifford, at 38.

[56] Gifford, at 39.

[57] Blackett, at 294.

[58] Gifford, at 39.

[59] Blackett, at 305. The *African Repository*, November 1855 issue (Vol. 31, No. 11, at 322) contains a lengthy discussion about the quality of the iron ore in Liberia, which was said to be "some of the best iron ore in the world…and of a purer quality than the purest refined iron of Europe and America." Iron ore deposits were especially prevalent in the Bassa Cove area of Liberia, which is the area that Bell's emancipated slaves settled in.

[60] Blackett, at 292-319.

[61] The author reviewed copies of these letters in the research materials compiled by Richard Blackett and deposited in the Vanderbilt University Archives, which are available for public review. They are found in Box 14, Folder 5 of Professor Blackett's materials.

[62] Journal of the ACS Executive Committee, Dec. 30, 1854, accessed at *www.fold3.com*, American Colonization Society, Business Papers, Board of Directors, Executive Committee Journal, 13 Dec 1838 – 4 Dec 1868, pages 736-738.

[63] Blackett, at 303.

[64] According to the July 1854 issue of the *African Repository* (Vol. 30, No. 7, at 193-194), the ACS originally intended to transport all these emancipated slaves on the *Sophia Walker*, but the ship did not have the capacity to take them all. As a result, the ACS chartered a small brig known as the *Harp* to take 21 of Bell's emancipated slaves. The total number of emigrants on the *Sophia Walker* was 252, and the total number on the smaller *Brig* was 25. *African Repository*, July 1854 issue (Vol. 30, No. 7, at 214-220); Journal of the ACS Executive Committee, June 16, 1854, accessed at *www.fold3.com*, American Colonization Society, Business Papers, Board of Directors, Executive Committee Journal, 13 Dec 1838 – 4 Dec 1868, pages 758-762.

[65] *African Repository*, September 1854 issue (Vol. 30, No. 9, at 287).

[66] *African Repository*, February 1855 issue (Vol. 31, No. 2, at 36).

[67] Journal of the ACS Executive Committee, June 23, 1854, accessed at *www.fold3.com*, American Colonization Society, Business Papers, Board of Directors, Executive Committee Journal, 13 Dec 1838 – 4 Dec 1868, pages 766-767.

[68] Incoming Correspondence, Domestic Letters, 6 May – 30 Sept 1854, June 30, 1854, accessed at *www.fold3.com*, American Colonization Society, pages 381-383.

[69] The use of honorary titles was common in the 19th century. Bell was often referred to as Col. Bell or by using the title Esq. after his name.

[70] Similar articles appeared in *The Shippensburg [PA] News* (January 28, 1854), *The Adams [PA] Sentinel* (January 16, 1854), and the *Pittsburgh Daily Post* (January 28, 1854).

[71] Wikipedia entry, "William Appleton: Politician"; Blackett, at 303. The May 1854 issue of *The African Repository* (Vol. 30, No. 5, at 158-159) documents the gift of $2,400 by Appleton, "to be expended in defraying one half of the expense of colonizing eighty of the slaves of Montgomery Bell, Esq. of Tennessee."

[72] Journal of the ACS Executive Committee, Jan. 24, 1854, accessed at *www.fold3.com*, American Colonization Society, Business Papers, Board of Directors, Executive Committee Journal, 13 Dec 1838 – 4 Dec 1868, page 744.

[73] Gifford, at 41.

[74] Blackett, at 313.

[75] Burin, at 2, 170 (Tables 2 and 3).

[76] Burin, at 170 (Table 2).

[77] Using ACS ship registers, one historian determined that 10,939 African Americans moved to Liberia during the antebellum period. Burin, at 175n.5.

[78] Blackett, at 313.

[79] Blackett, at 314.

[80] Ed Huddleston, "Fate of Freed Slaves Sent to Liberia Still Mystery" (*Nashville Banner*, May 17, 1955).

Chapter 16 – Montgomery Bell's Estate

[1] Letter from W. B. Leech to Mrs. Nannie Boyd, date November 20, 1928, on file at the Tennessee State Library and Archives.

[2] Watkins: *The Tennessean* (June 5, 1850); *The Nashville Union* (April 27, 1853). McRoberts: *Daily Nashville Patriot* (June 28, 1861); *The Tennessean* (May 10, 1867); *The Tennessean* (June 15, 1871)

[3] Davidson County Will Book 16 (1853-1855), pages 589-591.

[4] The Inventory of Bell's assets, including the list of his slaves, was filed with the Court on September 10, 1857 and is recorded in Davidson County Will Book 17, pages 191-194.

[5] *Lancaster Intelligencer* (April 15, 1856).

[6] These are the same properties that Bell had tried unsuccessfully to sell in 1854, as set forth in another chapter.

[7] Dickson County Deed Book L, page 142. The purchase price for 654 acres was $884.

[8] Dickson County Deed Book L, page 517. The purchase price for 392.5 acres was $1,505.

[9] *Nashville Union and American* (October 14, 1856); *Republican Banner* (October 21, 1856)

[10] Dickson County Deed Book L, page 512. The purchase price for 1,845.5 acres was not stated in the deed. The 5 buyers were Moses Tidwell, F. M. Caslin, John W. Sullivan, T. K. Grigsby, and W. M. Larkins. The land was located on the Beaver Dam Fork of Turnbull Creek and included the Jackson Furnace.

[11] *Nashville Union and American* (March 20, 1857).

[12] *Nashville Union and American* (May 7, 1857).

[13] Davidson County Chancery Court Minute Book E (November 1855-May 1857), pages 686-693.

Chapter 17 – Last Will and Testament of Montgomery Bell

No Endnotes recorded.

Chapter 18 – Montgomery Bell State Park

[1] Chapter 55, Tennessee Public Acts of 1925; Bevley R. Coleman, *A History of State Parks in Tennessee* (PhD Dissertation, George Peabody College for Teachers, 1963), at 27-35.

[2] Coleman, at 34.

[3] Coleman, at 35-36.

[4] Coleman, at 50-51. The Emergency Conservation Work Program act which created the CCC was the first piece of legislation passed by Congress as part of the New Deal. Almost 3.5 million men joined the CCC, performing a variety of conservation and reforestation activities. Approximately 70,000 of these individuals worked on projects in Tennessee. Ruth D. Nichols, *The Civilian Conservation Corps and Tennessee State Parks: 1933 – 1942* (M.A. thesis, Middle Tennessee State University, 1994), at 3; "Civilian Conservation Corps," Fact Sheet prepared by the National Association of Civilian Conservation Corps Alumni (Lewiston, Idaho).

[5] Coleman, at 50.

[6] Coleman, at 50.

[7] John C. Paige, *The Civilian Conservation Corps and the National Park Service, 1933-1942: An Administrative History* (National Park Service, 1985), at 118.

[8] Coleman, at 334.

[9] Ruth Nichols, "Montgomery Bell State Park" (Tennessee Encyclopedia, 2017).

[10] Tim Wheatley, "Hidden History of Montgomery Bell State Park" (*Tennessee Conservationist* magazine, July-August 2022), at 25.

[11] The CCC Companies working in Southern states were segregated by race in order to avoid conflict with local laws and mores.

[12] Nichols, "Montgomery Bell State Park".
[13] Dickson County Deed Book 69, pages 197-209.
[14] Wheatley, at 26.
[15] Paige, at 132.
[16] Wheatley, at 27. The replica of McAdow's cabin and the nearby chapel are located on land gifted to the Church by the descendants of ironmaster Richard Napier in 1856. *Email* from Gwen McReynolds (Dec. 26, 2023).
[17] Wheatley, at 27-28; Wikipedia entry, "Montgomery Bell State Park".
[18] Robert E. Dalton, "Montgomery Bell and the Narrows of Harpeth", *Tennessee Historical Quarterly, XXXV* (Spring 1976), at 25.
[19] *Email* from LinnAnn Welch, formerly a Ranger at Montgomery Bell State Park (Sept. 9, 2023).

Chapter 19 – Montgomery Bell Bridges

[1] Wikipedia entry, "Tennessee State Route 49".
[2] Robbie D. Jones, *Tennessee's Toll Bridges, 1927-1947: A Context Study* (New South Associates, prepared for the Tennessee Department of Transportation, Nashville, 2014), at 23.
[3] "New Span over Cumberland at Ashland City on Highway 49 Will Soon Be Opened to Traffic" (*Nashville Banner*, May 3, 1931) (hereinafter "1931 *Nashville Banner* article").
[4] Jones, at 1 and 14.
[5] Jones, at 30 and 34; Chapter 5, Public Acts of 1929.
[6] Senate Joint Resolution 28, Public Acts of 1929.
[7] Jones, at 191.
[8] Jones, at 192.
[9] 1931 *Nashville Banner* article.
[10] "To Let Road Contracts" (*The Tennessean*, February 21, 1932).
[11] "Harpeth Bridge Given Approval" (*Nashville Banner*, December 4, 1931).
[12] USGS map, Cheatham Dam, 1957.
[13] Jones, at 193; Chapter 118, Tennessee Public Acts of 1939.
[14] "Ashland City bridge to be dedicated Thursday" (*The Tennessean*, April 14, 1998); "Cheatham" (*The Tennessean*, November 21, 1996); Chapter 186, Tennessee Public Acts of 2013.
[15] "Lost Montgomery Bell Bridge": *www.flickr.com/photos/cmhpictures*.

Chapter 20 – Montgomery Bell Academy

[1] Inflation calculator: *www.officialdata.org/us/inflation/1855*.
[2] J.C. Rule, *History of Montgomery Bell Academy* (MBA Board of Trustees, 1954); John Edwin Windrow, *John Berrien Lindsley: Educator, Physician, Social Philosopher* (The University of North Carolina Press, Chapel Hill, NC, 1938), at 22; Lucius Salisbury Merriam, *Higher Education in Tennessee* (Government Printing Office, Washington, 1893), at 21; Chapter 29, Acts of North Carolina General Assembly (1785).
[3] Rule, at 8-9; Thomas Perkins Abernethy, *From Frontier to Plantation in Tennessee: A Study in Frontier Democracy* (The University of North Carolina Press, Chapel Hill, NC, 1932), at 197; Paul K. Conkin, *Peabody College: From a Frontier Academy to the Frontiers of Teaching and Learning* (Vanderbilt University Press, Nashville, 2002), at 1.
[4] Chapter 31 of the Acts of the Ninth Congress of the United States (April 18, 1806). This legislation granted 200,000 acres of federally owned land to the State of Tennessee for the support of education. Congress intended that the State sell the land to settlers and use the revenue to fund an academy in each Tennessee county and two colleges, one in east and one in middle Tennessee. Conkin, at 17; Merriam, at 23.
[5] Rule, at 13-14; Windrow, at 22-23; Abernethy, at 204; Chapter 7, Tennessee Public Acts of 1806. Chapter 7 stated that the petition to the General Assembly had been made by the Trustees of Davidson <u>Academy</u>. This nomenclature is confusing because Chapter 72, Tennessee Public Acts of 1803 seemed to change the name of the school to Davidson <u>College</u>. At any rate, after 1806 the name was Cumberland College.
[6] Rule, at 15-16; Windrow, at 23.

[7] Rule, at 17; Windrow, at 25; Chapter 47, Tennessee Public Acts of 1826.

[8] Chapter 52, Tennessee Public Acts of 1827.

[9] Rule, at 17-18; Windrow, at 26.

[10] Rule, at 20; Windrow, at 28-29; Conkin, at 30, 62-67.

[11] Conkin, at 73-80; Merriam, at 41.

[12] Rule, at 20-22; Windrow, at 29-43; Merriam, at 47.

[13] Chapter 124, Tennessee Public Acts of 1854; Merriam, at 47.

[14] Rule, at 26-30; Windrow, at 44-45; Conkin, at 80-88; Merriam, at 48.

[15] Rule, at 37-39; Windrow, at 53-54; Conkin, at 95-96; Merriam, at 50.

[16] Montgomery Bell's Will is recorded in Davidson County Will Book 16, Page 589.

[17] In order to make the school financially viable, the Trustees determined that Montgomery Bell Academy would also accept students whose parents could afford to pay tuition. "Had this not been done, it would have been confined to a very narrow sphere and never expanded … into a school offering advantages equal to those of many so-called colleges." Merriam, at 50.

[18] Ridley Wills II, *Gentleman, Scholar, Athlete: The History of Montgomery Bell Academy* (The History Factory, Chantilly, VA, 2005), at 1.

[19] Wills, at 3.

[20] Wills, at 14.

[21] *From the Hill to the Horizon: Montgomery Bell Academy 1867-2107* (Turner Publishing Co., Nashville, 2017).

[22] Ridley Wills II, *Nashville Streets and Their Stories* (Plumbline Media, LLC, Franklin, TN, 2012), at 70.

Chapter 21 – Bells Bend

[1] Davidson County Deed Book M, page 199.

[2] "History", Bells Bend Conservation Corridor, *www.bellsbend.squarespace.com/history*, at 2; David Price and Julie Coco, *Beaman Park to Bells Bend: A Community Conservation Project* (Report prepared by New South Associates for the Land Trust of Tennessee), at 27-28.

[3] LinnAnn Welch, "The Cultural Significance of Bells Bend", *Tennessee Conservationist* (Sept.-Oct. 2021), at 7.

[4] Davidson County Deed Book 14, page 44; Sarah Foster Kelley, *West Nashville…Its People and Environs* (Self-published, Nashville, 1987), at 93.

[5] Price and Coco, at 28.

[6] Metro Parks brochure on The Battle of Bell's Mill, created by Jeremy Childs, 2016; Welch, at 7.

[7] TRC Environmental Corporation, *Phase I Archaeological Survey of Two Parcels Proposed as Wetlands Mitigation Areas and the Bell's Mill Site, Harpeth Valley Utility District Property, Bells Bend, Davidson County, Tennessee* (Nashville, 2011), at 26-30, 38-47.

[8] TRC report, at 38.

[9] Price and Coco, at 45.

[10] Welch, at 7.

[11] The Nashville Bible School was renamed David Lipscomb College after Lipscomb's death.

[12] Davidson County Deed Book 26, page 163; Robert E. Hooper, *Crying in the Wilderness: A Biography of David Lipscomb* (David Lipscomb College, Nashville, 1979), at 61.

[13] Hooper, at 173-174.

[14] Hooper, at 82-83, 264. Their home on Granny White Pike is the present location of David Lipscomb University.

[15] Hooper, at 85.

[16] Price and Coco, at 29.

[17] Price and Coco, at 51.

[18] Nancy Vienneau, "Bend in the Road", *Nashville Lifestyles* (June 2016), at 62.

[19] Price and Coco, at 115.

[20] John P. Graves, a long-time resident of Bells Bend, wrote and published in 1985 a book entitled *Northwest Davidson County: The Land – Its People*. Graves mentioned the house repeatedly in his book (pages 74-76 and 113-117), but never explained who John Bell was. Members of the

Buchanan family lived in the house for many years in the 20th century. Plans are underway for restoration of the house by the Metropolitan Government.

[21] Vienneau, at 64-65.

[22] Price and Coco, at 6.

[23] Vienneau, at 65-66.

Chapter 22 – Rhodes College

[1] Chapter 8, Tennessee Public Acts of 1806.

[2] Chapter 25, Tennessee Public Acts of 1811.

[3] Chapter 112, Tennessee Public Acts of 1825.

[4] Wikipedia entry, "Rhodes College"; Waller Raymond Cooper, *Southwestern at Memphis: 1848-1948* (John Knox Press, Richmond, VA, 1949), at 2.

[5] Cooper, at 5.

[6] Cooper, at 6.

[7] These names appear on a marble slab described in this chapter.

[8] Chapter 196, Tennessee Public Acts of 1848.

[9] James E. Roper, "Southwestern at Memphis: 1848-1981", *Tennessee Historical Quarterly*, Vol. XLI (Fall 1982), at 207.

[10] Cooper, at 9; Chapter 12, Tennessee Public Acts of 1851.

[11] Like Montgomery Bell, William M. Stewart had migrated to Tennessee from Pennsylvania. In Tennessee, his "superior scientific attainments had enabled him to accumulate a considerable fortune in the iron business." Cooper, at 10.

[12] Roper, at 207; Cooper, at 9-11; Chapter 138, Tennessee Public Acts of 1856.

[13] Roper, at 208.

[14] Roper, 208-209.

[15] Roper, at 209; Cooper, at 74.

[16] Roper, at 210.

[17] Roper, at 210-212.

[18] Roper, at 215.

[19] Wikipedia entry, "Rhodes College."

[20] Richard Halliburton was a world adventurer and best-selling author who drowned in 1939 while trying to sail a Chinese junk boat across the Pacific Ocean. The Tower was financed by a gift from his parents. According to the Rhodes College website, the Tower is 140 feet in height and is listed on the National Register of Historic Places. The History Press has published an excellent biography of Halliburton. R. Scott Williams, *The Forgotten Adventures of Richard Halliburton: A High-Flying Life from Tennessee to Timbuktu* (The History Press, Charleston, S.C., 2014).

[21] The author gratefully acknowledges the assistance of Rick Hollis, who first brought this slab to his attention, and of William Short, Associate Director of Rhodes College's Barret Library, who dispatched a drone to take a good photograph of the slab.

Chapter 23 – Montgomery Bell's Legacy

[1] Vaughn and Mary Elizabeth Fults, *Bellsburg* (1976), at 3.

[2] Larry L. Miller, *Tennessee Place Names* (Indiana University Press, Bloomington, 2001), at 17.

[3] Wikipedia entry, "Bellsburg, Tennessee".

[4] Wikipedia entry, "Bell Town, Tennessee".

[5] The years of birth and death of Evelina's children are drawn from several family tree lists on *www.ancestry.com*, as well as from information provided by Jay Swafford, the Bell family researcher.

[6] Percy Hogan Woodall, *A Manual of Osteopathic Gynecology* (Jno. Rundle & Sons, Nashville, 1902).

[7] The years of birth and death of Lucy's children are drawn from the Nikki Swett-Smith family tree list on *www.ancestry.com*.

Bibliography

Books

Abernethy, Thomas Perkins. *From Frontier to Plantation in Tennessee: A Study in Frontier Democracy*. Chapel Hill: University of North Carolina Press, 1932.

Agnew, Jeremy. *Healing Waters: A History of Victorian Spas*. Jefferson, NC: McFarland & Co., Inc., 2019.

Ambrose, Stephen E. *Undaunted Courage: Meriwether Lewis, Thomas Jefferson, and the Opening of the American West*. New York: Simon & Schuster, 1996.

Amphlett, Hilda. *Hats: A History of Fashion in Headwear*. Mineola, NY: David Publications, 2003.

Bergeron, Paul H., Ash, Steven V., and Keith, Jeanette. *Tennesseans and Their History*. Knoxville: University of Tennessee Press, 1999.

Bining, Arthur Cecil. *Pennsylvania Iron Manufacture in the Eighteenth Century*. Harrisburg: Pennsylvania Historical Society, 1938.

Black, Archibald. *The Story of Tunnels*. Whittlesey House, 1937.

Bower, Billy Jackson. *A History of the Ash Grove Pike, Catnip Hill Pike and Other Byways of Jessamine County, Kentucky*. Nicholasville, KY: Jessamine County Historical Society, 2002.

Bower, Billy Jackson. *Mills, Murders and More in Early Days of Jessamine County, Kentucky*. Nicholasville, KY: Jessamine County Historical Society, 1998.

Bowman, Virginia McDaniel. *Historic Williamson County: Old Homes and Sites*. Nashville: Blue & Gray Press, 1971.

Burchard, Ernest F. *The Brown Iron Ores of West-Middle Tennessee*. Washington: U. S. Geological Survey Bulletin 795-D, 1927.

Burin, Eric. *Slavery and the Peculiar Solution: A History of the American Colonization Society*. Gainesville, FL: University Press of Florida, 2005.

Canellos, Peter S. *The Great Dissenter: The Story of John Marshall Harlan, America's Judicial Hero*. New York: Simon & Schuster, 2011.

Carey, Bill. *Runaways, Coffles, and Fancy Girls: A History of Slavery in Tennessee*. Nashville: Clearbrook Press, 2018.

Caruso, William C. *Out Franklin Road: The Oak Hill Home of Nashville's First Presbyterian Church*. Nashville: First Presbyterian Church of Nashville, 2023.

Chernow, Ron. *Grant*. New York: Penguin Books, 2017.

Coleman, J. Winston, Jr. *Lexington's First City Directory: Published by Joseph Charless for the Year 1806*. Lexington, KY: Winburn Press, 1953.

Conkin, Paul K. *Peabody College: From a Frontier Academy to the Frontier of Teaching and Learning*. Nashville: Vanderbilt University Press, 2002.

Cook, Michael L. and Cook, Bettie A. Cummings. *Fayette County, Kentucky Records, Vol. 2*. Evansville: Cook Publications, 1985.

Cooper, Waller Raymond. *Southwestern at Memphis: 1848-1948*. Richmond: John Knox Press, 1949.

Corlew, Robert E. *A History of Dickson County, Tennessee*. Greeneville, SC: Southern Historical Press, Inc., 1956.

Corlew, Robert E. *Tennessee: A Short History*, 2d. Knoxville: University of Tennessee Press, 1981.

Creighton, William F., Jr. and Johnson, Leland R., editors. *The First Presbyterian Church of Nashville: A Documentary History*. Nashville: First Presbyterian Church of Nashville, 1986.

Dieffenbach, Susan. *Cornwall Iron Furnace*. Mechanicsburg, PA: Stackpole Books, 2003.

Doyle, Don H. *Nashville in the New South: 1880-1930.* Knoxville: University of Tennessee Press, 1985.

Durham, Walter T. *Before Tennessee: The Southwest Territory.* Piney Flats, TN: Rocky Mount Historical Association, 1990.

Egerton, John. *Nashville: The Faces of Two Centuries 1780-1980.* Nashville: Plus Media, 1979.

Eggert, Gerald G. *The Iron Industry in Pennsylvania.* Pennsylvania Historical Society, History Studies No. 25, 2012.

Fults, Vaughn and Mary Elizabeth. *Bellsburg,* 1976.

Futhey, J. Smith and Cope, Gilbert. *History of Chester County, Pennsylvania, with Genealogical and Biographical Sketches.* Philadelphia: Louis H. Everts, 1881.

Graf, Leroy P. and Haskins, Ralph W., editors. *The Papers of Andrew Johnson, Vol 6 (1862-1864).* Knoxville: University of Tennessee Press, 1983.

Graves, John P. *Northwest Davidson County: The Land – Its People.* Nashville: 1985.

Hannah-Jones, Nikole. *"Democracy," The 1619 Project.* New York: One World, 2021.

Harper, Douglas R. *West Chester to 1865: That Elegant and Notorious Place.* West Chester, PA: Chester County Historical Society, 1999.

Harrison, Lowell H. and Klotter, James C. *A New History of Kentucky.* Lexington, KY: University Press of Kentucky, 1997.

Heathcote, C. W., Sr. *A History of Chester County, Pennsylvania.* Harrisburg: National Historical Association, Inc., 1932.

Heller, J. Roderick, III. *Democracy's Lawyer: Felix Grundy of the Old Southwest.* Baton Rouge: Louisiana State University Press, 2010.

Hooper, Robert E. *Crying in the Wilderness: A Biography of David Lipscomb.* Nashville: David Lipscomb College, 1979.

Hopkins, James F., editor. *The Papers of Henry Clay: The Rising Statesman: 1797-1814, Vol. 1 and 2.* Lexington, KY: University of Kentucky Press, 1959 and 1961.

Jackson, George E. *Cumberland Furnace: A Frontier Industrial Village.* Donning Co. Publishers, 1994.

Johnson, Leland R. *The Parks of Nashville.* Nashville: Metropolitan Nashville and Davidson County Board of Parks and Recreation, 1986.

Kalman, Bobbie. *The Gristmill.* New York: Crabtree Publishing Co., 1993.

Kashatus, William C. *Just Over the Line: Chester County and the Underground Railroad.* Chester County Historical Society in cooperation with Penn State University Press, 2002.

Kelley, Sarah Foster. *West Nashville...Its People and Environs.* Nashville: 1987.

Kilgore, Sherry J. *The History of Dickson County, Tennessee: 1803-2006.* Walsworth Publishing Co., 2007.

Killebrew, J. B. *Iron and Coal of Tennessee.* Nashville: 1881.

Klotter, James C. and Klotter, Freda C. *A Concise History of Kentucky.* Lexington, KY: University Press of Kentucky, 2008.

Knowles, Anne Kelly. *Mastering Iron.* Chicago: University of Chicago Press, 2013.

Livingston, John. *Portraits of Eminent Americans Now Living, with Biographical and Historical Memoirs of Their Lives and Actions, Volume IV.* New York: Cornish, Lamport & Co., 1854.

Lovett, Bobby L. *The African-American History of Nashville, Tennessee: 1780-1930.* Fayetteville, AR: University of Arkansas Press, 1999.

Merriam, Lucius Salisbury. *Higher Education in Tennessee.* Washington: Government Printing Office, 1893.

Miller, Larry L. *Tennessee Place Names.* Bloomington: Indiana University Press, 2001.

Moore, John Trotwood. *The Volunteer State 1769-1923, Vol. II.* Nashville: S. J. Clarke Publishing Co., 1923.

Ockerman, Foster, Jr. *A New History of Lexington, Kentucky.* Charleston, SC: The History Press, 2021.

Paige, John C. *The Civilian Conservation Corps and the National Park Service, 1933-1942: An Administrative History.* National Park Service, 1985.

Peter, Robert. *History of Fayette County, Kentucky.* Chicago: O. L. Baskin & Co., 1882.

Raines, Ben. *The Last Slave Ship.* New York: Simon & Schuster, 2022.

Remini, Robert. *The Life of Andrew Jackson.* New York: Harper & Row Publishers, Inc., 1988.

Rightmyer, Bobbi Dawn. *A History of Harrodsburg: Sarasota of the South.* Charleston, SC: The History Press, 2022.

Rule, J. C. *History of Montgomery Bell Academy.* Nashville: MBA Board of Trustees, 1954.

Sandstrom, Gosta E. *Tunnels.* New York: 1963.

Scott, William R. *The Forgotten Adventures of Richard Halliburton: A High-Flying Life from Tennessee to Timbuktu.* Charleston, SC: The History Press, 2014.

Spence, W. Jerome and Spence, David L. *A History of Hickman County, Tennessee.* Nashville: Gospel Advocate Publishing Co., 1900.

Stanton, Lucia. *"Those Who Labor for My Happiness": Slavery at Thomas Jefferson's Monticello.* Charlottesville: University of Virginia Press, 2012.

Staples, Charles R. *The History of Pioneer Lexington: 1779-1806.* Lexington, Ky: University of Kentucky Press, 1939.

Steele, Damaris Witherspoon. *First Church: A History of Nashville First Presbyterian Church, Vol. 1 (1785-1900).*

Swank, James M. *History of the Manufacture of Iron in All Ages.* Philadelphia: 1892.

Wilcox, R. Turner. *The Mode in Hats and Headdress.* Mineola, NY: Dover Publications, 2008.

Willis, Laura. *Dickson County, Tennessee Will Book, Vol. 1 (1838-1847).*

Wills, Ridley, II. *Gentleman, Scholar, Athlete: The History of Montgomery Bell Academy.* Chantilly, VA: The History Factory, 2005.

Wills, Ridley, II. *Nashville Streets and Their Stories.* Franklin: Plumbline Media, 2012.

Windrow, John Edwin. *John Berrien Lindsley: Educator, Physician, Social Philosopher.* Chapel Hill: University of North Carolina Press, 1938.

Woodall, Percy Hogan. *A Manual of Osteopathic Gynecology.* Nashville: Jno. Rundle & Sons, 1902.

_____. *From the Hill to the Horizon: Montgomery Bell Academy 1867-2017.* Nashville: Turner Publishing Co., 2017.

_____. *Dickson County History.* Chicago and Nashville: The Goodspeed Publishing Co., 1887.

_____. *The History of Tunneling in the United States.* Society for Mining, Metallurgy & Exploration, 2017.

Journals

Anonymous, "Furnaces and Forges," *Tennessee Historical Magazine*, Vol. IX, No. 3 (October 1925).

Bach, Mrs. William Everett, "Fayette County, Kentucky Records," *The Register of the Kentucky Historical Society*, Vol. 47, No. 160 (July 1949).

Bezis-Selfa, John, "A Tale of Two Ironworks: Slavery, Free Labor, Work and Resistance in the Early Republic," *William and Mary Quarterly*, Third Series, Vol. LVI, No. 4 (October 1999).

Blackett, Richard J. M., "Montgomery Bell, William E. Kennedy, and Middle Tennessee and Liberia," *Tennessee Historical Quarterly*, Vol. 69, No. 4 (Winter 2010).

Bradford, S. Sydney, "The Negro Ironworker in Ante Bellum Virginia," *The Journal of Southern History*, Vol. XXV, No. 2 (May 1959).

Dalton, Robert E., "Montgomery Bell and the Narrows of Harpeth," *Tennessee Historical Quarterly*, Vol. XXXV (Spring 1976).

Dew, Charles B., "Disciplining Slave Ironworkers in the Antebellum South: Coercion, Conciliation, and Accommodation," *American Historical Review*, No. 79 (1974).

Gavin, Michael Thomas, "From Bands of Iron to Promise Land: The African-American Contribution to Middle Tennessee's Antebellum Iron Industry," *Tennessee Historical Quarterly*, Vol. LXIV, No. 1 (Spring 2005).

Hoeflich, M. H., "John Livingston & the Business of Law in Nineteenth-Century America," *The American Journal of Legal History*, Vol. 44, No. 4 (October 2000).

Hoobler, James A., "Karnack on the Cumberland," *Tennessee Historical Quarterly*, Vol. 35, No. 3 (Fall 1976).

Isenhour, Judy, "When Nashville Was 'Lawsuit City'," *Nashville Business Advantage*, Vol. 7, No. 9 (January 1985).

Patton, James W., "The Progress of Emancipation in Tennessee: 1796-1860," *The Journal of Negro History*, Vol. XVII, No. 1 (January 1932).

Roper, James E., "Southwestern at Memphis: 1848-1981," *Tennessee Historical Quarterly*, Vol. XLI (Fall 1982).

Van Arsdall, Mai Flourney Van Deren, "The Springs at Harrodsburg," *The Register of the Kentucky Historical Society*, Vo. 61, No. 4 (October 1963).

Vienneau, Nancy, "Bend in the Road," *Nashville Lifestyles* (June 2016).

Warren, Louis A., "The Lincolns of Berks County," *Historical Review of Berks County* (April 1949).

Welch, Linn Ann, "The Cultural Significance of Bells Bend," *Tennessee Conservationist* (September-October 2021).

Wheatley, Tim, "Hidden History of Montgomery Bell State Park," *Tennessee Conservationist* (July-August 2022).

_____, "Sketches and Anecdotes of the Family of Brown," *American Historical Magazine*, Vol. VII, No. 2 (April 1902).

Newspapers

Adams [PA] Sentinel, January 16, 1854
Clarksville Jeffersonian, May 7, 1851
Daily Nashville Patriot, June 28, 1861
Lancaster Intelligencer, April 15, 1856
Nashville American, June 21, 1901
Nashville Banner: May 3, 1931; May 18, 1932; May 9-21, 1955; December 25, 1996
Nashville Daily American: August 17, 1882; May 6, 1883
Nashville Gazette, September 23, 1825
Nashville Union and American: October 14, 1856; March 20, 1857; May 7, 1857
Nashville Union, April 27, 1853
Nashville Whig: December 20, 1824; August 6 and 17, 1825
Pittsburgh Daily Post, January 28, 1854
Pittsburgh Weekly Gazette, August 19, 1825
Republican Banner, October 21, 1856
Shippensburg [PA] News, January 28, 1854
South Cheatham Advocate, November 20, 2000 through January 20, 2001
Tennessee Gazette, June 8, 1803
Tennessean: June 5, 1850, May 10, 1867; June 15, 1871; February 21, 1932; March 12, 1978; November 21, 1996; April 14, 1998

Tennessee Encyclopedia of History & Culture Entries

Corlew, Robert E., "Montgomery Bell"
Jackson, George E., "Cumberland Furnace"
Mielnik, Tara Mitchell, "Early Horseracing Tracks"
Nichols, Ruth D., "Montgomery Bell State Park"

Wikipedia Entries

Township (United States)
Chester County, Pennsylvania
Mason-Dixon Line
Lincoln University (Pennsylvania)
John Bell II (1705-1796)
Tanning

Fayette County, Kentucky
Pottstown, Pennsylvania
Province of North Carolina
Dickson County, Tennessee
Frank G. Clement
Overbrook
Harrodsburg, Kentucky
Gwen Shamblin Lara
Slavery in the United States
Bushrod Washington
American Colonization Society
Liberia
James G. Birney
William Appleton: Politician
Montgomery Bell State Park
Tennessee State Route 49
Rhodes College
Bellsburg, Tennessee
Bell Town, Tennessee

Other Sources

Adams, Carolyn T. Entry in *Encyclopedia of Greater Philadelphia*, "Chester County, Pennsylvania."

African Repository, issues between 1825 and 1855.

American Colonization Society Business Papers, 1838-1968, accessed at *www.fold3.com*.

Boyd, Nannie, "Montgomery Bell: Iron Master and Liberator." Unpublished manuscript in Tennessee State Library and Archives.

"Chester County, PA." *www.EXplorePAhistory.com*.

Childs, Jeremy. Metro Parks brochure on the Battle of Bells Mill (2016).

"Civilian Conservation Corps." Fact Sheet prepared by National Association of Civilian Conservation Corps Alumni. Lewiston, Idaho.

Coleman, Bevley R., "A History of State Parks in Tennessee." Ph.D. dissertation, George Peabody College for Teachers (1963).

Daniel, Buena Coleman, "The Iron Industry in Dickson County, Tennessee." M.A. thesis, Austin Peay State University (1970).

Faith and Works of Middle Octorara since 1727.

Ganier, Albert F., "Brief History of Montgomery Bell Park." Unpublished paper in Tennessee State Library and Archives.

Gifford, James M., "Montgomery Bell: Tennessee Ironmaster." M.A. thesis, Middle Tennessee State University (1970).

Hammerquist, Gail, "National Register of Historic Places Nomination: Drouillard House." National Park Service (March 1977).

"History," Bells Bend Conservation Corridor, found at *www.bellsbend.squarespace.com*.

Hollis, Rick, "Iron Master Montgomery Bell." Dickson County Bicentennial (2003).

Jones, Robbie D., "Tennessee Toll Bridges: 1927-1947: A Context Study." Prepared by New South Associates for the Tennessee Department of Transportation (2014).

Koontz, Russell Scott, "An Angel Has Fallen: The Glasgow Land Frauds and the Establishment of the North Carolina Supreme Court." M.A. thesis, North Carolina State University (1995).

Lange, Robie S., "National Historic Landmark Nomination: Montgomery Bell Tunnel." National Park Service (October 1993).

"Lost Montgomery Bell Bridge" photograph, accessed at *www.flickr.com*.

Mollow, Thomas. First plat of downtown Nashville, at *www.nashvillehistory.blogspot.com*.

National Archives and Records Administration, Miscellaneous Letters Received by the Secretary of Navy, 1801-1884. Washington.

National Park Service Handbook No. 124: *Hopewell Furnace* (1983).

Nichols, Ruth D., "The Civilian Conservation Corps and Tennessee State Parks: 1933-1942." M.A. thesis, Middle Tennessee State University (1994).

Pennsylvania Governor's Center for Local Government Services: *Township Commissioner's Handbook, 5ᵗʰ ed.* Harrisburg (2018).

"Phase I Archeological Survey of Two Parcels Proposed as Wetlands Mitigation Areas and the Bell's Mill Site., Harpeth Valley Utility District Propery, Bells Bend, Davidson County, Tennessee." Prepared by TRC Environmental Corporation for the Harpeth Valley Utility District, Nashville (2011).

Price, Daniel and Coco, Julie, "Beaman Park to Bells Bend: A Community Conservation Project." Prepared by New South Associates for the Land Trust of Tennessee.

Smith, Samuel D., Stripling, Charles P., and Brannon, James M., "A Cultural Resource Survey of Tennessee's Western Highland Rim Iron Industry: 1790s-1930s." Tennessee Department of Conservation, Division of Archeology, Research Series No. 8 (1988).

Troost, Gerard, "Third Geological Report to the Twenty-First General Assembly of the State of Tennessee." Nashville (1835).

United States Geological Survey map, Cheatham Dam (1957).

U.S. Census Records, 1820-1850.

Westminster Magazine (August 1780).

Websites

www.ancestry.com – Ancestry

www.transy.edu – Transylvania University

www.hbcheritage.com – Hudson Bay Company

www.amusingplanet.com – Amusing Planet

www.tfcg.com –French-Canadian Genealogist

www.ncpedia.org – North Carolina Encyclopedia

www.rsc.org – Royal Society of Chemistry

www.onsiteworkshops.com – Onsite

www.mountvernon.org – Mount Vernon

www.battlefields.org – Revolutionary War battlefields

www.phmc.state.pa.org – Pennsylvania historical markers

About the Author

John P. Williams

John P. Williams is a graduate of Montgomery Bell Academy, Davidson College, and Vanderbilt Law School. He has practiced law in Tennessee since 1972 and is currently Of Counsel with the firm Tune, Entrekin & White. He is a frequent contributor to legal and historical journals. This is his first book.

Index